The university is n‹
broadcasting moc‹

CW00544692

Eight episodes b‹
Joaquim Moreno

In conversation with
Tim Benton
Nick Levinson
Adrian Forty
Joseph Rykwert
Stephen Bayley

With contributions by
Nick Beech
Laura Carter
Ben Highmore
Joseph Bedford

Published by
Canadian Centre for Architecture
Jap Sam Books

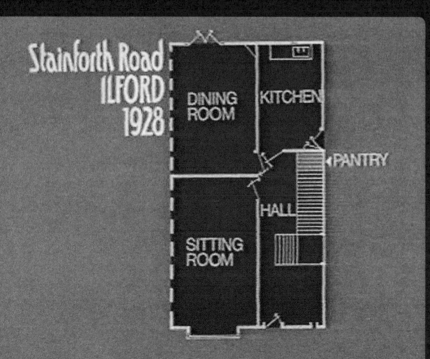

Stainforth Road
ILFORD
1928

DINING
ROOM

KITCHEN

►PANTRY

HALL

SITTING
ROOM

The Mutable Campus
— Mirko Zardini

Why a project for an open university?
And why examine this project, today?

A 2009 article in *The New York Times* labelled graduate education "the Detroit of higher learning," responsible for generating "a product for which there is no market."[1] Alongside a chorus of other voices, the headline of the article demanded an "End [to] the University as We Know It."[2]

The twenty-first century has witnessed growing skepticism towards the merits of higher education. For decades, doctorate programmes have been especially criticized for training students too narrowly and for ignoring a necessity for professional skill sets and collaborative, interdisciplinary ways of working.

Today we are part of a moment of large-scale change in education, synchronous with a crisis and mass criticism of a long-established academic model. In her recent article "What Are We Doing Here?" Marilynne Robinson wrote of the "pressure on [universities] to change fundamentally, to equip our young to be what the Fabians used to call 'brain workers.' They are to be skilled laborers in the new economy, intellectually nimble enough to meet its needs, which we know will change constantly and unpredictably."[3]

New distance-learning platforms continue to operate inside this Fabian model, producing "skilled laborers" for a precarious, ever-expanding knowledge economy. Massive Open Online Courses (MOOCs) especially, have been criticized as an opportunity for venture capitalists inside this knowledge economy and as a form of marketing and branding.[4] They have been cast as a best-case scenario in the context of austerity policies and as an institution that ignores questions of pedagogy or academic labour, positioning lesser-privileged students at an even greater disadvantage.[5]

In this context, it is becoming increasingly necessary to resurrect the mandate of the university—not to build a knowledge economy, for which knowledge and learning become commodities for the private good, but instead to use knowledge for the public good.[6]

There was a moment in 1969 in the United Kingdom when a new project, The Open University, recalled this mandate with a certain preponderance, advocating for the university as an element of social and political change. In one of the five conversations included in this volume, Tim Benton will speak of the emerging "conspiracy of education to change, especially the position of women, but also the position of working-class people."

1
Mark Taylor, "End the University as We Know It," *The New York Times*, 26 April 2009.

2
Headlines in Europe expressed similar attitudes. See for example, "Il fallimento dell'università," *Il Post*, 28 July 2010; Eric Marty, "La réforme de l'université, une catastrophe," *Le Monde*, 10 April 2012; Daniel Korski, "Britain's universities must change to survive. Higher education reform is the way forward," *The Telegraph*, 23 January 2017.

3
Marilynne Robinson, "What Are We Doing Here?" *The New York Review of Books*, 9 November 2017.

4
These criticisms are easily reinforced by slogans such as, "Black Friday Indulgence: Indulge and Learn Something New With Our Biggest Sale of the Year!" as advertised on Udemy, a global marketplace for online courses, https://www.udemy.com, 23 November 2017.

5
Ian Bogost, "MOOCs and the Future of the Humanities (Part One): A Roundtable at the LA Review of Books," 14 June 2013, http://bogost.com/writing/moocs_and_the_future_of_the_hu/.

6
See Andy Hargreaves, *Teaching in the Knowledge Society: Education in the Age of Insecurity* (New York: Teachers College Press, 2003), 1.

A305, History of Architecture and Design 1890–1939, the case study explored in depth by this project, was exemplary of The Open University's radical approach to the sharing of knowledge—one that reached a broader public and entered into new domestic learning environments. The course produced new ways of reading and understanding architecture for an audience previously in the margins of higher education. In 1975, at the time the course was first offered, over half of newly registered Open University students were from varied working-class occupations: 15 percent were housewives, 3 percent were tradesmen, 2 percent were farming, mining, and manufacturing labourers, 11 percent were clerical and office staff, 4 percent were salesmen and personal assistants, and 2 percent were retirees and non-employed persons. In the same year, the ratio of women among all new students reached 43 percent.[7]

The idea of education open to everybody translated into experimentations with methods and tools of communication. Raymond Williams, for example, spoke of The Open University as a "remarkable demonstration of some of the true possibilities of television."[8] Engaging with this course material—at risk of disappearing into a black hole of media obsolescence—has again launched the CCA into a project of media archaeology, an addendum of sorts to its recent *Archaeology of the Digital* project.[9]

At the root of these efforts is a conviction of the necessity to recuperate ideas and values from this historical moment, to promote the use of knowledge for the public good, and to recall again what it meant for The Open University to be

open to people, to places, to methods, and to ideas.[10]

7
British Broadcasting Corporation, *The BBC and the Open University* (Northampton: Belmont Press, November 1982), in "Open University Policy: File 4, 1980–,"file R126/81/1, BBC Written Archives.

8
Raymond Williams, *Television: Technology and Cultural Form*, 2nd ed. (London: Fontana, 1974; London and New York: Routledge, 2003), 51. Citation refers to Routledge edition.

9
From 2004 to 2017 the CCA developed a research programme that included exhibitions, publications, lectures, seminars, and acquisitions, to investigate the cultural shift that occurred with the emergence of the digital in architecture in the late twentieth century.

10
Geoffrey Crowther, Lord Crowther of Headlingley, first Chancellor of The Open University (1969–1972), from the first meeting of the Congregation of the Open University, 3 July 1969.

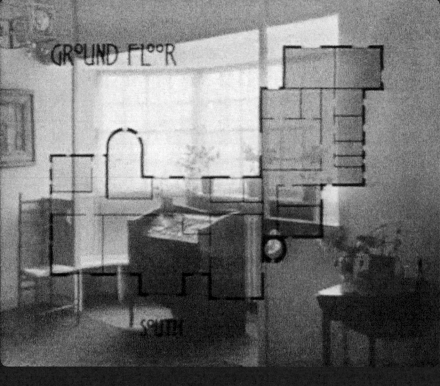

GROUND FLOOR

SOUTH

Visual prologue of A305 television programmes

The university is now on air,
broadcasting modern architecture

Episodes by Joaquim Moreno

1

Shared Audience, Open Education

Joaquim Moreno

Open,
wireless,
of the air,
at a distance,
door-to-door,
by correspondence,
extramural,
remedial,
continuing and adult education
—when these notions collided in postwar Britain,
the tensions between them reorganized the relationship among
media,
geography,
and education,
transforming the very idea of a university. This
transformation manifested in The Open University
(OU), a new kind of decentralized institution
founded in 1969.

In his 1976 book *Open University: A Personal Account by the First Vice-Chancellor*, Walter Perry highlights the key ideas that underpinned this endeavour:

> The concept of the Open University evolved from the convergence of three major postwar educational trends. The first of these concerns developments in the provision for adult education, the second the growth of educational broadcasting and the third the political objective of promoting the spread of egalitarianism in education.

According to this vision, the OU would mobilize mass media to expand mass education beyond the walls of conventional universities and to open up access to higher education to parts of the population that had typically been excluded from conventional systems—especially working adults.

[A]

In doing so, The Open University positioned itself as a supplement to, rather than a replacement for, existing institutions, operating through different channels. This was part of an ambitious political project captured by future Prime Minister Harold Wilson in his 1963 Labour Conference speech, *Labour's Plan for Science*, which introduced the party's plan for a "university of the air":

> It is designed to provide an opportunity for those who, for one reason or another, have not been able to take advantage of higher education, now to do so with all that TV and radio and the State-sponsored correspondence course, and the facilities of a university for setting and marking papers and conducting examinations, in awarding degrees, can provide.

[B]

As opposed to the methods used in traditional universities, this new kind of university could develop new formats of dissemination and new ways of learning and teaching that were mediated by interactions with technologies not commonly used for higher

education at the time. Content would be presented through a blended system that combined
television and radio broadcasts,
correspondence courses,
programmed tutorials,
and examinations,
as well as group study
at regional and local centres.

Such a project, a conspiracy to fuse
culture,
education,
and media
was, from the outset,
based on sharing resources
and sharing education.
The university of the air would share the space created by television and radio in order to broadcast higher education and make it more accessible to students as well as the general public.
The student and the everyday viewer
would become the same audience,
such that the OU,
rather than simply supplementing higher education, could potentially have a much greater effect on Britain's cultural life and technological progress. It was during the time that elapsed between Harold Wilson's 1963 Party Conference speech,
his subsequent 1964 electoral speech,
and his 1966 election manifesto speech

—he was then running for re-election—
that the idea of
a university of the air transformed
into the idea of an *open* university.

[C]

The phrase "of the air" was considered derogatory
because it implied that
   the association between
   education and entertainment
somehow made the former less substantive. And
given that it centred on the way content would be
disseminated through mass media rather than on
the educational aims being pursued, the phrase
also only partially explained the blended system
of the new institution and the wider social benefits
associated with it.
   By contrast, the word "open"
   made a very different point:
   an open university would breach
   entrenched social boundaries

and welcome those for whom
higher education might have been
inaccessible up to that point. As
Wilson stated in the 1966 manifesto:

This open university will obviously extend the best
teaching facilities and give everyone the opportunity
of study for a full degree. It will mean genuine equality
of opportunity for millions of people for the first time.

This was the first official political commitment of
the Labour Government to the idea of The Open
University, and it provides evidence of the impact
of the Ministry of Education White Paper titled
"A University of the Air,"
also published in 1966,
under the leadership of
the Minister for the Arts, Jennie Lee.
Lee had been tasked by Wilson to guide
the development of The Open University within
the newly formed Department of Education
and Science.
She led the Advisory Committee that
produced the 1966 White Paper,
which outlined various ways in which
the new institution would be more
open than others:

Enrolment as a student of the University should be open
to everyone on payment of a registration fee, irrespective
of educational qualifications, and no formal entrance
requirement should be imposed.

To fulfill this mandate,
the OU catered most particularly to working adults

who had to study part time, sharing their schedule with work and other responsibilities.

The OU therefore scheduled the television and radio programmes for its courses accordingly, inserting them into the flow of prime-time programming at the British Broadcasting Corporation (BBC),

which was already designated as the OU's broadcasting partner:

The television programmes will be broadcast for forty weeks a year at peak viewing time, i.e. in the early or mid-evening on week days, and, to meet the needs of shift workers and others who are not free in the evenings, programmes will also be broadcast during the day, including early morning, and at late night and week-ends.

The 1966 White Paper made clear that to be open, the OU also had to be public
—a shared cultural resource—

using media to share its content with a wider audience. As a result, the expected social and cultural impact of the OU would reach well beyond its enrolled students; the success of the university's openness would be measured by its total audience. But the White Paper also reaffirmed that even if only a small portion of the OU's potential viewers would graduate, this would nonetheless represent an increase in higher education participation nationally, and that the achievement would be momentous for individual students and for communities at large:

If the present rate of technological and cultural advance is to be sustained, it will depend not only on those who have reached the highest educational level, but on a population that is generally literate and well-informed.

[E]

Having published the White Paper, the next step in the development of this new form of mass higher education was to materialize the idea of a decentralized university.

To do this, Sir Peter Venables, the Chair of the Planning Committee for the OU, brought together a combination of

> several vice-chancellors
> from both new and well-established
> traditional universities,
> faculty with experience
> in adult education,
> and technologists and experts
> in educational broadcasting.

One of the objectives of the OU outlined in the Committee's report, published in 1969, was to redress past shortcomings of the educational system,

> plainly reinforcing
> the responsibility of the OU
> to provide a second opportunity
> for the postwar generation.

The report reinforced the OU's openness to students who enrolled without formal academic qualifications by introducing a series of foundation courses

> "designed as a means of familiarizing
> mature students with the modern
> concepts of the main 'lines' of study"

—the first four courses offered were

> Mathematics,
> Understanding Science,
> Literature and Culture,
> and Understanding Society.

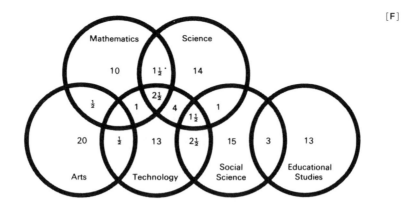

But the report was truly novel in the way it outlined the role of broadcasting in higher education:

Broadcasting, then, can most effectively be used as a component part of a fully integrated teaching system which also makes use of printed material, including specially written textbooks and directions for further reading; of correspondence tuition; of part-time face-to-face teaching, and of group discussion.

Broadcasting was a means for disseminating educational content quickly, but such speed came at a steep cost:

using television,
an expensive media,
obligated the OU to ensure the efficacy of its presentations and their universal appeal,
as well as the social and cultural interest of their contents to a broader audience than its enrolled students.
For the Planning Committee, this new education strategy was too expensive to be narrow in its focus and poor in its presentation. Broadcasting during prime-time hours maximized the audience

which, in turn, justified the OU's approach of
bringing together leaders in various fields
        to share their expertise
        and skilled presenters
        to ensure effective communication.

The Committee's report also pointed out that broadcasting was a way of returning in cultural value the
expense incurred by multimedia production while
also allowing prospective students to sample
various courses, browse different fields of study,
and measure their own capacities against the
demands of the OU before deciding to enroll.

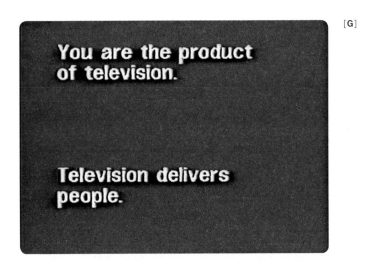

[G]

Diffusion through broadcasting meant that the
OU was advertised through the very medium of
its pedagogy and expertise. By being broadcast
during coveted prime-time slots, the OU was
getting the same exposure as expensive commercial advertising,

which made for accidental discoveries;
it was a way for viewers to find the OU
without searching.

Finally,
the Planning Committee's report contained an
important appendix that laid the ground rules for
the partnership between the nascent university
and the BBC. The OU would share both the BBC's
audience and its infrastructure, a relationship
that made the inception of the university possible
but also had a profound impact on its institutional
structure.

Inevitably,
this became a point of friction
between the two institutions,
which had very different operational
structures and overarching goals.
The appendix of the Planning Committee's
report clearly stated the complexity inherent in
this sharing of resources:

> The University will prescribe the academic objectives and
> general character of the broadcasts, in relation to the other
> component parts of each course, while the B.B.C. will
> provide the necessary presentation and production skills.
> In the overlapping area—where the inter-relationship of
> content and presentation is worked out—a reasonable
> degree of flexibility on both sides is essential in order to
> secure the proper concern of the academic staff and the
> fullest use of the experience of the broadcasting staff.

Once the groundwork for the operation of The
Open University was established, the new
university was awarded its Charter during the

first meeting of the Congregation of The University in July 1969.

On the occasion, Lord Crowther, the newly appointed Chancellor, pronounced the many ways of being open that remain part of the OU's mission statement to this day:

We are open as to places. This University has no cloisters —a word meaning closed. We have no courts—or spaces enclosed by buildings. Hardly even shall we have a campus. The rest of the University will be disembodied and air-borne. From the start, it will flow all over the United Kingdom.

Open to people,
to places,
to methods,
and to ideas:
an all-encompassing openness that would make decision-making processes, which were typically internal to an institution, more difficult.

This new university without boundaries —airborne, disembodied, and flowing throughout the United Kingdom— was not only sharing the audience, airtime, and production machinery of the BBC but also the infrastructure of other universities and community services like post offices, libraries, and halls, the latter of which provided spaces for collective tutorials.

Episode One

These networks enabled the OU to operate as a decentralized university, addressing every student at home.

At the same time, the OU and the BBC engaged in complex negotiations over the OU's need to broadcast courses outside working hours and the BBC's desire to reserve prime-time hours for entertainment and news. The BBC's expectation that all public programming fulfill its mandate to inform, educate, and entertain competed with the demand of the smaller OU audience to finally be able to participate in higher education.

[1]

While both OU students and BBC viewers could appreciate the opportunity to engage with cultural content through radio and television, the latter audience did not necessarily want to sit through specialized educational broadcasts during their leisure time. With the multiplication of broadcasting channels,

both public and commercial, viewers were now faced with choosing among the multiple programmes reaching their private television sets simultaneously. Given that multiple broadcasters were now sharing the same audience, it was increasingly difficult to conceive of a single flow of programming that could achieve social synchronization through mass media.

By intervening in the domestic sphere, the OU was sharing higher education well beyond the cloisters of conventional universities, to an unseen and unspecified audience. However,

because it lacked a dedicated
channel,
space,
and audience,
the OU was forced to constantly compromise

between the institution,
the public,
and the media through which
openness could be achieved.
This commitment to a principle of openness thus limited the freedom of each one of the stakeholders:

political decisions informed
academic freedom,

personal opinion,
social conventions,
and ideological positions,
while the collective institutional voice of the OU and the BBC further restricted the individual academic freedom of members of the OU course teams, the groups of specialists responsible for designing each course.

[J]

The mechanics of course design required a more collegial and less personal approach, and the academic views presented would only be allowed as much freedom as was fit to be broadcast in publicly accessible media.
By entering the homes of a general audience, academic discourse was being domesticated.
The accessibility of courses and their materials —in print, visual, and aural formats— to a broader public outside the confines of the traditional

academy implied great scrutiny of OU educational content. As Walter Perry remarked in his 1976 personal account:

> What is taught to the students is open not only to their criticism, but also to that of students in other institutions, of professional broadcasting critics, of politicians and of the general public. This very openness results in the academic staff responsible for designing the courses taking greater pains over what is offered than they would if they were presenting such materials behind the closed doors of the classroom. Statements will tend to be hedged in with reservations and qualifications, rather than made boldly and vested in the authority of the pedagogue.

To exist through mass media the university therefore had to speak not to cloistered students but rather to everyone who could receive its broadcasts at home,
in their living room,
through the special window of television.

Soon after Perry's publication, Robert Rowland, then head of BBC's Open University Production Centre,
also noted the friction
caused by the principle of openness
in his 1977 article,
"The University in a Palace,"
published in the The Listener,
a weekly magazine to supplement broadcast programmes by the BBC that ran from 1929 to 1991. On one hand, Rowland outlines the scope of the operation, stating that in that year the BBC would transmit, from its studios at Alexandra Palace in London, "over 1,500 television programmes

and 1,500 radio programmes, over four channels, covering about 100 'courses'" for the OU.

'This is the place where real television began' [K]

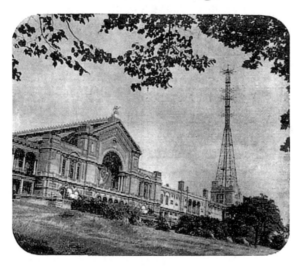

On the other, he clearly frames the perils of broadcasting public education on such a scale:

> No university has ever had so much potential access to the eyes and ears of a vast concourse of people as The Open University. This wedding of academic freedom with public responsibility works for most of the time, but sometimes throws up problems and difficulties which are the essence of adventure, particularly a shared one.... If "access" is "giving," The Open University is "sharing," both have their place in the walk into the future. I might just be forgiven at the moment for suggesting that to share is as difficult and complex as to "give" — perhaps more so.

As the OU course catalogue continued to expand beyond what was viable for the BBC to air during prime time, the friction between the OU and the BBC was eventually mitigated by the commercial dissemination of home video recording devices. Within the decade following the first OU broadcasts in 1971, these devices, the new media memory of television, were becoming increasingly available to the public.

At the same time, the OU began mailing videocassette tapes to its students while continuing to air its regular public programmes. Before private copies of television broadcasts could be produced in the home, the ephemeral character of television had required that broadcasters, like the BBC, synchronize programming with audience availability. This had not only carved out a space for educational television during prime-time hours, but also resulted in a substantial community of viewers for Open University programmes.

By contrast, the ability to view videocassette recordings off air not only enabled unprecedented spectator agency, allowing students to pace their own viewing schedules, but also provided a rationale for pushing educational programming to less popular time slots.

One OU course which was gradually pushed out of prime time was the third-level arts course A305,

Episode One

History of Architecture and Design 1890–1939.
Over the course of its life on air, from 1975 to 1982,
A305's television broadcasts were rescheduled
from 8:55 a.m. on Saturdays
to 6:25 a.m. on Sundays
and its radio broadcasts were rescheduled
from 6:05 p.m. on Tuesdays to
11:00 p.m. on Tuesdays or Wednesdays.
A305, like other OU programmes, was thus eventually being broadcast directly to insomniacs and
recording machines, demonstrating the difficulty
of retaining airtime for educational content. At the
same time, such changes in schedule jeopardized
the sense of community engendered by synchronized listening, heightening the perception that the
OU experience was one of studying alone rather
than of being part of a collective.
Soon, as prime-time audiences
were no longer being shared
between the OU
and general BBC programming,
accidental encounters between casual viewers
and OU broadcasts were less likely, diminishing
the openness of the university.

The epicentre of the conspiracy of education
shared between The Open University and its
audience eventually shifted to the distributed
nodes,
the regional and local study centres,

which had,
since the university's early years,
operated at an intermediate scale
between the OU's centralized
broadcasting and its domesticated
reception.
At study centres, students could interact among
themselves and with tutors on a regular basis,
sharing a physical space within which to debate
topics covered in OU courses.

[M]

The OU also held summer sessions on conventional
university campuses, where students could take
intensive courses during vacation periods and
share in a collective student learning experience.
Together, these two points
of interaction provided a counterpoint
to the OU's otherwise individualized
and domesticated model of higher
education through broadcasting;
a model which sometimes

fell short of the openness it purported to achieve.

The blended network established by the OU combined the centralized production of content
for television,
radio,
and print
with the local and regional centres and summer sessions, distributed across the United Kingdom.

The Open University thus mobilized a complex array of tools and modes of operation deployed at various scales, to reach multiple audiences, both at home and in collective environments.

[A]
Advertisement for The Open University, published in *Radio Times*, 6 February 1975: 50. The Open University. © Immediate Media

[B]
Harold Wilson addressing the Labour Party Conference. Photograph by Edward Miller, Scarborough, England, 30 September 1963. © Getty Images

[C]
Politicians at closing of Labour Party Conference, including Prime Minister Harold Wilson and Jennie Lee (far right), Scarborough, England, October 1967. © Getty Images

[D]
Advertisement for The Open University. Reproduced from *The Open University: A History*, written by Daniel Weinbren, 2015: 118.

[E]
The first Open University graduation ceremony. Alexandra Palace, London, England, 23 June 1973. The Open University. F1077-96

[F]
Diagram outlining The Open University's focus on inter-faculty courses. Reproduced from *Open University: A Personal Account by the First Vice Chancellor*, written by Walter Perry, 1976: 74.

[G]
Still from *Television Delivers People*, directed by Richard Serra, 1973. © Richard Serra/SODRAC 2018

[H]
An early BBC studio broadcasting Open University productions, London, England. The Open University. 200969_60045

[I]
Open University presenters working on the set of a programme for module TS282, Electromagnetics and Electronics, 1972. The Open University. TVC1012-15

[J]
Still of title card from television programme 2 of *Open Forum*, "An Open University Discussion," 1971. The Open University. 00521_2702

[K]
Detail from "Farewell to Ally Pally: This is the Place Where Television Began," written by Robert Rowland, published in *The Listener*, 2 July 1981: 12. © Immediate Media

[L]
Student watching an Open University programme at home. Reproduced from *The Open University: A History*, written by Daniel Weinbren, 2015: 160.

[M]
A tutor talking to a group of science students in a laboratory at The Open University Summer School, 1974. The Open University. 000000700078

Culture, Education, and Class in 1960s Britain: New media, New Universities, and the New Left
— Nick Beech

The Open University—as an institution, both imagined and realized—emerged in a period of pronounced cultural and social transformation in Britain, such that any debate on the expansion or quality of higher education rebounded upon a deeper, longer, and more fraught debate on class, culture, and power. If it is common in Britain today to assume that "upward mobility," "equal opportunity," and "a level playing field for all" are the normative conditions for a free and democratic society, then the prevailing attitudes and agendas about class of the 1950s and 1960s now seem startlingly different. Just as there was a general agreement that class structures and relationships in Britain were changing—whether because of the legacy of World War II, the introduction of the welfare state, or the collapse of the British Empire—there was very little agreement as to what that change consisted of, or whether any change could possibly be a good thing.

> Ever since I suffered in (almost) complete silence at
> the London University Institute of Education in 1954–55,
> I have carried around a shameful burden of disagree-
> ment with almost every professional "progressive"
> educationalist, sociologist, and Left Wing politician
> … How can anyone learn or impart knowledge in a
> screaming mass of children or adolescents who don't
> even know they don't know everything?[1]

For June Wedgwood Benn, as she expressed in this 1969 reflection on her experience as a teacher since the mid-1950s, education in Britain had taken a terrible turn in the postwar period. Benn understood herself as—and was widely acknowledged to be —a liberal, open, and morally sound individual, and her views on education reflected her understanding of how to care for and educate all members of society. However, while Benn wanted all children to enjoy a secondary education, she also believed that not all children required, or could respond positively to, the same education. In this argument, Benn was far from unique.

The form of extended education established under the Butler Act of 1944—a key arm of the welfare state—was widely acknowledged to be progressive because it provided, for the first time, secondary education for all regardless of income. Yet, the tripartite structure of this system—a mass of Secondary Moderns,

1
June Wedgwood Benn, "Letter to the Black Paper Editors," in "Black Paper Two: The Crisis in Education," eds. C. B. Cox and A. E. Dyson, special issue, *Critical Quarterly* 4, no. 3 (1969): 93.

a minority of Grammar Schools, and an even smaller minority of Technical Schools—demonstrably reproduced class hierarchies in British society, in particular through the results of an exam for all eleven-year-olds (the "Eleven Plus") according to which children were distributed within the structure. The allocation of a Grammar School place to a girl or boy from a working-class background was a peculiar enough phenomenon to excite a great deal of commentary; and, for many of the commentators, this phenomenon was no bad thing. Indeed, as social scientist and pioneer of market research, Mark Abrams, stated in a debate on class, social equality, and mass education, broadcast on the BBC Third Programme in 1961: [2]

> The outcome of the 11-plus is determined at the age of three, four, five, six, according to the child's parental background, home background. And this is an important explanation, I think, of why British society is so stable. The essence of the whole British class system is to stabilise it as early in life as possible, and the earlier you can do that the more stable, the more comfortable a class society you're going to have. [3]

Popular opinions about the Eleven Plus varied widely. For some, the exam provided both equality of opportunity and the grounds for a meritocratic class system (as the Conservative Member of Parliament and imperialist, Enoch Powell, asserted). For many others—encompassing the broad coalition of the left that included both wings of the Labour Party—the Eleven Plus served as an iniquitous tool of class reinforcement. The exam system, which allocated the small number of Grammar School places available, would always identify an elite tier, and many pointed out that the construction of the exam favoured those raised within middle-class households. Those few from working-class backgrounds who attended Grammar Schools—such as the literary and cultural critic Richard Hoggart—experienced a shock upon realizing that their own family cultures were, when not ridiculed, ruthlessly condemned by their new classmates and teachers. Finally, as indicated in Abrams's remarks, a third perspective suggested that the educational system was ultimately uninfluential in relation to entrenched class structures and could therefore only be understood in relation to economic changes, such as a rise in family income. But regardless of how one understood the Eleven Plus, it was *class* that remained the target of educational reform and anxieties.

As with debates about class, there was also a continuous discussion taking place, among civil servants in Whitehall as much as among vicars and teachers in village halls, not only about how British culture was changing, but about the ways in which it could or should change. Irrespective of the level of government, the general agreement was that a distinctly British culture—the product of a peculiar, exceptional, and heterogeneous but coherent island people [4]—was under assault from a commercial culture emanating from the United States. Through mass media forms such as cinema, television, vinyl records, pulp fiction, and comics, as well as "milk bars" and coffee shops, a traditional culture—or a tradition of distinct class cultures—was disintegrating. [5]

2
The BBC's Third Programme was a radio broadcast channel created in 1946. Whereas the Home Service offered discussion, news, and "middle-brow" cultural content, and the Light Programme offered popular music and entertainment ("low-brow" culture), the Third Programme specifically targeted a minority elite, offering less popular classical and contemporary music, and thought pieces by leading philosophers and social commentators. The Home, Light, and Third channels were all replaced between 1967 and 1970 by Radio 4, Radio 1 and Radio 2, and Radio 3 respectively.

3
Mark Abrams, "Social Equality —The Class System," radio broadcast (BBC: Third Programme, July 1961), quoted in David Kynaston, *Modernity Britain: A Shake of the Dice, 1959–1962* (London: Bloomsbury, 2014), 192.

4
For examples of how Britain as a landscape and as a people was conceived in the 1950s, see Nikolaus Pevsner, *The Englishness of English Art* (London: Penguin, 1993), a lecture series first broadcast by BBC Radio in 1955; and Sir Hugh Casson and Patrick O'Donovan, *Brief City: The Story of London's Festival Buildings*, directed by Jacques Brunius and Maurice Harvey (London: Richard Massingham Films, 1952).

5
Both "milk bars" (which sold milkshakes, targeting teenagers who could not go to pubs and did not want to go to cafés) and the new "coffee shops" were heavily criticized by cultural commentators at the time (and since) for their interior design, music, atmosphere, and even smell. For a more generous historical perspective, see Matthew Partington, "The London Coffee Bar of the 1950s—Teenage Occupation of an Amateur Space?," (lecture, *Occupation: Negotiations with Constructed Space* conference, University of Brighton, 2–4 July 2009), http://arts.brighton.ac.uk/__data/assets/pdf_file/0004/44842/33_Matthew-Partington_The-London-Coffee-Bar-of-the-1950s-.pdf.

For some, such as Hoggart, the members of youth sub-cultures harboured the collapse of a long-standing, authentic, communitarian, and morally-robust working-class culture.[6] Groups such as the "mods"—teenagers who constructed their identities by spending their unprecedented, disposable incomes on French jeans, American jazz records, and Italian scooters—were, in the process, inventing their own vocabulary, sensibility, and style of physical bearing. For imperialists like Enoch Powell, such cultural changes were symptomatic of a failure to invest in empire, defend free trade, police society, and resist immigration.[7] But what was to be done? While the answer to that question was always tempered by political positioning—whether radical, reformist, progressive, or reactionary—ultimately, the new commercial, or mass, society was to be resisted at all costs, either by censorship, the police, or through the establishment of robust alternatives.

Only a small number of commentators and creative practitioners associated with the broad New Left—such as Reyner Banham, Stuart Hall, or Cedric Price—had the capacity to think both critically and positively in regard to the popular cultural changes then occurring.[8] These critics were not united by a shared political position, but rather by the fact that they all considered that the definition of culture was up for debate. The basis for reformulating new cultural experiences (both aesthetic and cognitive) was established by new media forms and types of content that provided a powerful antidote to regressive and reactionary cultural tendencies in Britain. This shift suggested not a moment of regret or anxiety, but rather of hope and possibility.[9] In turn, these positive (if frustrated and often angry) critics offered answers to the question, "What is to be done?" that were distinct from those of conservative commentators, resulting in proposals that went further than simply asking "What?" (that was being answered by the youth themselves). Instead, they questioned where and how—in what institutions, forms of research, and academic disciplines, and through what means, technologies, and programmes—the critical potential of popular, mass-media culture would be expounded and explored. This enquiry necessarily touched on the role of education and its relationship to a broadened definition of the term culture. If culture was no longer understood as a selection of the best words and ideas from history, but rather as a way of life, then how, where,

6
Richard Hoggart, The Uses of Literacy: Aspects of Working-Class Life (London: Chatto & Windus, 1957).

7
Enoch Powell, Still to Decide: Speeches, ed. John Wood (London: Elliot Right Way, 1972).

8
The New Left remains a very open-ended political category. Artist and intellectual groups and wider social movements identified themselves as part of the New Left during the Cold War, as an alternative to either the "actually existing socialism" of the Soviet Union and its satellite states or to the various forms of mixed-economy or social-democracy of the United States and its European allies. Whether in Britain, North America, or Western Europe, the New Left was defined by an anti-imperialist and radically democratic politics, and a consistently cultural, rather than economistic, language. It therefore typically engaged artists, writers, and students, as much as purely political actors. For an account of the American New Left, see Van Gosse, Rethinking the New Left: An Interpretative History (New York: Palgrave Macmillan, 2005); for an account of the British New Left, see Stuart Hall, "Life and Times of the First New Left," New Left Review 61 (January–February 2010): 177–96.

9
See Reyner Banham, A Critic Writes, ed. Mary Banham et al. (Berkeley: University of California Press, 1996); Stuart Hall, Selected Political Writings: The Great Moving Right Show and Other Essays, ed. Sally Davidson et al. (London and Durham, NC: Lawrence & Wishart and Duke University Press, 2017); and Cedric Price, Opera, ed. Samantha Hardingham (Chichester, UK: John Wiley & Sons, 2003).

and who might teach (or learn about) culture as a subject that included the full breadth of communicative experience? There were two assumptions that made this programme for educational reform distinct: first, that education was a mechanism for working-class emancipation and empowerment; but second, that the nature of working-class culture was historically conditioned, and neither essential nor fixed.

Communications

> [It] is disciplined freedom, rather than absolute liberty, which most youngsters want and expect from school … The only discipline worth having is the discipline of *purpose*, in the context of love.[10]

As revealed in Hall's 1959 essay "Absolute Beginnings"—in which he delivers a sustained critique of the Secondary Modern and its effects on working-class teenagers—the question for many within the broader left in relation to education and media was really a question of power. Implicit in their approach to education and media was the fundamental debate about who should control educational institutions and mass media: to whom should they be directed? To what ends should they be used? And what form should they take?

With these questions in mind, Raymond Williams—another major contributor to New Left thought in the period who, like Hall, maintained an open and critical (but ambivalent) position toward popular culture and its effects—set out, from the mid-1950s, to analyze and make sense of the changing structures of British culture. In his 1962 publication, *Communications* (which both provided an index to the intellectual form and content of the debate and made a significant contribution to that debate), Williams discerned at least four systems of "control of communications" (communications being a term which tangentially included education): "authoritarian," "paternal," "commercial," and "democratic."[11] Williams presented the authoritarian control of communications as a historical category in British society: an exercise of state or institutional power, by a minority over a majority, through possession of the means of communication—such as theatres, churches, and printing presses—strict censorship, and policing.[12] It was rather in describing the combination between the paternal and commercial systems of communications control that Williams presented an account of mid-century British media and education. And finally, Williams offered a vision of the conditions necessary for a democratic control of communications—which remained a political aspiration.

The paternal system of control designated, for Williams, the same extension and exercise of power as in an authoritarian system, but less explicitly so. In the paternal system, the means of communication was monopolized but this was justified in order to ward against corruption by a radical minority (as opposed to a benign, elite minority) who would otherwise be able to corrupt members of the majority population. Censorship, both direct and indirect, was extensive but, again, was not exercised in defence of an authority or power per se, but rather on moral grounds as a form of guardianship and protection. Such a system of communications control

10
Stuart Hall, "Absolute Beginnings," *Universities and Left Review* 7 (Autumn 1959): 17.

11
Raymond Williams, *Communications*, 3rd ed. (Harmondsworth, UK: Penguin Books, 1976), 129–37. *Communications* can be understood as an extension of Williams's earlier works *Culture and Society, 1780–1950* (London: Chatto & Windus, 1958), and *The Long Revolution* (London: Chatto & Windus, 1961).

12
Williams, *Communications*, 130–1.

necessarily restricted the field of possibilities for the individual artist or a mass audience—subject as both were to the authority of the paternal elite.

Williams presented the commercial system of control as clearly antithetical to a moralizing, paternalistic authority: the commercial system was liberal, determined by market forces, uninterested in content or meaning, and in pursuit of market extension and penetration. This system provided the individual content provider—the artist—with, on the one hand, absolute freedom to say whatever they wanted in whatever manner but, on the other hand, absolute limitation if the subject was only of interest to a small minority or if they did not have the capital to command the means of communication. So too (by definition), was the audience subject to commercial control—any special interests, regional concerns, or minority or marginal tastes were provided with little or no supply, unless supported by specific demand (which certain performing arts, such as opera, always enjoyed).

The democratic model proposed by Williams, though grounded in observations of small-scale interventions in the communications landscape, was clearly a projective vision rather than a diagnosis of the times. In his projection Williams dissolves any clear-cut distinction between technical and professional producers on the one hand, and a mass audience on the other, proposing instead that expertise be utilized more broadly. Priority over such expertise was not to be offered to either a paternal, cultural elite or to commercial interests, and ownership was to be distributed at regional levels to elected councils of broadcast and print media. While commercial charges were to be maintained through licence fees and advertising revenue, the direct link from revenue to production was to be severed.[13] Advertising space was to be sold centrally and the funds were to be redistributed evenly to these autonomous regional organizations. Content was also to be organized according to the needs, aspirations, and desires of the people of those regions—drawing on, developing, and extending professional and technical expertise.

Though Williams presents each system in succession, and with hints at a historically sequential development (from authoritarian, through paternalistic and commercial, to democratic control), he underscores that all four were present within contemporary British communications. However, Williams clearly also regarded British media and education as a peculiar mixture of paternalistic and commercial control. In his terms, there were autonomous but paternalistic institutions—the BBC and the ancient and civic universities—that both monopolized their respective means of communication—higher education and broadcast media—and understood their Royal Charters in terms of moral obligation.[14] But these institutions operated within a more general and, perhaps, more pervasive commercial communications system—including print media, cinema, theatre, and live and recorded music—and were thus subject to private interests and market imperatives. Furthermore, there was no escaping the paternalistic motives of major private enterprises—such as Allen Lane's Penguin imprint or the photo journal *Picture Post*—nor the pursuit of dominance over commercial space by institutions such as the BBC. Caught within the hybrid system of

13
Whereas commercial broadcasters secured their revenue from advertising, the BBC has always been funded by a direct licence fee, paid annually by anyone in Britain who has private access to a receiver (television or radio). While the BBC is autonomous from the state (hence, its independent charter), the cost of the licence fee (and whether there should be one at all) is set by Parliament. It remains a highly contentious issue to this day.

14
The ancient universities were the medieval institutions of Oxbridge and Scotland and the civic universities were those established in the industrial provinces (such as Birmingham, Bristol, and Manchester) in the nineteenth century, by non-conformists.

paternal-commercial control of communications, author and audience, and producer and consumer, were left caged, resistant, and, at times, militant.

In his considerations of a possible democratic system of control, Williams identified a privileged role for education by proposing that knowledge of the practice, theory, and critique of communications (in all its forms) be developed in education at primary, secondary, and tertiary levels; that the tripartite division of secondary education be abolished and replaced by a comprehensive education system for all; and that the reach of higher education be radically expanded through new universities accessible to all regardless of age, gender, or ability to pay. He also proposed that the content of tertiary education be developed to include the study of communications as a subject (so called cultural studies rather than English literature), driven by the needs and aspirations expressed by students.[15] Williams's radical vision was shared by others within the broader New Left of the late 1950s and 1960s, as expressed in such works as *May Day Manifesto*, the first version of which Williams edited in collaboration with Edward Thompson and Stuart Hall.[16]

These calls from the New Left to institute a more democratic communications system also manifest in a broader set of proposals by left wing cultural producers who were dissatisfied with either Conservative or Labour government policies on culture and education. For example, Joan Littlewood and Cedric Price's Fun Palace project of 1964 proposed a centre for the free development of artistic production and performance, in which London's East End residents would not *receive* cultural education (typical of missionary cultural programmes of the nineteenth century) but rather *produce* their own, new forms of culture.[17] Price's Potteries Thinkbelt project, ongoing from 1963, imagined to transform the West Midlands with an open transportation and communications structure that would house a mega-polytechnic, in which science, engineering, and design education would be integrated into a constant, entrepreneurial, student-run experiment.[18] Finally, in their 1969 project Non-Plan, Banham, Peter Hall, and Price proposed to strip local and national government of their powers through a "bonfire of the planning system." Rather than emerging out of neoliberal ideas of market efficiency or pricing knowledge, Non-Plan

15
These changes in the content of tertiary education marked the birth of cultural studies as a field in Britain. For an account, which takes on board both the political motivations for cultural studies and its relationship to traditional humanities subjects, see Stuart Hall, "The Emergence of Cultural Studies and the Crisis of the Humanities," *October* 53 (Summer 1990): 11–23.

16
Raymond Williams, ed., *May Day Manifesto*, reissue with introduction by Mike Rustin (London: Lawrence and Wishart, 2013), https://www.lwbooks.co.uk/sites/default/files/free-book/Mayday.pdf.

17
See Stanley Matthews, *From Agit-Prop to Free Space: The Architecture of Cedric Price* (London: Black Dog, 2007).

18
See Kester Rattenbury and Samantha Hardingham, *Cedric Price: Potteries Thinkbelt (Supercrit no. 1)* (London: Routledge, 2007).

was a radically democratic model that would provide localities with autonomy and freedoms from both state and market.[19] These proposals all maintained the assumptions about working-class emancipation and transformation embedded within New Left educational reform—assumptions not shared by the mainstream political parties responsible for mass education policy in Britain.

Conservative and Labour Party Policy

Williams's visions of a democratic control of communications (to use his terms) were in stark contrast to mainstream, parliamentary policy proposals for tackling class power structures, culture, and education. The early 1960s marked a watershed moment for broadcasting in Britain as major institutions, including the BBC, faced scrutiny regarding their purpose and future. Beginning in 1954, an experiment had been conducted in commercial television broadcasting, launching an Independent Television (ITV) channel which was funded by advertising revenue and delivered via thirteen regional contractors who were free from the moral obligations felt by the BBC. ITV was overseen by the Independent Television Authority (ITA), which took a light touch to regulating the channel. The thirteen contractors soon realized the popularity of American television (particularly Westerns and game shows) such that the network predominantly aired derivatives, or indeed reruns of American commercial content. The experiment of ITV as an institution was, however, always due to end in 1962. At the same time, the BBC's Royal Charter was also due for renewal, and its monopoly on radio broadcasting was increasingly under debate.[20] Ongoing questions about the structure and content of broadcasting were consistently posed in terms of the protection of a high (superior) culture under assault from a low (commercial American) culture; a perspective which influenced later arguments about the transformation of mass education.

The 1957–1963 Conservative government of Harold Macmillan was overtly optimistic about prosperity—indeed Macmillan famously celebrated that Britons "ha[d] never had it so good"[21]—but always, naturally, struggled to balance market imperatives with an ideology fixed on maintaining the status quo. Media institutions, too, were caught between a desire to respond to commercial interests in television and a desire to protect the paternalistic BBC and its values. In 1960, Macmillan established an independent committee, chaired by the industrialist and (later) baron, Sir Harry Pilkington, to review the state of broadcasting. The Pilkington Committee's report, published in 1962, understood the situation of communications in a similar way to Williams. However, while Williams understood a complex structural relationship operating between commercial and paternal systems of control, the Committee brought together a spectrum of critics who understood commercial, or "mass-appeal," culture as a corrosive force that should be constrained, if not abolished.

As historian Jeffrey Milland has argued, the Pilkington Committee was responding to much more than simply the direct question of licence and charter renewals. In addition, it addressed the debate over whether there should be a third channel and whether it should be a public (delivered through the BBC) or commercial

19
See Jonathan Hughes and Simon Sadler, eds., Non-Plan: Essays on Freedom and Change in Modern Architecture and Urbanism (Oxford: Architectural Press, 2000). Both Potteries Thinkbelt and Non-Plan were published in the magazine New Statesman which was, through-out the 1960s, a forum for radical proposals across the left, both within the Labour Party and beyond.

20
There was no commercial or independent radio broadcasting until the early 1970s in Britain.

21
Harold Macmillan, speech at a Conservative rally, Bedford, United Kingdom, July 1957. See Peter Hennessy, Having It So Good: Britain in the Fifties (London: Penguin, 2006).

channel; a growing unease with the massive profit increase of commercial broadcast contractors since ITV's trial launch in 1954; and finally, a widespread perception of an erosion of British culture and values through contact with commercial communications.[22] For example, even Richard Hoggart (a key member of the Pilkington Committee), though certainly not condescending of the working class, nonetheless feared for the destruction of working-class values under the influence of American cultural products.

As a result, the Pilkington Committee recommended that any third television broadcast channel should be awarded to the BBC; that the ITV network should be restructured so that advertising revenue could not be directly linked to programme production and broadcast; that ITV should be subject to greater oversight through the ITA; and that no commercial licences for radio should be offered. Though unable to fully endorse the Committee's recommendations, the Macmillan government nevertheless responded to the spirit of the report: a third channel was awarded to the BBC; the powers of the ITA were strengthened; and commercial radio was resisted (leading to the blossoming of pirate radio stations in the 1960s). In other words, the Pilkington Committee, and the Conservatives, had produced precisely that peculiar mix of paternalism and commercialism analyzed and critiqued by Williams—and the Labour Party produced no clearer response.

Harold Wilson—champion of The Open University and the expansion of tertiary education—understood the power of broadcasting, both for political practice and economic growth. Indeed, within his larger strategy for Britain's industrial development, Wilson drew no distinction between engineering, transportation, and energy, on the one hand, and mass communications, on the other. His administration understood Britain's technological lag in broadcasting—characterized by a small number of broadcast channels, minimal or no satellite and cable networks, and a lack of colour transmission—as both a symptom and a cause of a lack of economic competitiveness.

Yet, if these conditions seemed to suggest that Wilson would preside over the vitalization of broadcast communications in Britain, such was not the case. While he was committed to intervening in the broadcast industry, Wilson was caught between the contradictory poles of commercial and paternal instincts—both within the existing broadcast institutions and the Labour Party itself—and, in the end, his policies were evasive and achieved little more than constricting the BBC's finances as part of wider public service cuts.[23]

The Labour Party during the Wilson governments (1964 –1970) found itself at the mercy of a set of forces that it was singularly ill-equipped to navigate: a working class fragmented by new industries and forms of consumption that ushered in new cultural identities, mores, and codes; mass immigration from former colonies bringing hopes, desires, and challenges that came into confrontation with the conditions of the imperialist "home" nation; and the development in women's political consciousness, and the subsequent strong interventions in domestic, industrial, and communications structures. How might a party organization respond when it was dependent on aging, white, male members who came from heavy industry and had lived through unemployment and austerity?[24]

22
Jeffrey Milland, "Courting Malvolio: The background to the Pilkington Committee on Broadcasting, 1960-62," Contemporary British History 18, no. 2 (2004): 78–9.

23
D. Freedman, "Modernising the BBC: Wilson's Government and Television, 1964–1966," Contemporary British History 15, no. 1 (2001): 21–40.

24
For a full account of such problems facing the Labour Party, see Steven Fielding, The Labour Governments 1964–1970, Volume 1: Labour and Cultural Change (Manchester: Manchester University Press, 2003).

For Labour revisionist Anthony Crosland, these changed circumstances required a change in the Party itself—in terms of both ideology and policy. Crosland argued that the introduction of the welfare state in 1945 had neutralized the antagonism between labour and capital, effectively disintegrating the historic form of capitalism to which the Labour Party had been opposed.[25] Within the managed economy of social democracy, introduced by the Labour government of 1945–1951, the working class gained access to more widespread affluence—evident in better housing, and easier access to commodities, motor cars, and a consumer life-style—thereby losing definition as a meaningful political category, let alone as a polity.[26] The Labour Party abandoned its historic goal of commanding the means of production and bringing private enterprise and industry under state control, precisely because this failed to harness the dynamic properties of capitalism. Instead, as Crosland argued, the Labour Party should aim for redistributive economic and social policies in favour of a technocratic manage-ment of the economy and of social services—such as education, cultural provision, and health care—to bolster equality of not only opportunity but also outcome.

For Crosland, a new education strategy would target social mobility, cultural identity, and autonomy of lifestyle all at once; a revision of the Labour Party's position which had lasting effects on policy developments in the 1960s.[27] Higher education had already been expanded under the conservative government of Harold Macmillan, a process which was further reinforced by the cross-party Robbins Report of 1963. This expansion was to be bolstered, in particular, by the development of "polytechnics"—further education for professional and vocational programmes of education—which would reinforce the ability of education to eradicate class division and ensure a lasting, prosperous social democracy.

The Labour Party's policy developments for education in the 1960s ran parallel to its approach to culture, specifically to the broader field of communications: broadcasting and education were to be extended, the rigidity of the British class structure was to be challenged, and education and culture were to be harnessed for commercial and industrial-capitalist dynamism. In some respects, these goals reflected many of the proposals of the New Left. But, in other crucial respects, these goals fell far short of the New Left's ambitions: they were developed and executed under the auspices of a rationalized, centralized, and paternalistic elite; they preserved a fixed notion of what was "best" in cultural terms; and they were driven by economistic, not cultural, imperatives. A highly contra-dictory fusion.

Crisis

Throughout the period, progressive models of education were consistently criticized by an intellectually conservative group of commentators, academics, and politicians. These figures attacked the introduction of comprehensive education, the expansion of higher education, and the investment in vocational and profes-sional fields. In principle, they were in agreement that more stu-dents was a positive indicator—after all, who would not relate an

25
Anthony Crosland, "The Transition from Capitalism," in New Fabian Essays, ed. R. H. S. Crossman (London: Turnstile Press, 1951).

26
Anthony Crosland, The Future of Socialism (London: Jonathan Cape, 1956).

27
See various articles from between 1951 and 1968 in Socialist Commen-tary, the monthly journal published by the Socialist Vanguard Group. Anthony Crosland's positions were supported by other major political operators such as Hugh Gaitskill, former Chancellor and Leader of the Labour Party from 1955 to 1963.

increasingly educated population with a rise in economic and social prosperity—but they disagreed on, and expressed constant anxiety about standards, quality, value, and discipline.

How were standards to be maintained? Given the lingering suspicion (made overt in the Robbins Report) over the proposed provision of higher education to all those who were able, who would judge this ability and what criteria would distinguish the "cream" from the "milk"? How would quality be assured outside of the long-established and respected universities? What would guarantee that new students would not be submitted to second-rate teaching or fashionable, ill-conceived discourse? What value would there be in introducing degree programmes on agriculture, engineering, architecture, art, or, even worse, television? Was the workplace, surely, not the appropriate environment for such technical and skilled (trade) work? Finally, how was discipline—both as social conduct or order and as established field of professional or scholarly enquiry—to be maintained?

To all these questions, conservatives found mid-century British developments in education grossly inadequate and disturbing. They were particularly concerned by the growing militancy of students in higher education from the mid-1960s that reached a peak in the student revolts of 1968.[28] Students were calling for greater transparency in university governance, involvement in the management of their universities, and changes to curricula—calls that mixed with radicalized feminist and Black politics, and a resurgence of Marxism. Yet, as Enoch Powell argued in 1970:

> There is no more sense in the students participating in the management of the universities than there would be in a union of housewives participating in the management of Marks & Spencer's stores. The students are there, strange as it might seem, to study and (I will go so far as to say) to be taught ... They may, or may not, like those who teach them, or what they are taught, or the way in which the institution is arranged. If they do not, they have the same remedy as other free men, and as a dissatisfied customer at a supermarket, and that is to take themselves and their custom elsewhere.[29]

Though his ability to link everyday market transactions to complex social phenomena remained unique (until the rise of Margaret Thatcher), Powell was otherwise not alone in his opinions. June Wedgewood Benn's earlier commentary on children's education appeared in an open letter in the second of two "Black Papers" on education, published by the literary journal Critical Quarterly.[30] The editors, Brian Cox and A. E. Dyson, were shaped by the same intellectual formation as Raymond Williams, but where Williams had radicalized English literature and tried to understand popular culture as a complex way of life, Cox and Dyson sought to continue the tradition of protecting the best words and ideas from history (even if they admitted that these might now be said and thought through film and radio rather than theatre and books).

The Black Papers were named in reaction to the government's White Papers on education in the late 1960s. In two volumes,

28
While the student protests and revolt of 1968 never achieved the same magnitude in Britain as in France or the United States, significant sit-ins, teach-ins, and demonstrations were conducted. See Sylvia Ellis, "'A Demonstration of British Good Sense?' British Student Protest During the Vietnam War," in Student Protest: The Sixties and After, ed. Gerard J. DeGroot (London: Routledge, 1998), 54–69.

29
Enoch Powell, speech, Northern Universities Dinner, Federation of Conservative Students, 7 March 1970, York, http://www.enochpowell.net/sd-07.html.

30
See "Fight for Education: A Black Paper," eds. C. B. Cox and A. E. Dyson, special issue, Critical Quarterly 4, no. 1 (Winter 1969); and, "Black Paper Two: The Crisis in Education," eds. C. B. Cox and A. E. Dyson, special issue, Critical Quarterly 4, no. 3 (1969).

Cox and Dyson gathered together some of the leading figures in education, social science, history, and English literature to reassert a rational and universal set of standards. The Black Papers argued for rigorous testing and measurement at primary school level—condemning the idea of play; streams of education rather than a comprehensive system at secondary school level—distinguishing academic and non-academic pupils; and a restriction in the growth and nature of tertiary education—keeping vocational and technical training absolutely distinct from general education in humanities and sciences. The Black Papers repeatedly offered up an earlier goal of education: that of the achievement and sustenance of the highest standards in culture. Though the various authors never made simple assumptions about what constitutes culture—they often developed careful interrogations—they nonetheless largely relied on the assumption that the purpose of education was to produce human beings who can access, reproduce, and support a common culture of moral virtues and standards.

In making these arguments, the Black Papers informed and reflected the mood of education ministers, both Conservative and Labour, in (and since) the 1960s. At the same time, those ministers have continued to operate within the systems of paternal and commercial communication control that have dominated British society throughout the twentieth and early twenty-first centuries. As a result, they have made a constant series of attempts to exert authority and regulate the standards of education and media, while trying to appropriate responsibility for the delivery of communications from the state to the market. Subsequently, British public discourse and government policy have also sustained, with great fervour, notions of cultural decline and fragmentation.

The democratic system of communications advocated by Williams and others in the New Left was never instituted or accepted by British political operators. The closest example one can identify is, perhaps, the Scottish political and Labour Member of Parliament Jennie Lee, whose work within the Ministry of Arts during the Wilson administration led to the foundation of The Open University. The OU set no qualification barriers to enrolment in its undergraduate courses and it was at the forefront of curricula design, developing courses in arts and cultural studies previously unheard of in either the ancient and civic universities or the new universities and polytechnics. Neither purely vocational nor a bastion of so-called high culture, Jenny Lee's Open University offered curricula designed to provide students with critical tools for assessing and consciously engaging everyday life, based on the same emancipatory ambitions that the New Left had for cultural studies. In establishing a university based on the principle of access to tertiary education for all, regardless not only of class but also of a student's educational background or their individual motivations, Lee offered a glimpse of the kind of institution that such a democracy of communications might entail.

A305 3-4

THE OPEN UNIVERSITY

Arts: a third level course
History of architecture and design 1890-1939
Units 3-4

Art Nouveau

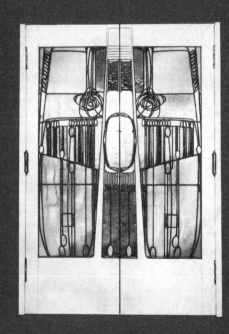

A305 9-10

THE OPEN UNIVERSITY

Arts: a third level course
History of architecture and design 1890-1939
Units 9-10

Expressionism

A305 11 and 12

THE OPEN UNIVERSITY

Arts: a third level course
History of architecture and design 1890–1939
Units 11 and 12

The New Objectivity

A305 19-20

THE OPEN UNIVERSITY

Arts: a third level course
History of architecture and design 1890-1939
Units 19-20

British Design

A305 21-22

THE OPEN UNIVERSITY

Arts: a third level course
History of architecture and design 1890-1939
Units 21-22

Mechanical Services

Broadcasting the Modern Movement

Joaquim Moreno

From 1975 to 1982, The Open University innovated in its use of print media, radio, and television broadcasting to offer the groundbreaking course A305, History of Architecture and Design 1890–1939.

 [A]

Through the course,
students of arts and architecture,
architects,
educators,
and, most importantly,
the general public
were invited to participate in a massive effort to make modern architecture accessible to a wider audience through broadcasting.

The course materials included, in their entirety,
roughly eight hours of film,
ten hours of audio recordings,
and almost two thousand printed pages
produced specifically
for the A305 curriculum.

[B]

Like all Open University courses, A305 had to
find its place within the OU's allotted BBC airtime,
balance its content across radio and television,
and coordinate its media programming with
the distribution of other course materials by mail.

While other OU courses typically involved
            thirty-two weeks of coursework
            paced by televised broadcasts,
            A305 devoted eight weeks
            of its curriculum
            to a hands-on research project,
            consequently reducing
            its television programming
            to twenty-four broadcasts
            directly related
            to twenty-four course units,
            complemented by
            thirty-two radio programmes.

This was a particularly hybrid manner of organizing
the teaching of architecture history to
            an unknown and unseen audience
            rather than
            to a conventional classroom.
Instead of a syllabus, A305 had a broadcasting
schedule prefaced with precise specifications
about the different structures of its television and
radio programmes and their accompanying course
materials. The television programmes were mostly
dedicated to the experience of visiting buildings;
            typically, the presenter
            would move through a building,
            ask basic questions
            about the ways of living it facilitated,

TELEVISION

1 *What is Architecture? An Architect at Work*, Geoffrey Baker (Sat. 15/2 08.55 R Wed. 19/2 17.25)

2 *The Universal International Exhibition, Paris, 1900*, Tim Benton (Sat. 1/3 08.55 R Wed. 4/3 17.25)

3 *Charles Rennie Mackintosh: Hill House*, Sandra Millikin (Sat. 8/3 08.55 R Wed. 12/3 17.25)

4 *Industrial Architecture: AEG and Fagus Factories*, Tim Benton (Sat. 15/3 08.55 R Wed. 19/3 17.25)

5 *Frank Lloyd Wright: The Robie House*, Sandra Millikin (Sat. 5/4 08.55 R Wed. 9/4 17.25)

6 *R. M. Schindler: The Lovell Beach House*, Sandra Millikin (Sat. 12/4 08.55 R Wed. 16/4 17.25)

7 *Eric Mendelsohn: The Einstein Tower*, Dennis Sharp (Sat. 19/4 08.55 R Wed. 23/4 17.25)

8 *The Bauhaus at Weimar, 1919-23*, Tim Benton (Sat. 3/5 08.55 R Wed. 7/5 17.25)

9 *Berlin Siedlungen*, Tim Benton (Sat. 10/5 08.55 R Wed. 14/5 17.25)

10 *The Weissenhof Siedlung, 1927 Stuttgart*, Tim Benton (Sat. 17/5 08.55 R Wed. 21/5 17.25)

11 *The International Exhibition of Decorative Arts, Paris, 1925*, Tim Benton (Sat. 31/5 08.55 R Wed. 4/6 17.25)

12 *Adolf Loos*, Tim Benton (Sat. 7/6 08.55 R Sun. 8/6 07.40)

13 *Le Corbusier: Villa Savoye*, Tim Benton (Sat. 14/6 08.55 R Thurs. 19/6 18.40)

14 *English Flats of the Thirties*, Tim Benton (Sat. 12/7 08.55 R Wed. 16/7 17.25)

15 *English Houses of the Thirties*, Geoffrey Baker (Sat. 19/7 08.55 R Wed. 23/7 17.25)

16 *Hans Scharoun*, Tim Benton (Sat. 26/7 08.55 R Wed. 30/7 17.25)

17 *English Furniture*, Jessica Rutherford (Sat. 9/8 08.55 R Wed. 13/8 17.25)

18 *Edwin Lutyens: Deanery Gardens*, Geoffrey Baker (Sat. 16/8 08.55 R Wed. 20/8 17.25)

19 *The London Underground*, Geoffrey Baker (Sat. 30/8 08.55 R Wed. 3/9 17.25)

20 *'Moderne' and Modernistic*, Geoffrey Baker (Sat. 13/9 08.55 R Wed. 17/9 17.25)

21 *The Other Tradition*, Geoffrey Baker (Sat. 20/9 08.55 R Wed. 24/9 17.25)

22 *Mechanical Services in the Cinema*, Stephen Bayley (Sat. 27/9 08.55 R Wed. 1/10 17.25)

23 *The Semi-detached House*, Stephen Bayley (Sat. 11/10 08.55 R Wed. 15/10 17.25)

24 *The Housing Question*, Stephen Bayley (Sat. 18/10 08.55 R Wed. 22/10 17.25)

RADIO

1 *What is Design?* (sound only) Tim Benton (Tues. 18/2 18.05 R Sat. 22/2 15.40)

2 *The Magazines of Decorative Art in the 1890s* (radiovision) Tim Benton (Tues. 25/2 18.05 R Sat. 1/3 15.40)

3 *Gaudí's Architecture and Design* (radiovision) Tim Benton (Tues. 4/3 18.05 R Sat. 8/3 15.40)

4 *Hector Guimard* (radiovision) Francine Haber (Tues. 11/3 18.05 R Sat. 15/3 15.40)

5 *Tony Garnier: La Cité Industrielle* (radiovision) Dr. Dora Wiebenson (Tues. 18/3 18.05 R Sat. 22/3 15.40)

6 *Ferro-concrete: Hennebique to Perret* (radiovision) Prof. Peter Collins (Tues. 25/3 18.05 R Sat. 5/4 15.40)

7 *Louis Sullivan* (radiovision) Richard Chafee (Tues. 8/4 18.05 R Sat. 12/4 15.40)

8 *Frank Lloyd Wright: Architecture and Democracy* (sound only) introduced by Sandra Millikin (Tues. 15/4 18.05 R Sat. 19/4 15.40)

9 *Glass Architecture* (sound only) Dennis Sharp (Tues 22/4 18.05 R Sat. 26/4 15.40)

10 *Futurism* (radiovision) Charlotte Benton (Tues. 29/4 18.05 R Sat. 3/5 15.40)

11 *The Debate between Van de Velde and Muthesius* (sound only) Dr Marcel Franciscono (Tues. 6/5 18.05 R Sat. 10/5 15.40)

12 *Walter Gropius before 1923* (sound only) Dr Jacques Paul (Tues. 13/5 18.05 R Sat. 17/5 15.40)

13 *'The People deserve their colonnades': Soviet Architecture* (radiovision) Charlotte Benton (Tues. 20/5 18.05 R Sat. 24/5 15.40)

14 *Berthold Lubetkin: Art, Ideology and Revolution* (sound only) Berthold Lubetkin (Tues. 27/5 18.05 R Sat. 31/5 15.40)

15 *Pierre Chareau: Maison de Verre* (radiovision) Tim Benton (Tues. 3/6 18.05 R Sat. 7/6 15.40)

16 *Oriental Lacquer and French Design in the 1920s* (radiovision) Charlotte Benton (Tues. 10/6 18.05 R Sat. 14/6 15.40)

17 *Villa Savoye: Preliminary Drawings* (radiovision) Tim Benton (Tues. 17/6 18.05 R Sat 21/6 15.50)

18 *Basil Ward on Connell, Ward and Lucas* (sound only) interviewed by Dennis Sharp (Sat. 28/6 15.40 R Sat. 12/7 15.40)

19 *Gordon Russell and Modern British Craftsmanship* (radiovision) Sir Gordon Russell introduced by Tim Benton (Tues. 15/7 18.05 R Sat. 19/7 15.40)

20 *The Labour-saving Home* (radiovision) Adrian Forty (Tues. 22/7 18.05 R Sat. 26/7 15.40)

21 *Alvar Aalto: The Failure of Total Design* (radiovision) Ranulph Glanville (Tues. 29/7 18.05 R Sat. 2/8 15.40)

22 *Germany: The Second Tradition of the Twenties* (radiovision) Prof. Julius Posener (Tues. 5/8 18.05 R Sat. 9/8 15.40)

23 *Project Case Study: 66 Frognal, Part 1* (radiovision) Tim Benton (Tues. 12/8 18.05 R Sat. 16/8 15.40)

24 *Project Case Study: 66 Frognal, Part 2* (radiovision) Tim Benton (Tues. 19/8 18.05 R Sat. 30/8 15.40)

25 *Frank Pick: London Transport Design* (sound only) Sir Nikolaus Pevsner (Tues. 2/9 18.05 R Sat. 6/9 15.40)

26 *London Transport Design* (radiovision) Bridget Wilkins (Tues. 9/9 18.05 R Sat. 13/9 15.40)

27 *Berthold Lubetkin: A Commentary on Western Architecture* (sound only) Berthold Lubetkin (Tues. 16/9 18.05 R Sat. 20/9 15.40)

28 *The Mars Group and the 1930s* (sound only) Sir John Summerson (Tues. 23/9 18.05 R Sat. 27/9 15.40)

29 *The Reform of the Skyscraper* (radiovision) Prof. Reyner Banham (Tues. 30/9 18.05 R Sat. 4/10 15.40)

30 *The Work of Isokon* (radiovision) Jack Pritchard (Tues. 7/10 18.05 R Sat. 11/10 15.40)

31 *The International Style Fifty Years After* (sound only) Prof. Henry-Russell Hitchcock (Tues. 14/10 18.05 R Sat. 18/10 15.40)

32 *Conclusion* (sound only) Tim Benton (Tues. 21/10 18.05 R Sat. 25/10 11.20)

TEXTS

1-2 *Introduction*, Tim Benton and Geoffrey Baker

3-4 *Art Nouveau*, Tim Benton and Sandra Millikin

5-6 *Europe 1900-1914*, Tim Benton, Stefan Muthesius and Bridget Wilkins

7-8 *U.S.A. 1890-1939*, Geoffrey Baker, Lindsay Gordon and Sandra Millikin

9-10 *Expressionism*, Tim Benton, Charlotte Benton and Dennis Sharp.

11-12 *The New Objectivity*, Charlotte Benton, Tim Benton, John Milner and Aaron Scharf

13-14 *The International Style*, Charlotte Benton and Tim Benton

15-16 *Design 1920s*, Charlotte Benton, Tim Benton and Aaron Scharf

17 & 18 *Le Corbusier/English Architecture*, William Curtis

19-20 *English Design*, Adrian Forty and Geoffrey Newman

21-22 *Mechanical Services*, Reyner Banham and Stephen Bayley

23-24 *The Garden City*, Stephen Bayley and Tim Benton

SUPPLEMENTARY MATERIAL

Documents (a collection of source material)
Images (illustrated source material)
Radiovision Booklet (illustrations to radiovision programmes)
Radiovision Sheet (a separate sheet of illustrations for radio programmes 17 and 23)

SET BOOKS

R. Banham, *Theory and Design in the First Machine Age*, Architectural Press, (paperback) 1972. £1.75.
Le Corbusier, *Towards a New Architecture*, trans. F. Etchells, Architectural Press, 1970. £1.50.
H. R. Hitchcock, *Architecture: Nineteenth and Twentieth Centuries* (The Pelican History of Art), Penguin, 1971. £6.00.
H. R. Hitchcock and P. Johnson, *The International Style*, W. W. Norton, New York, 1966. £1.50.
N. Pevsner, *Pioneers of Modern Design*, Penguin, 1972. £1.00
A305 Course Anthology, *Form and Function*, ed. C. A. and T. J. Benton with D. Sharp, Crosby Lockwood Staples/The Open University Press. 1975. £5.00.

* Any of the above books can be obtained from booksellers or from the RIBA Bookshop.

and present
other documentary evidence about it.
Radio programmes were, for the most part,
interviews and recorded presentations
by prominent architects,
designers,
and architecture historians
from A305's period of analysis.

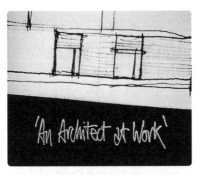

While television concentrated on objects and object lessons, radio recorded and broadcast the voices of the protagonists of the modern movement. The programmes were accompanied by a range of printed materials produced by the Course Team—consulted only by registered A305 students or those who had acquired course unit booklets in bookshops—in which the course's research and didactic texts were compiled. These included

        twelve course unit booklets
        each accompanied by a film strip
        of colour photographs
        with a plastic viewer,
        five supplementary booklets,
        and one anthology
        of primary source texts called

Form and Function: A Source Book for the History of Architecture and Design 1890–1939.

[E]

The supplementary booklets published for A305 included *Radiovision Booklet*, with sequences of selected images to enrich most of the radio programmes;

 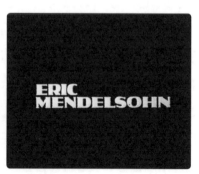

[F]

Broadcasting Supplement, *Part 1* and *Part 2*, with brief guiding texts and questions to allow students to experience media unencumbered by note taking;

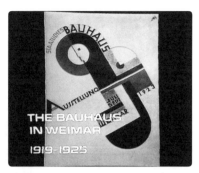

Documents, with reproduced extracts from primary source materials that were either referenced in the course broadcasts or that could help students inform themselves about particular debates within the course; and *Images*, a series of facsimiled translations of important written and visual sources that were otherwise unavailable in English. Finally, the A305 syllabus included a selection of so-called set books, complementary references on theoretical and historical topics:
Le Corbusier's 1923
Towards a New Architecture;

Henry-Russell Hitchcock
and Philip Johnson's 1932
The International Style;
Nikolaus Pevsner's 1936
Pioneers of Modern Design;
Hitchcock's 1958
*Architecture Nineteenth
and Twentieth Centuries*;
and Reyner Banham's 1960
*Theory and Design in the First
Machine Age.*

By both producing and assembling this complex
and compelling web of cross references across
multiple formats,
        A305 was in turn producing
        a layered panorama
        of modern architecture and design.

Although broadcasting was only one of the means
through which A305 was being taught,
        the course was indeed made to be
        broadcast and not simply transmitted.

The course was reaching out to a wider audience than would typically engage with architecture culture, and that audience was being invited to participate in the experience of visiting notable buildings at the turn of a knob on a television set.

[1]

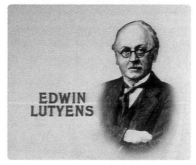

The course was addressing society at large, simultaneously as an educational project aimed at individual development, as a broad mobilization of media for collective cultural transformation, and as a deployment of new broadcasting channels to convey the social meaning of modern architecture. A305 was made open to everybody by the common denominator of broadcasting as a form of teaching, which reached a mass audience at home, individual by individual.

THE LONDON UNDERGROUND

As Raymond Williams argued in his 1974 book *Television, Technology and Cultural Form*, modern society was increasingly one of "mobile privatization" in which

> the idea of the centrality of the home
> became synonymous
> with physical mobility
> and an immaterial connection
> to the outside world.

For Williams, another one of the specificities of new media was that the means of broadcasting were considered more important than the purpose or content of broadcasting:

In broadcasting, both in sound radio and later in television, the major investment was in the means of distribution.... Unlike all previous communications technologies, radio and television were *systems primarily devised for transmission and reception as abstract processes, with little or no definition of preceding content.*

Around the same time,
broadcasting itself was moving into
what Brian Wenham,
a prominent BBC executive
from the 1970s through the 1990s,
called
a "third age of broadcasting,"
as in the title of his 1982 book.
Cable television promised the tailored content of narrowcasting to differentiated audiences, as opposed to the coherent body of content offered by broadcasting to a single, general audience —finally giving use to the four channel buttons of most television sets. Specialized channels were now offering
music,
news,
entertainments,
and sports,
thus making more difficult
the dissemination through mass media
of a unified social narrative.

But A305 was proposing a form of resistance to the rushed replacement of a single channel with a proliferation of specialized channels. It did not conform to an approach of what Williams had called
a "technology of specific messages to specific persons,"
and instead used one of
a "technology of varied messages to a general public."
In 1975, around the same time as the course was first aired, Tim Benton introduced A305 in an article titled "Broadcasting the Modern Movement,"
published in *Architecture Association Quarterly* (AAQ), the journal of the AA School of Architecture in London.

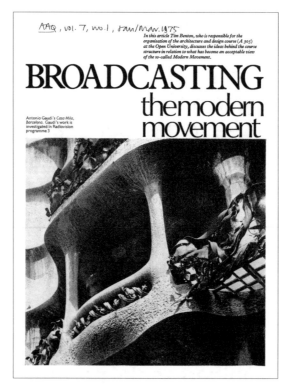

[K]

AAQ, vol. 7, no. 1, Jan/Mar. 1975

In this article Tim Benton, who is responsible for the organisation of the architecture and design course (A 305) at the Open University, discusses the ideas behind the course structure in relation to what has become an acceptable view of the so-called Modern Movement.

BROADCASTING
themodern
movement

Antonio Gaudi's Casa Milo, Barcelona. Gaudi's work is investigated in Radiovision programme 3

Broadcasting was written in capitals across the entire title page

       seemingly to emphasize the course
       as an invitation to tune-in
       to the history of the modern movement.

Benton's article concluded with a full-spread layout of the timetable of A305 broadcasts for the year 1975 and of the scope of its printed materials, pointing to the double commitment of the course.

       On one hand,
       it would reach its students
       through encapsulated study materials
       sent through an intricate mailing service,
       but on the other,
       it would also reach
       a wider public audience
       by using the common language
       of broadcast media,
       even if at the risk of being received
       in the homes of its audience
       like an uninvited guest.

In addition to OU students and the general public, Benton's article was expanding A305's audience to include the architecture community

       —practitioners, students,
       and educators—
       as a third constituency.

AAQ was therefore inviting its readers to be part of a larger body of spectators, to merge with the flow of mass media.

"Broadcasting the Modern Movement" was an attempt to synchronize multiple audiences and mobilize them around the debates framed by the course.

Nevertheless, although A305 was not directed at a limited audience of architects and architecture students, its role within the profession and how it reacted to the changes then occurring within the architecture community were still made explicit by Benton in the strong opening statement of his article:

> Re-interpreting the architecture of the past is a parallel activity to architectural creativity and helps us to understand the ideological and aesthetic framework of our own culture, as much as that of the period under study.

By further proposing
> that "a proper understanding
> of the modern movement"
> was a "necessary feature
> of a healthy architecture climate,"
Benton was inviting the architecture community to critically reflect on the myths of the modern movement before rushing to a quick dismissal of its legacy under the influence of the eclecticism and historicism of the growing postmodern movement.

> Above all, it is a pity to reject the prime tenets of the participants in the Modern Movement without realising in what ways they were wrong, or when they should not be challenged for holding views they did not hold. It's absurd to accuse the International Style in general, for instance, of functionalism. There is no more symbolic or associative statement than that the house is a machine for living in. This is about imagery, not about functions. No one argued for very long that things were beautiful because they performed a function.

This challenge to *AAQ* readers signalled a parallel
between the transformation
of mass media
from single-channel broadcasting
to multi-channel narrowcasting,
and the shift in architecture culture
from the unified discourse of modernity
to the eclecticism of postmodernity.
The field of broadcasting was changing, and so
were the things everybody could watch. But, as
Benton warned, simplifying and rejecting outright
the tenets of the modern movement was a wasted
opportunity to learn from them and would not
produce a newer, fuller perspective on that historical moment. The history of architecture offered
by A305 thus came after the modern movement
but was not postmodern in its perspective or
method. Following in the path of Reyner Banham's
Theory and Design in the First Machine Age,
which Benton describes
as the first "account in English
of the real intellectual background
of the architectural avant garde,"
A305 was paying close attention to other modern-
ities in architecture culture. But it was also rec-
ognizing the "continuance of the classical tradition and the influence of the Beaux-Arts" in the
profession at the time. As Benton clearly states:

Part of the stress in the course is on the alternative
traditions to the One True Path of the Modern Movement.

Episode Two

A305's presentation of various narratives of the modern movement was enabled by television, because it made travelling less-trafficked routes possible and allowed the exploration of previously unseen points of view.

Paradoxically, television also offered
a medium for attending empirically
to buildings that
had otherwise been subjected
to judgments and assumptions
not founded
on direct and careful observation.
The main objective of A305's television programmes was to convey an understanding of built architecture through movement. Photography could suffice to capture the static image of a building,

but the modern viewer
engaged architecture through motion,
and only moving images
could fully capture this relationship.

The range of televisual techniques mobilized by A305 to reframe modern architecture can be understood through two A305 broadcasts:

TV 4,
"Industrial Architecture:
AEG and Fagus Factories,"
written by Tim Benton,
and TV 7,

"Erich Mendelsohn: The Einstein Tower,"
written by Dennis Sharp.
The first was filmed on location,
while the second,
given that the Einstein Tower on the East side
of the Berlin Wall and therefore inaccessible at
the time,
was recorded
in the Alexandra Palace studios.
TV 4 is a strong example of how media brought into
the home both direct observation and the experience of moving through a building, while in TV 7 the
experience of the building had to be dramatized
and made tangible through technological
staging. Though different in approach,
both television programmes shared an
ambition which could only be enacted
through the medium of television.

In TV 4, the A305 Course Team took the opportunity
of elaborating on the almost canonical historiographical exercise of comparing two examples of
early-modern architecture from Germany:
Peter Behrens's AEG Turbine Hall,
built in 1909,
and Walter Gropius' Fagus Factory,
built in 1913.
Rather than simply contrasting the massive yet
thin corner of the AEG Turbine Hall with the
dematerialized glass corner of the Fagus Factory,

A305 used television to turn its analysis into an experience of the two buildings as complex assemblages of moving parts.

The A305 television programmes that were filmed on location were scripted to capture the relationship of the body to space:
> the presenter would typically
> enter through the main door,
> turn their head around,
> go up and down stairs and ramps,
> and position their body in relation
> to the size of various parts of
> the building.

[M]

In the case of TV 4, the eye of the camera pans across an aerial view of German industrial sites, hangs from the gantries that move the heavy parts on the production line in the AEG Turbine Hall, and captures the continuous circular motion of the machines carving shoe lasts at the Fagus Factory.

Other times, the camera simply renders the almost sublime scale of industrial buildings and their structural details —what Tim Benton calls, in the case of the AEG Turbine Hall, Behrens's "functional romanticism"— by filming a small child perched alongside the gigantic hinges at the base of the Hall columns. The AEG Turbine Hall and the Fagus Factory were thus monumental machines, reframed for a general audience as the mechanized cathedrals of the future.

In the case of TV 7, Dennis Sharp brought to life both Mendelsohn's Einstein Tower, built in Potsdam in 1921, and the pathos of Expressionism, by mobilizing the full extent of the BBC's studio production resources and the artificiality of television. TV 7 combines animated tracings of Mendelsohn's design sketches, rotating shots of a scale model of the tower built specially for the programme, a drama-tized voice over of Mendelsohn's words by actor Gabriel Wolf, and archival footage of World War I trench warfare, all accompanied by excerpts from J. S. Bach's *Magnificat*.

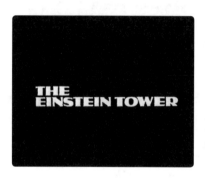 

[0]

Using such an array of media and physical sources was a very efficient way of communicating com-plex ideas to a wide audience from the confines of a recording studio. In *Broadcasting Supplement, Part 1*, Sharp clearly outlines the use of montage as a narrative tool for TV 7:

> This programme tries to trace the conceptual develop-ment of the Einstein Tower starting with an exploration of Mendelsohn's drawing technique and his inspiration in music, especially that of J. S. Bach. The growth of the idea is traced through the war years in the letters and sketches which Mendelsohn sent home from the trenches. After this, a short extract from a recording of a lecture by Mendelsohn in March 1953 describes something of the building of the Tower. Finally we analyse the finished building and see how closely it follows the early writings and sketches.

A305 students would have prepared before watching the programme and, having watched it, were required to go back to the broadcasting notes and respond to the question:

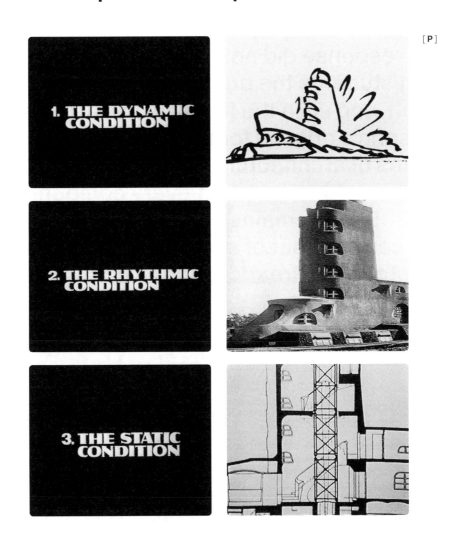

"Do you think that the Einstein Tower can be seen to fulfill Mendelsohn's three conditions of architecture?"

Evidently, this was not an open-ended question and, for the purpose of study, Sharp thoroughly answers his own question:

I think it's possible to see the play between the horizontal and vertical elements in the building as creating the dynamic condition. The 'contours' or outlines of the building correspond to the linear elements in the sketch. The rhythmic condition is created by the surface recessions and protrusions which modify the vertical/horizontal conflict. The static condition can be seen in the reconciliation of these conflicts in a symmetrical, axial plan.

Sharp's response did not preclude the necessity of giving students the primary source for this assertion, and so in the footnotes Sharp presents Mendelsohn's original formulation of his three conditions of architecture from a 1917 publication. Furthermore, to ensure that every component of the A305 unit remained self-contained, Sharp reproduces a full set of scale drawings of the Einstein Tower in *Broadcasting Supplement, Part 1.*

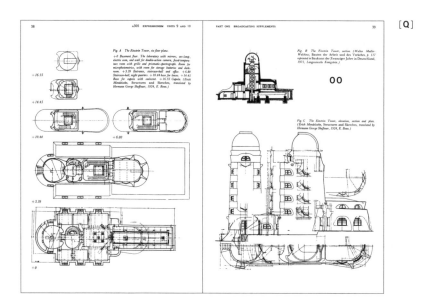

[Q]

As TV 4 and TV 7 show, the doors of many modern buildings were being swung open to a mass audience by A305 and, when that was not possible, the BBC's technical resources were being mobilized to fabricate a visual experience that could emulate an actual visit.

A305's television and radio programmes were intended for multiple audiences. This implied that broadcasts had to be widely accessible and mutually independent from the elaborate web of study materials distributed through complex networks, while remaining part of a coherent whole.
Despite its attempt to use media
in ways that could satisfy
a wide range of viewers,
A305 was gradually losing
ground to narrowcasting,
as were other OU courses.
As a result, it became dislocated from the flow of BBC prime-time programming, further jeopardizing its ability to reach a general audience serendipitously.

By broadcasting the modern movement, A305 was nevertheless inserting architecture history into a wider flow of media,
while also immersing the viewer
in the complex system
of technological,
cultural,
and social forces

that shaped changes
in both the tools of broadcasting
and perspectives
on the modern movement.

Enabled by television, the course was thus an
artifact of a complex interplay
between an emergent
third age of broadcasting
and a modern movement
that was fading from view.
A305 reframed the normative timeline of modern
architecture—bound between the avant-garde
and postmodernism—by rereading modernist
icons through different narratives, perspectives,
and architecture cultures, presented simultaneously through the ever-multiplying channels
of mass media.

[A]–[B]
All stills from television programme
1 of A305, "What is Architecture?:
An Architect at Work," presented by
Geoffrey Baker, 1975. The Open
University. 00525_3167.

[A]
Still of slate board

[B]
Stills of title cards

[C]
Complete list of course materials from
promotional leaflet for A305, History
of Architecture and Design 1890–1939,
1975. Wells Coates fonds, CCA.

[D]–[J]
Stills of title cards from television pro-
grammes 1 through 24 of A305, 1975.
The Open University.

[K]
Title page of "Broadcasting the Modern
Movement," written by Tim Benton,
published in *Architectural Association
Quarterly* 7, no.1, 1975. © Tim Benton

[L]
BBC/The Open University crew filming
the Siemensstadt Estate from Hans
Scharoun's "Battleship Potemkin"
housing block for television programme
9 of A305, "Berlin Siedlungen."
Photograph by Tim Benton, Berlin,
Germany, 1973. Image courtesy of the
photographer. © Tim Benton

[M]–[N]
All stills from television programme 4
of A305, "Industrial Architecture: AEG
and Fagus Factories," presented by
Tim Benton, 1975. The Open University.
00525_3149

[M]
Fagus Factory, by Walter Gropius
and Adolf Meyer, Alfeld, Germany,
1952.

[N]
AEG Turbine Hall, by Peter Behrens,
Berlin, Germany, ca. 1909.

[O]–[P]
All stills from television programme 7 of
A305, "Erich Mendelsohn: The Einstein
Tower," presented by Dennis Sharp,
1975. The Open University. 00525_3044.
© Estate of Erich Mendelsohn

[O]
(left) Title card; (right) Model built
by A305 Course Team of Einstein
Tower by Erich Mendelsohn,
Potsdam, Germany, 1921.

[P]
(left) Caption cards; (right)
Sketch, photograph, and
section of Einstein Tower by Erich
Mendelsohn, Potsdam, Germany,
1921.

[Q]
Floor plans, section, and elevation
of the Einstein Tower by Erich
Mendelsohn, Potsdam, Germany,
1921. Reproduced from *Broadcasting
Supplement, Part 1*, 1975: 38–39.
The Open University. © Estate of Erich
Mendelsohn

[R]
Still of closing credit from television
programme 24 of A305, "The Housing
Question," presented by Stephen
Bayley, 1975. The Open University.
00525_3168

Open University TIMETABLE

Television

The television programmes are detailed case studies of key buildings and design work, eg Le Corbusier's Villa Savoye, Wright's Robie House, Schindler's Lovell Beach House, the Weissenhof Siedlung in Stuttgart and Mackintosh's Hill House. These buildings and many others are filmed in colour and analysed with the help of plans, diagrams, models and historical material. Film offers a chance to visit these key buildings and go through the documentary evidence recording the architects' and clients' intentions and aspirations. It offers a much better analysis of the development of spaces and the quality of environmental siting and context than textbook photographs.

1 *What is Architecture?*
   An Architect at Work
   Geoffrey Baker
   Sat 15Feb 08.55 R Wed 19Feb 17.25
2 *The Universal International*
   Exhibition, Paris, 1900
   Tim Benton
   Sat 1Mar 08.55 R Wed 4Mar 17.25
3 *Charles Rennie Mackintosh*
   Hill House
   Sandra Millikin
   Sat 8Mar 08.55 R Wed 12Mar 17.25
4 *Industrial Architecture*
   AEG and Fagus Factories
   Tim Benton
   Sat 15Mar 08.55 R Wed 19Mar 17.25
5 *Frank Lloyd Wright*
   The Robie House
   Sandra Millikin
   Sat 5Apr 08.55 R Wed 9Apr 17.25
6 *R M Schindler*
   The Lovell Beach House
   Sandra Millikin
   Sat 12Apr 08.55 R Wed 16Apr 17.25
7 *Eric Mendelsohn*
   The Einstein Tower
   Dennis Sharp
   Sat 19Apr 08.55 R Wed 23Apr 17.25
8 *The Bauhaus at Weimar*
   1919–23
   Tim Benton
   Sat 3May 08.55 R Wed 7May 17.25
9 *Berlin Siedlungen*
   Tim Benton
   Sat 10May 08.55 R Wed 14May 17.25
10 *The Weissenhof Siedlung,*
   1927, Stuttgart
   Tim Benton
   Sat 17May 08.55 R Wed 21May 17.25
11 *The International Exhibition*
   of Decorative Arts, Paris, 1925
   Tim Benton
   Sat 31May 08.55 R Wed 4Jun 17.25
12 *Adolf Loos*
   Tim Benton
   Sat 7Jun 08.55 R Sun 8Jun 07.40

13 *Le Corbusier: Villa Savoye*
   Tim Benton
   Sat 14Jun 08.55 R Thu 19Jun 18.40
14 *English Flats of the Thirties*
   Tim Benton
   Sat 12Jul 08.55 R Wed 16Jul 17.25
15 *English Houses of the Thirties*
   Geoffrey Baker
   Sat 19Jul 08.55 R Wed 23Jul 17.25
16 *Hans Scharoun*
   Tim Benton
   Sat 26Jul 08.55 R Wed 30Jul 17.25
17 *English Furniture*
   Jessica Rutherford
   Sat 9Aug 08.55 R Wed 13Aug 17.25
18 *Edwin Lutyens: Deanery Gardens*
   Geoffrey Baker
   Sat 16Aug 08.55 R Wed 20Aug 17.25
19 *The London Underground*
   Geoffrey Baker
   Sat 30Aug 08.55 R Wed 3Sep 17.25
20 *'Moderne' and Modernistic*
   Geoffrey Baker
   Sat 13Sep 08.55 R Wed 17Sep 17.25
21 *The Other Tradition*
   Geoffrey Baker
   Sat 20Sep 08.55 R Wed 24Sep 17.25
22 *Mechanical Services in the Cinema*
   Stephen Bayley
   Sat 27Sep 08.55 R Wed 1Oct 17.25
23 *The Semi-detached House*
   Stephen Bayley
   Sat 11Oct 08.55 R Wed 15Oct 17.25
24 *The Housing Question*
   Stephen Bayley
   Sat 18Oct 08.55 R Wed 22Oct 17.25

Radio

Some of the radio programmes are interviews with famous architects, designers and architectural historians who played an important role in the period covered by the course. Twenty of the radio programmes employ the technique of 'radiovision', in which the speaker refers to specific illustrations by number during his talk. Each of the radiovision programmes is based on photographs, plans, original drawings and diagrams. These illustrations are printed in the *Radiovision Booklet* and special *Radiovision Sheet* for programmes 17 and 23, which are indispensable to an understanding of these programmes. Subjects covered include Antonio Gaudi, Hector Guimard, Alvar Aalto, Pierre Chareau's Maison de Verre, Soviet architecture in the 1920s, Le Corbusier's preliminary drawings for the Villa Savoye, Connell, Ward and Lucas's house at 66 Frognal and London Transport design.

1 *What is Design?* (sound only)
   Tim Benton
   Tue 18Feb 18.05 R Sat 22Feb 15.40

2 *The Magazines of Decorative Art*
   in the 1890s (radiovision)
   Tim Benton
   Tue 25Feb 18.05 R Sat 1Mar 15.40
3 *Gaudi's Architecture and Design*
   (radiovision)
   Tim Benton
   Tue 4Mar 18.05 R Sat 8Mar 15.40
4 *Hector Guimard* (radiovision)
   Francine Haber
   Tue 11Mar 18.05 R Sat 15Mar 15.40
5 *Tony Garnier La Cité Industrielle*
   (radiovision)
   Dr Dora Wiebenson
   (Tue 18Mar 18.05 R Sat 22Mar 15.40
6 *Ferro-concrete Hennebique to Perret*
   (radiovision)
   Professor Peter Collins
   Tue 25Mar 18.05 R Sat 5Apr 15.40
7 *Louis Sullivan* (radiovision)
   Richard Chafee
   Tue 8Apr 18.05 R Sat 12Apr 15.40
8 *Frank Lloyd Wright*
   Architecture and Democracy
   (sound only)
   introduced by Sandra Millikin
   Tue 15Apr 18.05 R Sat 19Apr 15.40
9 *Glass Architecture* (sound only)
   Dennis Sharp
   Tue 22Apr 18.05 R Sat 26Apr 15.40
10 *Futurism* (radiovision)
   Charlotte Benton
   Tue 29Apr 18.05 R Sat 3May 15.40
11 *The Debate between Van de Velde*
   and Muthesius (sound only)
   Dr Marcel Fanciscono
   Tue 6May 18.05 R Sat 10May 15.40
12 *Walter Gropius before 1923*
   (sound only)
   Dr Jacques Paul
   Tue 13May 18.05 R Sat 17May 15.40
13 *'The People deserve their*
   colonnades': Soviet Architecture
   (radiovision)
   Charlotte Benton
   Tue 20May 18.05 R Sat 24May 15.40
14 *Berthold Lubetkin*
   Art, Ideology and Revolution
   (sound only)
   Berthold Lubetkin
   Tue 27May 18.05 R Sat 31May 15.40
15 *Pierre Chareau: Maison de Verre*
   (radiovision)
   Tim Benton
   Tue 3June 18.05 R Sat 7June 15.40
16 *Oriental Lacquer and*
   French Design in the 1920s
   (radiovision)
   Charlotte Benton
   Tue 10June 18.05 R Sat 14June 15.
17 *Villa Savoye*
   Preliminary Drawings
   (radiovision)
   Tim Benton
   Tue 17June 18.05 R Sat 21June 15.

All television programmes are shown on
BBC 2

All radio broadcasts are transmitted
initially on BBC Radio 3 VHF
and are repeated on BBC Radio 4 VHF

18 *Basil Ward on Connell,*
Ward and Lucas (sound only)
interviewed by Dennis Sharp
Sat 28June 15.40 *R* Sat 12Jul 15.40
19 *Gordon Russell and*
Modern British Craftsmanship
(radiovision)
Sir Gordon Russell
introduced by Tim Benton
Tue 15Jul 18.05 *R* Sat 19Jul 15.40
20 *The Labour-saving Home*
(radiovision)
Adrian Forty
Tue 22Jul 18.05 *R* Sat 26Jul 15.40
21 *Alvar Aalto*
The Failure of Total Design
(radiovision)
Ranulph Glanville
Tue 29Jul 18.05 *R* Sat 2Aug 15.40
22 *Germany The Second Tradition*
of the Twenties (radiovision)
Professor Julius Posener
Tue 5Aug 18.05 *R* Sat 9Aug 15.40
23 *Project Case Study 66 Frognal,*
Part 1 (radiovision)
Tim Benton
Tue 12Aug 18.05 *R* Sat 16Aug 15.40
24 *Project Case Study 66 Frognal,*
Part 2 (radiovision)
Tim Benton
Tue 19Aug 18.05 *R* Sat 30Aug 15.40
25 *Frank Pick*
London Transport Design
(sound only)
Sir Nikolaus Pevsner
Tue 2Sep 18.05 *R* Sat 6Sep 15.40
26 *London Transport Design*
(radiovision)
Bridget Wilkins
Tue 9Sep 18.05 *R* Sat 13Sep 15.40
27 *Berthold Lubetkin A Commentary*
on Western Architecture
(sound only)
Berthold Lubetkin
Tue 16Sep 18.05 *R* Sat 20Sep 15.40
28 *The Mars Group and the 1930s*
(sound only)
Sir John Summerson
Tue 23Sep 18.05 *R* Sat 27Sep 15.40
29 *The Reform of the Skyscraper*
(radiovision)
Professor Reyner Banham
Tue 30Sep 18.05 *R* Sat 4Oct 15.40
30 *The Work of Isokon* (radiovision)
Jack Pritchard
Tue 7Oct 18.05 *R* Sat 11Oct 15.40
31 *The International Style Fifty*
Years After (sound only)
Professor Henry-Russell Hitchcock
Tue 14Oct 18.05 *R* Sat 18Oct 15.40
32 *Conclusion* (sound only)
Tim Benton
Tue 21Oct 18.05 *R* Sat 25Oct 11.20

Texts
The core of the course is contained in 12
books (each including around 180
figures and plates – 11 books also contain
colour filmstrips) which are linked to
the programmes. Although these books
are primarily designed as texts for Open
University students enrolled in the
course, they should be of considerable
interest to other students, architects,
town planners and the general reader.
1/2 *Introduction*
    Tim Benton and Geoffrey Baker
3/4 *Art Nouveau*
    Tim Benton and Sandra Millikin
5/6 *Europe 1900–1914*
    Tim Benton, Stefan Muthesius
    and Bridget Wilkins
7/8 *U.S.A. 1890–1939*
    Geoffrey Baker, Lindsay Gordon
    and Sandra Millikin
9/10 *Expressionism*
    Tim Benton, Charlotte Benton
    and Dennis Sharp
11/12 *The New Objectivity*
    Charlotte Benton, Tim Benton
    John Milner and Aaron Scharf
13/14 *The International Style*
    Charlotte Benton and Tim Benton
15/16 *Design 1920s*
    Charlotte Benton, Tim Benton
    and Aaron Scharf
17/18 *Le Corbusier English Architecture*
    William Curtis
19/20 *English Design*
    Adrian Forty and
    Geoffrey Newman
21/22 *Mechanical Services*
    Reyner Banham and Stephen Bayley
23/24 *The Garden City*
    Stephen Bayley and Tim Benton

Supplementry Material
In addition to the texts and the
Radiovision Booklet there are also two
ancilliary books. *Documents* contains over
one hundred pages of documentary
material, including contemporary
German reactions to the first major
manifesto of the International Style, the
Weissenhof Siedlung built in Stuttgart in
1927. *Images* reprints edited versions of
four important visual 'manifestos' by
German architects of the 1920s (the
Arbeitsrat fur Kunst's *Ruf Zum Bauen,*
Walter Gropius's *Internationale*
Architektur and Eric Mendelsohn's
Amerika and Russland-Europa-Amerika),
translated into English for the first time.
Documents
a collection of source material
Images
illustrated source material
Radiovision Booklet
illustrations to radiovision programmes

Radiovision Sheet
a separate sheet of illustrations
for radio programmes 17 and 23

Set Books
Theory and Design in the First Machine Age
R Banham
Architectural Press 1972
paperback £1.75
Towards a New Architecture
Le Corbusier *trans* F Etchells
Architectural Press 1970
£1.50
Architecture Nineteenth and Twentieth
Centuries (The Pelican History of Art)
H R Hitchcock
Penguin 1971
£6.00
The International Style
H R Hitchcock and P Johnson
W W Norton, New York 1966
£1.50
Pioneers of Modern Design
N Pevsner
Penguin 1972
£1.00
Form and Function
A305 Course Anthology
ed C A and T J Benton with D Sharp
Crosby Lockwood Staples
The Open University Press 1975
£5.00

Tim Benton
A305 Course Team chair

Alexandra Palace, London, UK
20 July 2017

Tim Benton [TB]
Joaquim Moreno [JM]

JM   Tim, you developed the A305 course for The Open University and were its main lecturer. How did the project come about?

TB   I joined The Open University at the age of twenty-five, in 1970, and two years later began working on the course A305. I knew nothing about modern architecture at that time. I was working on English eighteenth-century architecture and architectural drawings, but it was a great adventure for me to learn about, and create a learning experience out of, the teaching of modern architecture.

JM   I am curious about your role in The Open University interdisciplinary foundation course in arts. What made the foundation course different from other courses at the OU?

TB   I first contributed to the foundation course in 1970, within months of joining the University. The Open University was committed to interdisciplinary study for various reasons, some of them practical. In order to produce a well-funded course that would have all the support for students who had perhaps not done any advanced study before, we had to have a very large number of students. So the foundation course in the Humanities, A100, even from the beginning, had 3,000 students. That's about three million pounds worth of income. In 1971, over 6,000 students enrolled in the foundation course, and you needed those numbers to have the resources to support students in their first year.

The foundation course also introduced students to the different disciplines within the humanities. We had comparatively more students doing art history and architectural history at The Open University than you would find in Cambridge, or Oxford, or another university, and this was because they were introduced to these subjects in the foundation course.

There was also an ideological dimension to this, in the belief that culture is undivided, and that music, religious studies, history, literature, and art are all part of people's need for creative activity. The foundation course always had introductions to these different topics—I wrote an introduction to art, for example. And then there would be a case study that would bring everything together; in the first foundation course, the case study was industrialization—which fit with the ideology of The Open University and our good old leftist interest at that time, in the context of Workers Education Council evening classes and so forth. Industrialization was a way of looking at culture which was anti-elitist, anti-formalist, and which was to do with the fundamental changes that everybody could recognize in the cities, in the suburbs, and in the places where they lived.

JM You were overlaying mass culture with mass production.

TB Absolutely.

JM And The Open University was mass education, because it operated through mass media and had to be mass produced for radio, television, and print. I'm always taken by the set books for A305, which included *Pioneers of Modern Design* by Nikolaus Pevsner and *Theory and Design in the First Machine Age* by Reyner Banham, because they had to be made massively available for a constituency that couldn't attend or couldn't reach the normal channels of distribution.

TB Our slogan was: "The Open University is open to people, to places, methods, and ideas." We had no entrance examinations, anybody could join, and you could do our courses with what we sent you, or what you bought. The students had to buy the set books as part of the course, but the cost was restricted and a lively trade in second-hand books existed. The students could also buy recommended reading directly from The Open University. Anthologies were always a central part of our approach: read these texts, analyze them, and come to some sort of conclusion. We gave students the extra reading, but not in a direct teaching form. We were not telling them what to think but, rather, allowing them to make up their own mind about texts.

JM Was it you who put Ruskin's text on the opening of the Crystal Palace in the recommended readings?

TB I had a role in that, but it was Aaron Scharf, Professor of Art History, who was really the one involved in this. My connection with the foundation course was the Introduction to Art: my first television programme about cast iron, which we filmed in a foundry in the East End of London. The rest of the programme was done in the studio with black and white photographs and so forth.

This was a classic example of the whole idea behind the course: art applied in an industrial context using the media of the nineteenth century.

JM You wrote a piece in the *Architecture Association Quarterly* in 1975, inviting architects to tune in to the A305 broadcasts. To what extent was the OU replacing the course syllabus with a broadcasting schedule?

TB Timetables were produced for Open University courses and sent to students, while broadcasting schedules were going to anybody who wanted to watch or listen. The AAQ piece was trying to bring together the public audience and the teaching audience.

JM You took all the photos published in that article, is that right?

TB Yes. I've always taken photographs and I came to the history of architecture through taking photographs. When I was still at university I took photographs for two books by Anthony Blunt on Sicilian Baroque architecture and Neapolitan Baroque architecture. I have always taken photographs of whatever I'm doing, and the illustrations for the AAQ article were connected with programmes I had been involved with—I did a Radiovision programme about Gaudí, we filmed the Berlin-Britz housing estate, Behrens's AEG Turbine Hall, and so forth. My visual memory and photographs were an important part of how I worked. I've always believed that you can't teach visual subjects unless you capture the visual yourself. I wish I could draw, but I can't, I take photographs. But with architecture, photography is I think the best medium. The way that you analyze and understand something is by photographing it live, analyzing the building in your photographs, and taking pictures that communicate what you want to say about something.
I also did a huge amount of research for A305. I knew nothing about modern architecture when we started, so I was seeing things for the first time, and often before I really knew about the thing. When I first went to Barcelona and photographed works by Gaudí, I had read almost nothing about Gaudí. It was a complete adventure to be finding out about this material, and taking the pictures was

extremely important to me because it helped me try to understand Gaudí as an architect.

JM   The *AAQ* essay was also trying to place A305 within architectural culture and within the architecture conversation at the time.

TB   There were at least three audiences for the piece. There was the audience of our students: 718 students signed up for the course in 1975. And then there was another audience: the people who could watch the programmes at nine o'clock on a Saturday morning. Right from the start, we had 40,000 viewers of our programmes. These two audiences were extremely important, because in validating the programmes, there was dual approval. The BBC had to sign off on the programme, and they were thinking of the general audience; and the course team had to sign off on the programme too, and they were thinking of academic things —whether the external examiner would be happy with it, whether it was accurate, whether it was fair, and all those academic questions. And there was a tension between those two things.

And then there was a third audience: architectural and design historians who came to the course through the media and who, I realized very quickly, were watching the programmes a lot and were writing to complain about things they didn't like, and so on. It was the programmes that got teachers to look at the printed material, and to be frank, this course—A305—had a big impact on the way the history of architecture and design was taught in schools of architecture for the next ten or fifteen years. And not just in Britain, but in America as well.

JM   And in terms of what you were adding to the historiography, Banham's *Theory and Design in the First Machine Age* seems very important here. There is also a whole other strand of re-evaluating modernity, bringing in other traditions, including the work of Julius Posener.

TB   Julius Posener was very important on the other tradition in German architecture, but we also did television programmes on what, in England, was called the Moderne and which we now call Art Deco. We had a television programme on Lutyens, for example, and one on the semi-detached house.

There were really two different kinds of motors driving the historiography of the course. One was to try to tell the story of the development of modern architecture and design. Why was it that, by the end of the 1930s, every young architect or designer realized that modernism was there, that it was a challenge, and they had to design in order to change the way they worked? That was the first half of the course, through Units 3 to 16.

The second half of the course put together a series of elements that were kind of in the background of that history. The *Mechanical Services* unit, for example, looked at elevators, air conditioning, and all the things that made high-rise buildings possible. We also looked at things like housing, design, and so forth. These were like extra ingredients that the students could use for preparing and presenting their projects, because the whole course, from a teaching and learning point of view, led towards an eight-week project.

The whole point of the project was that the students would choose the subject. They would not be led by the ideology of the course, which was more or less modernist. They would choose a building, which they could visit—they had to be able to see it. They had to be interested in it. They had to be able to get hold of planning materials, and to relate that thing to the themes of the course. Three quarters of the projects were not about modern architecture, they were about semi-detached houses, churches, town halls—buildings that students could find and get access to, and about which they could find documents.

These other things that we did were all trying to support the students in that work, not just in the choice of subjects, but also in the approach. Deep learning is not about giving students a stock of visual images, information, and attitudes. It's about teaching them how to use systems of thought that are different from their own, and which are embedded in a period of time—how to deal with strange, new material.

JM   The OU used images differently in radio broadcasts than in television programmes or print publications. I'm thinking here of the colour film strips that were sent to A305 students with each course booklet, and that worked as visual aids to the radiovision programmes. Could you tell us more about those film strips?

TB We had one film strip of twelve images in each of the twelve books. That's an interesting story because I was reading some feedback on the course the other day, and a student asked, "Well, film strips are nice, but why didn't you print the pictures in colour? It would have been much better." And this is a wonderful example of internal politics. We were told that we were not allowed to print in colour because it was too expensive. However, there was a second budget for kits—the Science faculty sent students microscopes and things like that—so we made a kit with these slide film strips and a little plastic viewer, and we got a separate budget to produce them. A lot of the photographs we used in the film strips were mine and therefore didn't have copyright costs.

Early radio programmes in the 1930s and the 1950s, before The Open University, were already using this idea of radio with accompanying illustrations. I think there was a tradition in Britain for this kind of outreach, which was an important part of the background, if you like, to The Open University. John Summerson was a precursor, of course. Long before A305, he had done a series of radio programmes on the origins of architecture which became a bestselling book, *The Classical Language of Architecture,* in which the illustrations were magnificent. After A305 came to an end, the Pidgeon archive, done by Monica Pidgeon, the editor of *Architectural Design*, and Leonie Cohn, was an interesting tribute to the power of the kind of teaching The Open University was developing: mixing visuals and the spoken voice, which we were absolutely committed to as a form of teaching and of spreading the views of architects or historians.

JM Did the television programmes follow the same approach as the radio programmes?

TB Each one of the television programmes was a case study, and they were meant to be an analysis of how to interpret lodgings. The main aim of the course was to get students to open their eyes, look at things around them and understand them. Just like a music course is about trying to get people to listen to music that they wouldn't normally listen to and understand how it works. The students of A305 were not architects, and one of the difficulties, just like reading music, was teaching them how to read an architectural plan.

The trouble is that published architectural plans are all done in different formats and styles and, when reproduced, they are often small and illegible. So we had a policy of redrawing all the architectural plans in the course, and we provided a plan reading guide that explained, with a key, everything you saw written—the dashed lines, the dotted lines, the overhead beam, the change in level, and so forth—and what everything meant. An architectural plan is like a score. It has information about a building which is not immediately visible and the work of relating a plan to a photograph of an interior and an exterior is one of the fundamental skills of architectural history and this is how we taught it.

On the back of the *Introduction* booklet, as part of the whole idea of deep learning, we had some notes for reading plans with questions, so that students would be prompted to ask questions about any plan that they saw and really work with a plan, not just treat it as a picture. For example, we always had a triangle showing the entrance. We wanted students to go in through the front door, imagine what happens when you go into the hall, what do you see on the right? What do you see on the left? And this is a discipline that we used ourselves and always in our television programmes. We always went in through the front door. We tried to mimic the experience of visiting buildings, because it is the central experience of architectural history, and we tried to excite the students into how to do this in our television programmes.

JM Did this concept run aground among the students who weren't at home and couldn't visit buildings, for example because they were on an oil rig or in prison?

TB These were textbook Open University students, and this is why we had to provide everything students needed at a distance, including objects and things that they could be inspired by. I had a student in prison in Belfast who did his project on the prison, built in the 1890s, and the prison governor let him photograph the original watercolour plans of the prison with little bits of paper covering the security parts. So you can be almost anywhere and find a project. I had an Open University student in the army, who later became a tutor, who became fascinated with Margarete Schütte-Lihotzky and the Frankfurt kitchen. He was a tank commander stationed in Frankfurt and became a feminist. [Laughs] He became a very good tutor.

JM   When you verify the broadcasting times for A305 in 1975, you see that this is education after working hours, education for people who work.

TB   Absolutely. In that year, they typically went out in the morning on Saturdays, I think at nine o'clock, 8:55 or 8:50, and then in the evening during the week. So there were two transmissions of a programme each week, and of course students could record them as well. But later, unfortunately, the BBC drove us into the night-time trans-mission, from 12:30 at night to 5:30 in the morning, and we lost a large part of our casual viewers. Our students would set their video recorders.

JM   But this is the moment where broad-casting is a way of sharing the space with society at large and making a very different contribution.

TB   Yes. As teachers, we were sometimes upset that the popular vision of The Open University was the "university of the air," because a lot of our work went into writing the material, you know, doing a lot of research. But the transmission of television and radio reached an audience that became quickly habitual. The radio programmes were particularly successful in creating regular listening habits. The radio programme times were often better for people to listen to, and there's a whole tradition in the UK of listening to quality radio as a regular thing. The BBC in those days was fairly good, and many families were used to listening to high quality radio programmes in the early evening.

The Open University television programmes were a bit early and they often conflicted with Saturday morning chores and other things. The radio captured a big strand of regular listeners.

JM   In addition to the public television and radio programmes, how was The Open University reaching its students?

TB   The Open University was divided into thirteen regions, and within each region, there was a separate academic structure with a regional study centre that employed the tutors. It's very important to understand that The Open University was not a single point diffusion system. It was always a partnership between the tutors, who actually had contact with the students, and us, who wrote and produced the material.

The tutors had their own voices as well. For example, by the second year of the course, half the tutors were postmodernists who didn't agree with modern architecture. The dialogue between the course team that produced materials and the tutors who commented on the students' work and did the teaching was extremely important.

The system of diffused teaching is important to understand the way we reached our students. We didn't own our tutors and we didn't own our students. Our students were adults. They were not like groups of young people in schools of architecture whom you teach directly and whose work you then examine in terms of your own ideology. Most of the students had their own views about modern architecture. They lived in little Council houses and in semi-detached houses, and although they didn't like modern archi-tecture particularly, they were interested in finding out about it. That negotiation with the culture and interests of other people, of our students, was extremely important.

JM   You wrote, in 1975, in the pages of *The Architect*: "Any day now they're going to start demolishing Quarry Hill Flats, one of the biggest and most spectacular housing experiments of the 1930s. Quarry Hill housed 3,280 people in 938 flats, with an overall site density of thirty-six dwellings to the acre." In using Quarry Hill as a case study for television programme 14, "English

Flats of the Thirties," was A305 actually cutting really close to the bone of its own time?

TB   Using Quarry Hill as a case study for a television programme shows the levels we had worked into it. First, we had a unit about the flat. One of the prejudices most British people have is that they don't like flats, and in the 1970s the big scandal of postwar reconstruction in big cities was already becoming apparent: the disastrous use of high-rise blocks of flats was creating certain difficulties. To understand why flats became a dominant form of housing in Britain, one must go back to the 1920s and 1930s. The unit on the modern flat looks at the origins of apartments and tenement blocks in the great European examples, including the Karl-Marx-Hof of Red Vienna, by Karl Ehn, and the offspring of that building, which was Quarry Hill, in Leeds.

The Quarry Hill flats were also a kind of test of taste, because they were part of our programme on housing estates, the other half of which was Lubetkin's Highpoint 1, a beautiful modernist example. While Quarry Hill is popular housing, Highpoint 1 is expensive, modern, middle-class housing. The programme on the modern flat used these examples to bring into the foreground the social basis of architecture and the whole political question of housing. Quarry Hill was a model of socialist society with collective elements, like a collective garbage system that actually fuelled part of the central heating system. It had collective laundry. It had a whole defensive organization, like Karl-Marx-Hof, intended to give an idea of protection for a socialist community. And it was built by a socialist council.

And Quarry Hill was physically under attack at the time. It wasn't shelled by militia, like the Karl-Marx-Hof had been in the 1930s when artillery was actually fired at the Communists inside and it was part of a civil war in Vienna, but the Quarry Hill housing estate was being left to rot, and the postwar Conservative Council wanted to let it fall down and be destroyed.

To come full circle, when we did this whole unit on apartment buildings, we filmed Quarry Hill flats, and when it was being pulled down and destroyed, an Open University student did his project on it, took photographs,

and was able to show faults in the construction. I think it's a nice example of the way that The Open University did interact with real issues at the time, issues of taste, of social conscience, of why certain things became important after the War, and of events going on in the 1970s. There was a television series at the time, *Queenie's Castle,* with Diana Dors, which was set in the Quarry Hill flats. Of course the students watched *Queenie's Castle* and it would come up in discussions about Quarry Hill.

JM   I imagine that doing research at The Open University was always very complex. If we take Unit 17, *Le Corbusier; English Architecture in the 1930s,* it opens with a photo of Le Corbusier's Villa Savoye, and the back cover shows two alternative plans for the Villa.

TB   And this was something that changed my life.

JM   This booklet changed your life?

TB   Yes. William Curtis, who is a great scholar of Le Corbusier, wrote the two units on Le Corbusier and English architecture in the 1930s. These units were important because they linked what had gone on in the course up until that point to England, to Britain. Because the students lived in Britain, they were, of course, going to base their project essays on English architecture, and Le Corbusier was the main influence on English architects of the 1930s. But William couldn't do the television programme on the Villa Savoye that went with the booklet, because he was at Harvard. So I went to Paris, and we selected the Villa Savoye to make a film about it. And this was something that changed my life, and it's an interesting example of how something that began as a teaching exercise turned into research.

This was in 1973. Le Corbusier had died in 1965, and the Fondation Le Corbusier, which he set up, was just beginning to operate. The drawings for the Villa Savoye were in rolls in Le Corbusier's old apartment, unorganized and completely unsorted. I spent two weeks looking at these drawings and out of that I did a radiovision programme, with this big sheet in which we presented a certain number of drawings that came between the first project and the final project for the Villa Savoye, with this completely different project in the middle. The film won a silver medal at the International Union of Architects in Madrid in 1976, and I later published my research on Le Corbusier's drawings as a book, in 1984.

You might think that, between writing texts and doing television, radio, or radio-vision programmes, the media would be more lightweight, but in fact, in my experience, it was always the other way around. A lot of research that I later developed and that others who were involved in the course later developed, came out of television and radio, because every programme was primary research. You couldn't just reproduce what other people were saying in the secondary literature. For me, these drawings of the Villa Savoye were a complete revelation about how Le Corbusier's mind worked and how he changed it in rather unpredictable ways over the course of designing a house.

JM   How did A305, an architecture history course, end up being exhibited at the Venice Biennale in 1976?

TB   Well, this was a wonderful adventure. Our presence at the Biennale came about for two reasons. One, a young Italian researcher who worked at that time for Mondadori, named Daniele Doglio, came to The Open University and spent a year researching the University. He was an architect and came up with this idea of doing an exhibition at the Venice Biennale. This was also the moment in Italy with the end of the *numero chiuso*, the end of university recruitment numbers being closed by examinations, and there was a big debate about how to make mass, higher education available. The exhibition of A305 was part of that debate.

The question was: should Italy go the direction of The Open University and start teaching by distance teaching methods? There was a press conference, for example, with the Minister of Education and the Minister of Finance. All these people came and they debated this question about the direction of higher education. There was also another press conference with architects like Bruno Zevi and Tomás Maldonado.

JM   How was A305 shown?

TB   The exhibition was a metonymic representation of the course. It was divided up into a series of large screens, which reproduced the covers of the course. So you walked into the course, fortnight by fortnight, and behind the screens were little alcoves where the television programmes were shown on screens. There were radio programmes you could listen to on earphones, there were texts, there were examples of the film strips with the magnifying glass. Six of the programmes were translated into Italian and were then shown on RAI Television —for several years after that, in fact. It was uncritical in a sense.

JM   1976 was also the year Raphael Samuel launched the *History Workshop Journal,* although the Workshop itself had started in the mid-1960s, as an experiment in socialist history. Was Samuel an interlocutor for A305?

TB   The ideology of The Open University about the ownership of history was very much in line with that of Raphael Samuel, who set up the Oral History Society as an offshoot from History Workshop, but I didn't know Raph at the time of A305. History belongs to the people and history should be told out of memory and experience as much as from documents. This was fundamental in The Open University, as was teaching in small collectives that share experience and tell stories. How you transfer that kind of teaching to a distance teaching university is not easy.

There were two ways in which I think that The Open University did it. One was the self-help groups. It was nothing to do with us, students organized themselves. There was a huge students' union, they would meet quite regularly, have tea, talk about their assignments. That shared learning experience was very important.

The other thing was the summer schools. Courses like A305 had a summer school where for one week students would come in and be taught in person. A305 had a summer school in Brighton, at Sussex University. We taught together, we worked together and, the most important thing, we learned what the students were like and what kinds of questions they asked. Summer schools gave students the experience of

traditional university education. They were extremely intense for us too: you were teaching and involved with students from breakfast until two in the morning.
If I can tell an anecdote?

JM   Certainly.

TB   A formative experience for me was in the second year that I taught the foundation course in summer school. I was waiting to ring home—usual telephone on the wall with a long queue of people waiting to ring home—and there was a woman in front of me, on the phone, and she burst into tears. I asked what the matter was. She said that her husband, who was a long-distance truck driver, had just found out she was doing The Open University. She had kept it a secret because, in many working-class families, if a woman tried to improve herself through any learning, it was perceived as a kind of betrayal. And now, this woman had to go home to explain to her husband that, when he was away in his truck, she was doing The Open University.
       So I think that's extremely important: the whole solidarity between students and the conspiracy of education to change, especially the position of women, but also the position of working-class people. We never had as many working-class students as we would have liked, but our mission was there.

12 LB 8 OZ
5.7 KILOS

24"
16½"
11"

IF UNDELIVERED RETURN TO:-
THE OPEN UNIVERSITY WAREHOUSE,
PLOT 16, DENINGTON ESTATE,
WELLINGBOROUGH, NORTHANTS.

TAD 392

1980

CAUTION: When opening these packages
do not damage the cardboard outer cases
or any of the inner packing material —
You must have these to return the equipment
to the University.

The Factory of the Air

Joaquim Moreno

To dematerialize the university and open up the transmission of knowledge, The Open University paradoxically had to construct industrial-scale infrastructure:

> an assembly line
> to produce all the support materials
> for the broadcast courses,
> a complex mailing network
> to distribute those materials
> throughout the country,
> and a place to house
> sophisticated computers
> that could manage the entire system.

The OU thus operated as a kind of post-industrial factory, a mechanical assemblage for dissemination that relied on robust logistical networks and shared telecommunications infrastructure, both material and "of the air."

Although The Open University recorded its television and radio programmes at the BBC studios at Alexandra Palace, in North London, the symbolic centre of this decentralized university was in fact a logistical hub, a campus empty of students, located in Milton Keynes, Buckinghamshire.

Transmitting education through the airwaves
required a new form of network in which the campus
and the classroom were replaced by the operations
building and the studio
      —thus demanding
      a new hybrid space of production,
      a factory of the air.
The control node of the OU production network was
built as a part of the development of Milton Keynes,
one of the last and most well-known of the English
new towns, designated in 1967.

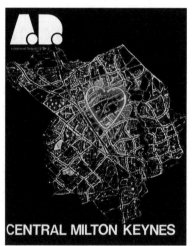

[A]

CENTRAL MILTON KEYNES

In *The Open University: A Personal Account*,
Walter Perry describes how, despite the Planning
Committee's intention that the OU be based in
proximity to Alexandra Palace, available property
within Greater London, mostly office blocks,
was prohibitively expensive and would limit future
development. In 1969, as the Committee was

A.D.

Architectural Design 6/1973   40p

Milton
Keynes

searching, the Milton Keynes Development Corporation offered the OU generous and affordable land upon which to develop a new campus within the boundaries of the new city. Indeed, the first volume of the *The Plan for Milton Keynes*, published soon after in 1970, was explicit about the important role education would play in the new town's development. The first point in the section on the strategy for education clearly states:

As Milton Keynes will be built in a period when knowledge is becoming the most important "industry" it is appropriate to regard it as a "city of learning." The city presents the need and the opportunity for great advance and innovation in education.

It seemed to be a perfect match: the Development Corporation wanted Milton Keynes to be based around an industry of knowledge production and therefore to have a university, which no other new town did; and the Committee needed a compromise
between distance
and expense,

which the satellite location seventy-four kilometres
north of London provided, and room to create a
different kind of infrastructure for higher education.
Thus, a new idea of a city of learning
and a new idea of a university campus
were being formulated simultaneously,
and both were advocating
for open-ended processes
as a counterproposal to more
conventional models of innovation.

[D]

The Open University campus at Milton Keynes
was designed by a team comprised of Fry, Drew &
Partners as site architects and Ove Arup & Partners
as structural engineers. Arup had been offered
the commission in March 1969, in a letter from
Anastasios Christodoulou, the first Secretary of

The Open University, at which point Fry and Drew had already been confirmed as the architects. Ove Arup & Partners showcased their importance in this venture into new modes of knowledge production and dissemination by boldly printing the OU logo on the cover of *The Arup Journal* issue of June 1974. As Frank Coffin, a structural engineer at Arup, writes in "The Open University," his article for that issue of the journal, the ground conditions of the site chosen for the OU campus, a piece of open countryside, posed no problems that could complicate the construction of the campus or its buildings.

It was rather the sense of urgency and the lack of references that forced Arup and the OU to think innovatively about the design process.

According to Coffin, two aspects became apparent from the outset of the project:

The first was that, having decided to embark on such an unusual adventure, everyone from Jennie Lee downwards was desperately anxious to get it off the ground or on the ground so far as the buildings were concerned, as quickly as possible. The second was that, since no one else had started an open university before, there was no previous experience to draw on and no-one really knew precisely what facilities were required for such a venture.

As such, the team decided to develop the campus in two phases, distinguishing between simple structures needed for immediate operations and larger structures to be designed as the work moved forward.

Because the OU produced and circulated educational content through both material and immaterial means, it set into motion a vast flow of information, moving back and forth from its students,
>which required new systems and facilities for processing and handling.

These facilities had to manage not only course materials, but also student information and other data that was processed both through computers
>—that took up entire rooms—
>and through masses of paper

—handled and stored in factory-sized warehouses. The combination of these systems led the OU to become one of the biggest
>printing,
>mailing,
>and publishing operations
>in the United Kingdom.

Additionally, the new types of spaces required for the material and immaterial production and circulation of knowledge exceeded those of conventional universities. According to Coffin, the focus on the institution as a logistical hub, with associated circulation and services, effectively left architects Maxwell Fry and Jane Drew
>"with the problem of incorporating what [were] basically industrial buildings within an academic setting."

They designed warehouses and circulation systems for delivery trucks rather than lecture theatres

Episode Three

and student parking lots, and reconceptualized
traditional campus programmes, such as the library, as spaces of knowledge production inhabited
by faculty instead of spaces mainly dedicated to
students. In order to accommodate
            both industrial and academic use,
            the plan of the OU campus had to
            separate different types of circulation:
for example, large trucks circulated around the
periphery of the site, forcing Arup to reinforce
and regrade these roads so they could withstand
such heavy traffic. Coffin writes that The Open
University project was ever-evolving because
            "the present [was] always quite different
            from the earlier forecasts," such that
            the character of innovation needed
            was always changing
            with respect to the site as a whole.
This new hybrid machine for education,
the factory of the air,
            was thus conceived of piece by piece,
            assembled almost through bricolage
            rather than designed
            as a preconceived whole.

To understand the scope and complexity of operations undertaken by the OU in Milton Keynes,
it is valuable to return to two sources: the significantly discrete chapters on "Course Production" and "Course Distribution" in Walter Perry's

personal account,
        and the descriptions of operations
        published in various issues
        of *Open House*,
        the OU's fortnightly staff magazine
        —the voice from the factory floor,
        so to speak.
Perry was making most of the decisions about the OU machine, and his retrospective view brings to light how unanticipated glitches and jams—administrative, logistical, and financial—were managed. On the other hand,
        the perspective of staff members,
        captured as new infrastructure
        was being put into place,
        better demonstrates
        just how challenging it was to make
        this new kind of assembly line
        run smoothly.
As Perry makes evident, the industrial scale and holistic logic of the OU's operation had a cumulative effect:

> As a publisher the university required not only to determine the methods to be used to control such variables but also to employ the staff to take all the decisions needed daily to implement them. For this purpose we set up a Publishing Division to handle copyright, house style and copy editing, and a Media Production Division to process all illustrations, graphic and photographic, and to be responsible for layouts and briefing the printers, including our own internal print-shop.

This cumulative growth of tasks not only spurred the need for more space but also resulted in ever-increasing building and operation costs. The Open University, which began with the goal of offering a manageable curriculum of four foundation courses soon expanded the scope of its academic output substantially, printing two hundred new publications a year and some ten thousand illustrations, with approximately as many requests to be cleared by the copyright officer. As Perry describes:

In 1971 copies of each foundation course unit were needed for 7,000 students and 1,500 part-time staff, so that almost the maximum economy of scale in printing costs could be obtained by running off only one year's supply, namely some 10,000 copies.... By 1975 we had in stock printed materials valued at about £1 million, and our total warehouse space had grown to some 10,000 square metres.

[F]

A similar level of logistical complexity, but in terms of the circulation of three-dimensional objects rather than printed matter, is expressed in *Open House* through the voice of the staff who managed the OU's distribution network on a hands-on, daily basis. One particular story from 1971 about a new warehouse described the size of the building and everything about its operation, from the loading docks to the boxes of home experiment kits used in science courses,

which were sent out from the new facility, received back at the end
of the academic year,
recycled and reconditioned,
and sent out again the next year
to a new cohort of students:

A visitor's first impression is one of size. At the back of the 20,000 square feet warehouse is a door large enough to admit the British Road Services vehicle which is being loaded with S100 kits in their newly designed cartons.... In October the S100 kits began coming in—returned by students at the end of their first year's course.... 200–300 kits were received back every day. These were then checked fairly rapidly, and later checked in detail.... Checking, re-furbishing and storing has since overlapped the other major task—dispatch. There are approximately 20,000 kits to dispatch in about four weeks.

While it was the television broadcasts that paced OU courses and established a rhythm compatible with part-time study, it was the course materials and home experiment kits delivered through the network of local post offices that truly facilitated distance education. The OU went so far as to manufacture new tools for its technical and scientific courses that would allow laboratory experimentation at home. One particular mechanism, the cheap, compact, and plastic McArthur field microscope, was exemplary of the design innovation that went into producing the home experiment kits. The material that arrived through the post into the homes of every student was

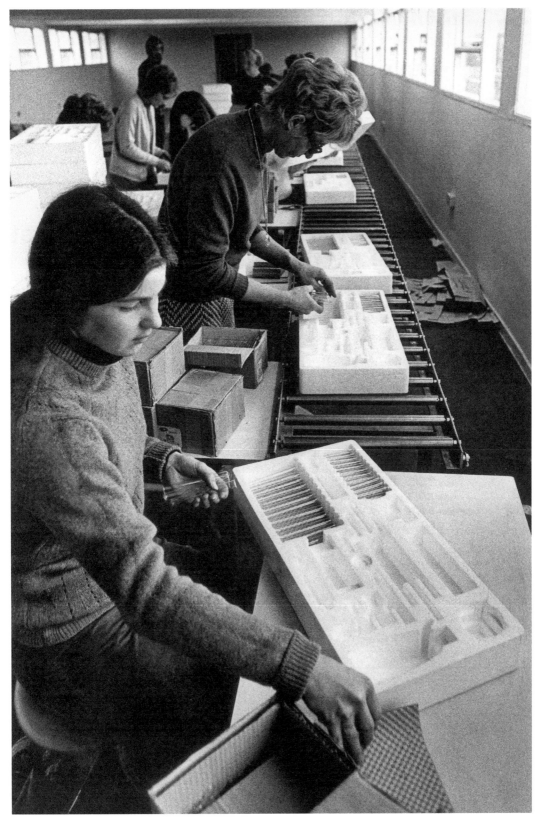

indeed a major component of each OU course, and
rather than overwhelm students
with a single, bulk delivery
at the beginning of their studies,
the OU divided the distribution
of course materials
into manageable packages.
Perry describes in detail the implications of this
decision for the mechanics of the OU within its first
few years of operation:

We therefore decided that we would not send out more than three or four weeks' work in one mailing. Since we were to work to a 36-week teaching year, this meant a total of about nine mailings for each course. In 1971, our first teaching year, there would therefore be 36 mailings covering the four foundation courses. Thus, if we could schedule our system properly (and this was very difficult in practice), we would have to arrange one mailing per week. With student numbers of between 7000 and 8000 in each course, plus all the part-time staff concerned with that course, this meant a dispatch of anything up to 10,000 packages in each mailing. To write out 10,000 names and addresses and to pack 10,000 envelopes, each containing up to nine or ten individual items, is not a job that can be tackled by hand without a very large staff. By 1975, we would be dealing not with four courses, but with something nearer 70. There would then be not one mailing per week, but four mailings per day in a five-day working week. The need for mechanisation was obvious.

[H]

This mechanization happened quickly: within the first year, as a bombastic article headline in *Open House* announced, the Open University had installed "the biggest automatic mailing machine in Europe." The machine, which had nine stations operated by four staff for packing envelopes and applying labels, was the only way to handle the intense frequency of mailings, which could reach "three mailings a week to up to 10,000 students, staff, and tutors." The division which kept this entire operation running, the correspondence service unit, employed a staff of about fifty, working out of a 10,000 square-foot space.

[1]

Computers were also an integral part of OU mechanics from an early stage, operating as gigantic, electronic brains to manage "administration, student computing service, computer-assisted instruction, and research," as another *Open House* article specified. In particular, computer-assisted instruction was evaluated through computer-marked assignments, which could be read and graded for a fraction of the price of tutor-marked assignments, which were assessed manually —and therefore more laboriously.

The combination of these two modes of evaluation established a hybrid system that allowed the OU to provide students with different types of feedback at different paces. For example, computer-marked assignments were used for multiple-choice exams and tutor-marked assignments were used for written submissions that required personalized comments. The balance between the two modes was thus decided based on the content requirements of each course.

However, while the automation of academic processes was advantageous for the OU, it was not necessarily so for the students. As Walter Perry details in his personal account, while the OU ensured that higher education could reach as widespread a potential audience as possible by tapping into existing communication infrastructure —broadcasting, telephone, and postal service networks— this also resulted in a heavily mediated relationship with the student body, which the OU counterbalanced by establishing local points of direct contact between faculty and students, and between students and books:

> It is based on the existence, in almost every town in Britain, of a conventional educational institution that is able to provide us with space for study centres and with part-time staff to use in teaching our students. It is also able to rely on the existence of a very highly developed system of public libraries and an inter-library loan system which allows our students to gain access to almost all the reading material that they require without great difficulty. We have been able to make increasing use of telephone for teaching purposes and telephone tutorials have been a growing feature of the teaching programme in some of our more advanced courses.

The OU thus employed a series of overlapping networks, with various densities and levels of interaction, to expand its campus to the edges of the country through dispersed study centres. As Perry explains,

> to support the broadcast components of its courses, the OU was "based on a centrally controlled system backed up by the provision of copies of the broadcasts in regional centres."

Study centres were stocked with both
the materials for the four foundation
courses as well as playback equipment
for viewing and listening to recordings
of the television and radio programmes
—such as the Hacker radio, which was rebranded
with the OU logo and included in the standard list
of supplies for local centres. Specifically, the OU
developed a non-recording audio cassette player
for listening to radio programme tapes, which could
only play and rewind, and used a compact table
projector that could replay television programmes
from their original 8mm film cassette format.

[K]

But the localized network was so extensive that,
although the OU sent recordings of the foundation
course radio programmes to every study centre,
it could only afford to supply the foundation course
television programmes to the fourteen study centres that were outside of BBC2 broadcasting range.

Other centres had to request copies from their respective Regional Offices, which held a full library of films that could be borrowed by a local tutor or counsellor, on behalf of students who might have missed the original broadcasts or wanted to consult them for study. For students not in synchronicity

        with the OU's broadcast programming,
        the study centres provided
        specific, localized moments
        of resynchronization
        of the learning experience.

The OU's 270 local study centres

        were open weekday evenings,
        and sometimes weekends,
        and they were typically staffed
        by a part-time tutor.

Given that part-time OU tutors were only expected to undertake 10 percent of a full-time workload, as Perry specifies, the OU "had to employ no less than 3380 part-time tutors and counsellors to cover the needs of [their] students in 1971." Local tutors and counsellors were the hinge between the overall OU network and the students;

        they were the interface between
        a centralized administration
        and production of knowledge,
        and a dispersed and often isolated
        student body.

In an article called "Networks in the Open University System," in *Open House*, Dennis Mills, a social sciences tutor, reinforces the importance of local infrastructure to the OU's reach:

> In unit 4 of "Understanding Society" our students are introduced to the concepts of networks and systems in the geographical context. The Open University has, of course, produced its own geographical network stretching across the country.... The study centres ... are the corner-stones of the network and are broadly in accordance with general population distribution in the region.

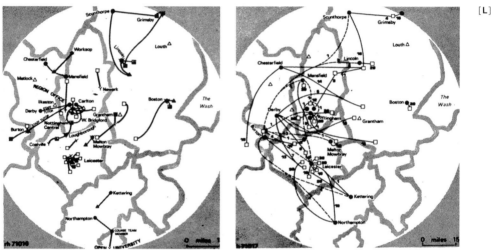

[L]

Mills maps the distribution of study centres in the East Midlands, both with and without tutors on location, and the movement of students and correspondence tutors between these centres and their homes or workplaces. In doing so, Mills visualized

the more concrete, fine-grained level at which the OU's teaching model was actually deployed.

As it turned out, the availability of high-quality local tutors throughout all the regions of OU operation was an unexpected resource. As Perry describes,

> initially,
> the OU had only planned to provide
> tutorials by correspondence,
> using the same postal networks
> to distribute knowledge
> and to evaluate its reception,
> but early evidence of tutor availability
> opened up the possibility
> of face-to-face teaching
> and encouraged the OU to adapt
> its strategy to include class tutorials.

Nevertheless, to avoid jeopardizing the mandate of distance learning and the operating budget of the university, the OU administration insisted that collective sessions be offered only as a supplement for students in need of more guidance, rather than as a fundamental part of a course's structure. This balance was the great innovation of the OU's blended system:

> combining distance education,
> centrally produced
> and locally distributed,
> with a network of mobile tutors
> answering the phone and interacting
> with students at local centres
> on a more personal basis.

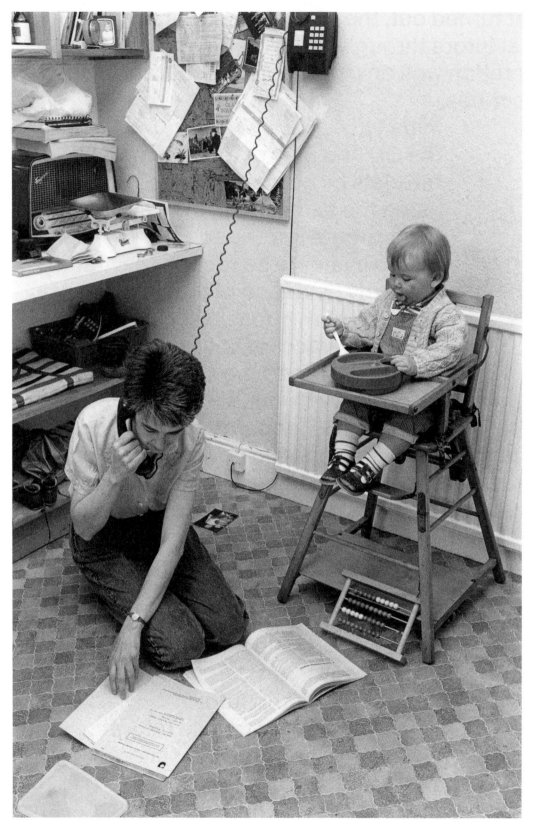

Episode Three

Despite the complexity of its infrastructure, The Open University still lacked the residential facilities and teaching spaces common in conventional campuses, and yet it occasionally needed them.

       This posed a particular logistical problem in the case of the OU's annual, intensive summer sessions,

in that neither the Milton Keynes campus nor the regional and local centres could provide the space the OU needed to offer its students a sample of campus life and of close interaction between faculty and students. The OU therefore had to rent spaces from other universities when their campuses were otherwise empty and available for several weeks of intensive learning.

       Contrary to the typical academic schedule, OU students only had the opportunity to dedicate an extended period of time to study, and in a location solely intended for study, during vacation periods.

The summer sessions therefore had to take place at the moment when the free time of working adults coincided with the free space made available by conventional students vacating campuses.

       OU students were thus borrowing, perhaps paradoxically,

from their time of rest and leisure
to participate in
an intensive collective
learning experience
in the space of
conventional classrooms.
The intricate interdependencies among these
superimpositions make evident the effects of
scale in the operation of The Open University's
"factory of the air" and the complex integration
of post-industrial machinery into the production
and dissemination of knowledge.

[A]
(left) Cover of "Milton Keynes," special issue of *Architectural Design*, no. 4, 1974; (right) Cover of "Central Milton Keynes", special issue of *Architectural Design*, no. 14, 1975. © John Wiley & Sons

[B]
Cover of "Milton Keynes," special issue of *Architectural Design*, no. 6, 1973. © John Wiley & Sons

[C]
Axonometric drawing of The Open University Campus by Fry, Drew & Partners, Milton Keynes, England, ca. 1972. Reproduced from *Open House*, no. 55, 27 January 1972: 21. The Open University. © Estate of Maxwell Fry

[D]
Cover of *The ARUP Journal*, June 1974, https://www.arup.com/publications/the-arup-journal/section/the-arup-journal-1974-issue-2. © ARUP.com

[E]
The Open University warehouse staff checking science kits before they are dispatched to students. Reproduced from *Open House*, no. 72, 25 May 1972: 4. The Open University.

[F]
The OU Printshop Manager and staff working on Media Development's 36 foot Macey Multibinder. Reproduced from *Open House*, no. 55, 27 January 1972. The Open University.

[G]
Open University home experiment kits being packed by staff in the University's warehouse. Wellingborough, England, 24 November 1970. The Open University. 591-9A.

[H]
The Open University mail room staff sorting incoming mail at Walton Hall. Photograph by Chris Ware, Milton Keynes, England, 1971. © Getty Images.

[I]
The Open University's £225,000 ICL 1902A computer being installed in the air-conditioned computer room at Walton Hall. Reproduced from *Open House*, no. 31, 7 January 1971. The Open University.

[J]
A computer tape machine at Walton Hall. Photograph by Peter Trulock, Milton Keynes, England, 9 February 1971. © Getty Images

[K]
Students attending an Open University study centre to watch a recording of an OU broadcast on a Technicolor 1300 projector. Reproduced from *The Open University: A History*, written by Daniel Weinbren, 2015: 79.

[L]
Dennis Mills, "Networks in the Open University System," *Open House*, no. 31, 7 January 1971. The Open University.

[M]
An OU student working on a course at home, looking through her course books while speaking on the phone. Nottingham, England, ca. 1988. The Open University. 000000700057

Nick Levinson
A305 Series Producer

Alexandra Palace, London, UK
18 July 2017

Nick Levinson [NL]
Joaquim Moreno [JM]

JM Nick, you were with A305 through the whole story: from the making and through the life of the course until its demise in 1982.

NL Well, I'm the only survivor of the BBC production team, so you didn't have much choice in who you could speak to. [Laughs] But I was producer of the A305 architecture and design course. Worked with the course team very closely, from… I don't know when we started working on it. It went live in 1974.

JM How did it all begin?

NL I remember talking to Tim Benton about it very early on, before the course was approved by the University. I knew very little about architecture of this period—modern architecture—and Tim and I talked a lot about architecture but mainly about Georgian and Victorian architecture. Then Tim worked on a proposal for the course and it was approved by the Arts Faculty and the Professor of Art History. It was then put forward and approved by the University as a course. The next stage was for the course to go, as all courses did, before the University's Broadcast Sub-committee that awarded—or didn't award—broadcasting resources to a course. We were bidding high, the maximum, because we were bidding for twenty-four television programmes and thirty-six radio programmes.

We weren't being modest and we—Tim and I—had got a lot of arguments together and a lot of outlines, and we went before this committee which was a bit of a make-or-break thing because we didn't know how it was going to go.

The members of the committee were from all over the University, but not from our Faculty, and it was chaired by Russ Stannard, who was, I think, Professor of Science or Technology. He looked at our proposal and said, "Well, why are you asking for film? Because buildings don't move." And it was a very good question. Buildings don't move so why film them? And we thought for a while—and I can't remember how we came up with it, but it was probably Tim, not me, I expect—and we explained that buildings don't move but humans move through buildings, and you experience buildings through moving through them. So that was accepted and we were rewarded a good amount of resources of studio and film to get on with the work.

And of course, it was clear from that moment on that our programmes were going to show the experience of moving through space as much as possible. Obviously, you could do that more in the film programmes for which you could go out on location. You could achieve it in a slightly less dramatic way in the studio, using stills, plans and models. It was a huge jump forward from the

125

architectural history courses I did when I was a student at The Courtauld Institute, which were based on a single photo per building in a book, black and white and grainy, taken in 1924, you know?

JM   I assume John Berger and the series *Ways of Seeing* were somehow the model of the way you wanted to do television.

NL   Well, it's a good starting point but he was never a model. I thought about this. His series went out in 1972, and, at the OU, we'd already started trying to work out our first art history programmes beginning in 1970. We were very much on the same lines and same communal interests, but of course Berger was trying to do something very, very different—less historical. He was making very successful programmes, produced by Mike Dibb, almost entirely about painting, and he was deconstructing the assumptions we have in the way of looking at art. With The Open University, we were trying to do something different. We were hoping students would be able to do this kind of deconstruction in the course of their careers, but we have the business of actually teaching what it was all about and trying to interrogate the works of art or buildings to find out what the intentions were historically. We weren't so interested in the accretion of what culture has applied to them, which is what I think John Berger was mostly concentrating on.
But—as you know—*Ways of Seeing* were very important programmes because they came out as antidotes to Kenneth Clark's *Civilisation*. I remember, when I worked in BBC Music and Arts in 1969, that Mike Dibb and more critical colleagues were told by the head of the department, Stephen Hearst, to stop making derogatory comments about *Civilisation* and stop mocking Clark. And Mike's response was to make this brilliant series.

JM   I thought the BBC wanted *Civilisation* as the model for OU?

NL   They may have, because *Civilisation* had its good points. It was a thoroughly enthusi- astic and educating series of programmes. It opened people's eyes to art, but it was very much presenting art as a manifestation of the triumph of the best in "civilization" in a way which nowadays we would question —and we had started questioning it then. We had tried to devise something different.
Peter Montagnon, the first head of Open University Productions, had been the co-producer of *Civilisation* and was very per- ceptive. He realized that we wouldn't make programmes that would interest students if we had academics speaking to the camera as if they were in a university lecture theatre. It could be very boring. So he encouraged us to use more televisual production values. For one thing, I remember that the very first programme I did for the Arts Foundation course was with an academic called Catherine King. She was working on Bernini's *Ecstasy of Saint Teresa*, looking at how the form functioned by expressing complex religious meanings.
It was a whole programme about one sculpture, which was very different from what John Berger was doing. I went to Peter Montagnon and said, "I don't know how to do this, I don't think we can afford to do film." So we thought, well, the way to do it was to take lots and lots of still photographs from all different angles, film them on a rostrum camera, and edit them together.
Another type of programme we did were Studio Programmes, like the A305 programme on the International Exhibition in Paris, in 1900.

JM   Yes, I remember. There's a lot of sound to it.

NL   We're talking about a twenty-four- minute programme. We used eighty-eight captions shot by studio television cameras in real-time. The captions were sheets of cardboard with black and white photos stuck to them. I can remember coming in at six in the morning, with a pile that high of captions. They all had to be copied from books before- hand in our photographic department downstairs, then mounted and arranged so that they would be divided up between four stands, and the four cameras would go from one to the other. And of course, we weren't supposed to stop and start once we started recording. If we did it more than once or twice, our bosses got very angry, because you had to physically cut the videotape with a splicer like you cut film and you glue it together, and you had to re-record and re-lay the sound over the cut. It was a hell of a lot of editing—time consuming and very expensive!

And then there were back-projections, which were slides the presenters stood in front of. And there was some music and an actor's voice that all had to be mixed together in real time.

The Universal International Exhibition, Paris, 1900 broadcast, it was all planned out, then recorded over two days: 9 and 10 August 1972. Four cameras. Three zooms. One boom. Tapes. One floor monitor. A TK—that's a telecine, a machine that splices in film, like archival footage. And I would be directing the cameras, to pan left or right, to zoom in or out, to track and so on, and my PA would be calling, "shot number 98 on camera 4, camera 3 next ... change caption on 3 ... on three ... caption 10 .... Standby TK," and so on. We were tightly packed into a gallery or control room, and chain smoking. It was nerve-wracking.

JM   Wow.

NL   That was the Studio Programme, one kind of programme we did. Later, there were hybrid programmes for which we were allowed to use a bit of film and introduce them into the studio. Very expensive to do, but you might shoot a building on location and cut that in.

And then All-Film Programmes came about. The programme on Charles Rennie Mackintosh was the first colour film we did for A305, and it was my first ever all-film, on-location programme. We had one day to film it.

JM   With Sandra Millikin.

NL   With Sandra Millikin. And it wasn't anything like enough time. I'd never done it before, and we ran out of time because we only had the crew for one day. I had to go back up to Scotland with our house photographer, David Amy, and he took lots and lots of 35mm slides which we then filmed on a rostrum camera and cut in.

Later on when we did all-film programmes, like the Villa Savoye—those we filmed in two days. But I think these limitations made us think about what the content could be. The best use of television was probably to concentrate on one building, rather than going around filming lots and lots of different ones. But in the Studio Programmes, ironically, you could use millions of stills and show more locations, because studio time was budgeted as a resource, whereas film was cash.

There were always huge controversies about production values. On one side were people who wanted to be more like BBC General Service. They would like to have music, to make it like *Civilisation*. On the other side was the idea to making the programmes more austere—austerity was a good word in those days [laughs]—to have it as simple as possible and to make the programmes concentrate on the evidence, have simple graphics, simple title sequences, no incidental music, and put all of the money which was available into locational filming.

And we never resolved these tensions, and they always kind of played off against each other. But they were also questions about what the programmes were really about. Were they about self-glorification? Were they about teaching? Who were the people we were addressing? What sort of education were we purveying? Did we want to show off to the general public? Did we want to be thought of and seen in the Sunday papers as rivals to the BBC? Did we not mind about publicity?

So all these questions came out. None of them were ever formally resolved. It was always a moveable discussion in each different subject areas.

JM   Perhaps we can try to reconstruct a little bit the universe that was being assembled, for example in the programme about the Einstein Tower by Erich Mendelsohn.

NL   Yes. Mendelsohn said that the idea of the Einstein Tower came to him when he was in the trenches in the First World War, listening to Bach and drawing. We tried to recreate that process using Mendelsohn's voice, read by Gabriel Wolf, who was a very well-known voice-over actor at the time. And we animated the drawings to make it look as if they were being drawn, developing to Bach's *Magnificat* as the music grew and swelled. It was cleverly done by a graphics artist called Pauline Talbot who transferred the drawings onto a sheet of acetate, enlarged them quite a bit and filmed them frame by frame as she scraped them away. So they went from full drawings to nothing. The animation was then played in reverse to give the effect of the drawings growing from a blank page. It was very good how the animation worked.

JM   You had a very short time anyway, to make the programme.

NL   Very short, you started recording at about 6 p.m. with a view to wrap up by 7 p.m. You have to plan it all, come in to rehearse it in the morning then record it without stopping and starting—unless you really had to. I mean, you'd probably get it wrong in a few tries, but you were supposed to get it right in nearly one go!

We had to make the Mendelsohn programme in the studio because we could not get permission to film in what was then the GDR. When we filmed Hans Scharoun's Mohrmann House in West Berlin, it was the last house before the Wall, and then somewhere on the other side, they said about half a kilometre, was the Einstein Tower. But we couldn't see it. For the programme, we used a scale model made by our Special Effects Designer, Jerry Abouath.

When we filmed in West Berlin—the Siedlungen programme, the Industrial Architecture programme, and the Scharoun programme—it was pouring rain the entire time we were there. We had our own BBC crew, but we used German electricians, grips, technicians, and a German fixer, borrowed from I'm not sure which German television channel.

JM   I was always very curious about how you produced drawings for A305. I saw a letter you received from the Frank Lloyd Wright Foundation, complaining about the drawing you had retraced. Did you do tracings to facilitate copyright permissions?

NL   If you were completely redrawing an architect's plan, you wouldn't need permission, but the reason we usually redrew or made models of plans was to make the plans easier to understand on television. Sometimes we wanted to use original drawings and

needed permission, it was very unusual to be turned down. The copyright owners often misunderstood how the images were being used because television was a different medium than print. Tim used the original Le Corbusier plans for the booklet about the Villa Savoye, and that was alright, but they were too faint to be shown on television so we had to redraw them for the programme. The Frank Lloyd Wright plans were also too finely drawn, so we redrew them as well.

Copyright was a big issue in all these things. You had to be on the right side of it otherwise it was a nightmare. For the Paris Universal Exhibition programme, the majority of the pictures came from a book which I think Tim bought in Paris from a *bouquiniste* on the Seine. It didn't have any photo credits, didn't have an author, so there was no worrying about copyright.

But for other things, we would have to write to the owners of the copyright to get permission, to use paintings and drawings by Scharoun for example. When we first started, there was just one man running BBC copyright, Mr. Walford, a solicitor and a most charming man who, if you had a copyright problem, would sort it out for you. But later on, with the modern art series, when all these works of art which we were filming had very closely guarded copyright, it became terribly complicated. When you're making programmes about modern art, there's a thing which you can do in British law called fair-dealing. If you film a work of art for the purpose of criticism or review and identify it, you can get away without paying copyright, but you have to make sure that you identify and review every picture you film.

JM   And how did it work with architecture? With the buildings?

NL   On the one hand, you do have a certain right to film a building from the public highway without getting permission. That may have changed now, but we used to do that quite a lot. Otherwise, the rights to film a building rest in the owner of the building, so you have to get permission from the owner to go on their property and film. You have either a contract or, if it's just, "Can I stand in your front garden and shoot film?" you just agree to a small facility fee on the spot.

But of course there was a problem when we tried to get the OU to agree to make the architecture and design series available for sale to other universities. The OU was balking, saying that it would be too costly to renegotiate third-party copyrights.

JM　How was The Open University sharing that particular inversion: television being the cultural media that introduced books rather than books simply going into programming?

NL　With the University, the publishing was done entirely by the OU. The BBC didn't publish any books for The Open University, They just had the agreement to give it so much time and production resources in return for money from the OU. As an organization, the BBC General Service did not care an awful lot about The Open University. The Government hung the University on the BBC, the BBC played the game and set it up, but they did not try to develop it.

The development of OU educational broadcasting was so much on a separate track than the BBC General Service that the two didn't really overlap. Our head of BBC Open University Arts faculty, Nancy Thompson, who was a brilliant producer, was very much in the rhythm of working with The Open University and sharing their values. She also had a lot of BBC production values, because she was someone who had cut her teeth in the 1960s on the arts series *Monitor,* and had even worked for Kenneth Clark during the War, at the National Gallery.

Nancy Thomas invited the BBC Music and Arts department for lunch at the Alexandra Palace Studios. The head of that department then was Alan Yentob, who said to me, "Well, how do you find it working at The Open University?" I said that one thing I really liked was the feedback we got. The Open University had a brilliant feedback department where someone was in charge of researching how our programmes were received by students. Yentob replied: "I don't care what people think of my programmes, as long as I know they're good. That's all I care about." And I think that showed me the real difference between the approaches between the BBC General Service and us at that time.

JM　Another difference was how you used radiovision. Could you tell us more about that?

NL　Radiovision is not purely radio because it is attached to pictures, in the same way videocassettes are not purely transmitted television because they are recorded and, therefore, available to be watched anytime. Radio programmes that work with visual aids, like radiovision, also go much further back than videocassettes. There even was a series about art done on BBC radio before the War, for which transparencies were sent to viewers who requested them. But it was a rather elite programme for educated people, probably for a rather specialized audience.

Then there was a radio producer at the OU Production Centre, Helen Rapp, who had done a series called *Picture of the Month.* They sent out a printed picture, like Degas's *Dancers,* which you could pin up on the wall, and then there would be a talk about it. For us, in A305, radio was a resource to get people talking about art, but it had poor visual content. So we came up with the radiovision booklet, which was extremely successful because we were able to refer the students to the pictures published in it before the programme, have them do certain exercises using the broadcast supplements, listen to the programme which referred to specific pictures, and then do follow-up exercises.

So to revise the course, you would go to the broadcast supplements: you have images, all the notes, and the questions. These questions weren't directorial in the sense that we said, "This is what the answer is," but, "This is how I would answer them." So the students were also being given models of how to ask questions about a building to use in their own projects, and then afterwards to answer them and justify their answers. We were able to use the ephemeral character of radio to really maximize the cognitive process by which people talk and think about art and architecture. Radiovision, I think was a great success. And it was used for other courses after this.

JM　So all those are strategies that came about because A305 was transitional: half of the course was film, some in colour, but most in black and white.

NL Yes.

JM So the film strips that came with the radiovision were bringing back the high definition of the image to the listener along with colour, creating a hybrid that breaks away from technical limits.

NL That's right. It was very much, as you said, transitional. At first, we had the old black and white film—the old black and white television camera equipment we'd inherited from other parts of the BBC that were switching into colour. We were eventually colourized. Everything was changing during the production of A305.

And I think that when A305 started, videocassettes possibly existed, but people didn't have the machines, and we didn't use them. By the time the course was half-way through, everyone had the machines, and people could copy the programmes from transmission and view them at home at different times, which made a huge difference.

At the time, the BBC and the OU resisted sending out videos to students because they insisted on something they had inherited from the beginning of the OU: that radio and television were not totally essential, that they were only there to interest students. I think they came to see the broadcasts as essential in the 1990s or something like that, for more specialized third-level courses.

Videotapes liberated people from tele-vision programming but, on the other hand, it sort of ended the dramatic excitement of live television and of people making the effort to capture the programmes with the help of broadcast supplements. It became something they could do much more on their own time.

In later courses, the evidence one could study with videocassettes was also different, because you could give students a view of a building with an exercise saying: "What questions would you ask about this building? View it and then stop. Read the notes. Then watch it again without commentary. And then what do you think of what our interpretation is? Have we got it right or are there other questions?" So you could do some much more complicated things with it.

JM I always thought about this as a moment in which The Open University was a bit less open. That's when the relation between The Open University and the general public changed: the time limits, the programming, the way The Open University was reorganizing the flow of the BBC, and the way the OU's way of teaching was reorganized by videocassettes.

NL In the days when Open University courses were transmitted publically, we had a different relationship with the public, and we got lots of letters from people who weren't students. They would write to us, BBC producers, rather than to the OU to say they watched the programming, or that they thought it was wonderful they got a chance to learn about architecture and other sub-jects. We got many letters like that, and they also wanted more information about how they could find out more, where they could see more of it, what the music was, whose voice they had heard. Things like that.

JM So the end of broadcasting you are speaking about was also the end of being responsible for speaking to everybody, in public, and of going through the BBC standards.

NL Yes, that's very true, and it was the openness of live transmission which was so exciting at the time. You really felt that people were out there—students and non-students—getting this material that they weren't getting from anywhere else. But with that, of course, came the responsi-bility of having to fit in with BBC values.

JM To entertain, educate, and inform?

NL Not so much that: I'm thinking of cen-sorship. The BBC had to keep a weathered eye on what was suitable for the time it was transmitted. If controversial content, usually bad language or sexually explicit content, was going out at a time that was considered unsuitable for that sort of programme, then the BBC could get very upset about it.

I was supposed to be a faithful BBC employee, but I was talking to the other side, to The Open University, who were appalled at this idea of the BBC censoring an academic course they had approved. When we did Jean Genet's *The Balcony* for a Drama Course (A307), the Controller of BBC 2 wanted cuts to the version the OU and BBC had already approved. Because the play is set in a brothel, we thought it was important to show that this was a not only a kind of brothel of the mind, a brothel full of fantasies. For instance, there's a Bishop who comes to confess to a girl played by a very beautiful black actress, who takes off her top. You briefly saw a bit of topless imagery. It was not dwelled on or anything. The BBC was very insistent that all that had to go. The OU refused, and the play wasn't allowed to be transmitted.

But *The Balcony* was always shown at the summer school. It was a big event. The students wanted to know all about censorship, talk about why the play was banned, and how the BBC had the right to do it. I used to go down to summer schools and do a talk about it.

JM   That's a very productive tension. This brings to mind Reyner Banham's work on Los Angeles, and his idea of a structure behind the city—or in this case, behind the scene.

NL   Yes, that's right. I think Banham was a big influence on the course, and he followed what was going on very closely, gave us a lot of support. He developed a complete socio-economic analysis of the structure behind Los Angeles, which is really a Marxist methodology, isn't it? Understanding something in its whole historical and cultural context. There are similar structures behind everything, including behind what was going on in the OU and the BBC. Some of the newspapers had got it into their heads that the OU was a Marxist organization, which of course it wasn't. There were complaints that some courses had Marxist bias, which they may have, but others didn't.

There may have been some old Marxists at the OU, but it wasn't a sort of crude example of Marxism taking over. Some of our courses were influenced by Marxist methodology, like the programme we did for the Modern Art and Modernism (A315) on The Beaubourg, presented by Michael Baldwin. It was based on Jean Baudrillard's analysis of The Pompidou Centre, or The Beaubourg, in Paris, and that

was the other high point of my life under censorship. The OU Course Team liked and approved the programme, but the BBC didn't want to transmit it because they didn't like its "tone." They said it was too critical. It was negative. It was disturbing. I remember the head of University Production Centre then, Bob Rowland, came up to me and said: "Nick, I just can't see why you can't make beautiful programmes about art. Why you have to say these horrible things." [Scoffs]

But of course we were able to turn that on its head by discussing with the students, the reasons for censorship, the nature of the art museum in the modern world, the values that prop it up, nationalist values, ideologies of French cultural supremacy, and everything. It was a good occasion to get a huge debate going.

JM   Did the BBC have a certain monopoly, both on cultural programmes and on music, which the OU was trying to break?

NL   Yes. Well, this takes us back—doesn't it?—to Kenneth Clark and John Berger. Kenneth Clark's *Civilisation* was the great proclamation of the BBC, the gatekeepers of culture, which John Berger's *Ways of Seeing* challenged. The Open University was there behind, occasionally challenging, occasionally falling back on triumphalism, depending on the different academics who were in the mix. It's interesting that the disclaimer printed by the OU on some of the written study material, "Opinions expressed in it are not necessarily those of the course team or the University," was the same disclaimer the BBC insisted on putting on the front of The Beaubourg programme, as a compromise to break the impasse about it not being transmissible in its present state. The disclaimer was wonderful because the students could ask: "What does the disclaimer mean? Why is it necessary? Why should anything be other than someone's own viewpoint and opinion?"

JM   That would make it open?

NL   Yes. So this is kind of opening up in order to close down.

JM   What are the most significant contributions you recall from that course?

NL   It was a very exciting period in my life, in my career, and in my experience with The Open University because it was the first major art history course I worked on, and it was innovative, really, and we felt we were doing new things. It reached out to the general public as well, because it went out on the airwaves where it got a lot of interest, from students, academics, and the general public. We felt that the OU and A305 were hitting the right notes.

And we were a terrific team. It was a great privilege to be part of it. We really enjoyed working together, traveling abroad, seeing interesting buildings, that sort of thing. I was the coordinating BBC producer. Another producer, the late Ed Haywood, did a lot of the programmes. There were one or two other BBC producers who came in, and then there was Helen Rapp, the Senior Radio Producer, and Nancy Thomas, the Senior Producer, Arts faculty, who had worked on the BBC *Monitor* arts series and had done a documentary on Le Corbusier. And there were a number of BBC production assistants, including Christine Jackson and Jane Bywaters. We all related very closely to the OU team, of course, headed by Tim Benton.

We realized we were doing something new and different: architectural history hadn't been taught like that before. A305 wasn't a great intellectual jump ahead like John Berger's *Ways of Seeing,* but this course was looking at the history of architecture and trying to understand what architects intended, what the circumstances were in which they designed and built, and how the buildings were created and adapted by them in the process—using documents and visual evidence and of course, film.

A 305 Im 1 2 3

THE OPEN UNIVERSITY

Arts: A third level Course
History of architecture and design 1890 - 1939
Images123

Images

Ruf zum Bauen	Walter Gropius	Eric Mendel sohn
	Internationale Architektur	Russland Europa Amerika and Amerika

A305 D

THE OPEN UNIVERSITY

Arts: A third level Course
History of architecture and design 1890-1939
Documents

Doc
uments

A collection of source material on the Modern Movement

Higher Education and the Pedagogies of Communicating Elite Knowledge in 1970s Britain
—Laura Carter

A Decade of Possibilities

When positioned amidst British higher education in the 1970s, it is clear that The Open University (OU) was a creature of its time. It was conceived and created at a juncture in the late 1960s when innovative educational ideas received robust political support, due to the technocratic promise of higher education and the burgeoning democratic demand from new constituents of students. In this climate, OU courses took shape, advancing radical approaches to teaching and learning traditional subject matter. The development of the OU's methodology was embedded within pedagogical debates that dominated educational circles in twentieth-century Britain. In order to communicate elite and vocational knowledge to uninitiated and remote learners, OU courses also drew on well-established methods, many of which had already been tested across a range of educational settings in the preceding decades, including at the BBC.

The 1970s in Britain, the OU's first decade, are perceived negatively in popular memory. Economic downturn and widespread unemployment, precipitated by domestic responses to global hikes in oil prices in 1973, suggested that Britain was in decline. Political rhetoric since then, notably that of Margaret Thatcher and Tony Blair, has reinforced this image of a chaotic and poorly managed decade.[1] The prevalent tendency has been to see events in the 1970s as a prelude to the Thatcher revolution of the 1980s which, through social and economic measures, replaced the social-democratic consensus of the post-1945 era with a new set of neo-liberal ideas and policies. However, economic historians are increasingly revaluating the so-called intellectual crisis of Keynesian political economy in the 1970s, revealing an alternative view of the decade as a time of multiple possibilities.[2]

Social and cultural historians, too, have recently advanced alternative ways of thinking about the 1970s. Two new frameworks help to explain the arrival and success of the OU much more so than the notion of Britain in crisis and decline. A first group of scholars have suggested that at the time Britain was "transitioning into the first post-industrial nation."[3] As the economy and the labour market deindustrialized, a range of new ideas, or products, were on offer

1
Lawrence Black, Hugh Pemberton, and Pat Thane, *Reassessing 1970s Britain* (Manchester: Manchester University Press, 2013).

2
Aled Davies, *The City of London and Social Democracy: The Political Economy of Finance in Britain, 1959–1979* (Oxford: Oxford University Press, 2017).

3
Black, Pemberton, and Thane, *Reassessing 1970s Britain*, 17.

to society. In adjusting to this new era, the education sector had to engender new skills, prepare people for the utilization of increased leisure time, and foster openness to private sector mentalities. Far from representing a lack of innovation and creativity, as the decline narrative suggests, the OU's adaptation to this new set of social and economic conditions epitomized the application of progressive pedagogical ideas to the higher education sector in 1970s Britain. A second set of historians have argued that during this period there was also a rise of "popular individualism." [4] This social shift was not as simple as the rise of the "greedy" individualism often associated with the Thatcher era, but was rather one in which ordinary people were making greater claims for personal equality and social justice. British men and, especially, women were becoming less deferential and growing more likely to demand fulfillment of their individual needs, including access to elite enclaves of academic knowledge. These demands were satisfied by the new ways of teaching and learning that the OU offered, particularly to students previously unserved by the higher education sector.

New Appetites for Higher Education

The OU was part of a suite of policies, shaped by the technocratic and modernizing impulses of Harold Wilson's 1964–1970 Labour government, which were designed to reconfigure Britain's industrial economy. [5] The eventual foundation of the OU in 1969 came at a highly optimistic moment for British education. During the 1960s the secondary education system underwent a series of reforms that geared educationists towards mass education and eventually created a generation of better-educated citizens. Beginning in the mid-1960s, most schools educating eleven- to fifteen-year-olds were converted into mixed-ability local schools, known as comprehensives. This dismantled the testing and selecting apparatus of secondary education that had existed since 1944. The process of so-called comprehensivization was completed by 1979, at which point just over 79 percent of pupils in state secondary schools in England were attending such schools. [6] These comprehensives also educated pupils for longer, given that the school-leaving age was finally raised to sixteen in 1972. [7] Simultaneously, higher education in Britain underwent a period of expansion: there were approximately 450,000 students in full-time higher education in the United Kingdom by 1970, not including OU and other part-time students, a figure which remained stable at between 400,000 and 500,000 throughout the following decade. [8]

4
Emily Robinson et al., "Telling Stories about Postwar Britain: Popular Individualism and the 'Crisis' of the 1970s," Twentieth Century British History 28, no. 2 (2017): 268–304.

5
Peter Dorey, "'Well, Harold Insists on Having It!'—the Political Struggle to Establish the Open University, 1965–67," Contemporary British History 29, no. 2 (2015): 241–72.

6
Brian Simon, Education and the Social Order, 1940–1990 (London: Lawrence & Wishart, 1999), Table 5b, 585.

7
Simon, Education and the Social Order, 422.

8
National Committee of Inquiry into Higher Education, The Dearing Report: Higher Education in the Learning Society, Report 1 (London: HMSO, 1997), 18.

These circumstances were the long-term consequences of the 1963 Robbins Report which had argued for a dramatic expansion in the provision of higher education in Britain. The Report stated that university degrees "should be available for all those who are qualified by ability and attainment to pursue them and who wish to do so."[9] The rest of the decade has been described by historian Peter Mandler as a period of Robbins "euphoria." The Report's recommendations stimulated greater supply as new polytechnic universities opened, which was met with a drastically increased democratic demand.[10] This pattern of increasing participation in higher education halted during the 1970s, picked up again in the early 1980s, and then continued to increase steadily across the late twentieth century. Mandler suggests that the early period of stagnation was due, in part, to a negative image of isolated universities and lazy students that was propagated by mass media. The university shifted from being a "space of modernity" and aspiration, embedded within a community, to being "a space apart from society."[11]

The OU began admitting students on a first come, first serve basis in 1970, precisely at the point when participation rates in higher education were dropping. In addition, popular representations of the new venture often mirrored the standard critique of lazy student life, and were exacerbated by the skepticism surrounding the delivery of OU courses via television.[12] Despite these circumstances, the OU grew rapidly: of the students who began courses in January 1971, over 900 participated in the first graduation ceremony in 1973, and by 1977 the total student body of the OU, including postgraduate students, was nearly 60,000.[13] By the end of the decade, 9 percent of the total 741,000 students in higher education in the United Kingdom, both full-time and part-time, were studying through the OU.[14]

However, a closer look at participation rates suggests that the increased demand for higher education captured by the OU in its first decade did not come from existing categories of learners whose potential participation had thus far not been maximized, such as mature or female students, but rather from a different type of student altogether. While the OU appealed to adult learners and admitted those with no formal educational qualifications, the proportion of mature students entering higher education (those over the age of twenty-one upon entry to an undergraduate programme) was already 41 percent of full-time undergraduates in 1962–1963, before the OU came into being, and had only reached 48 percent by 1979–1980.[15] And despite the increased participation of women, throughout various periods of their lives, in higher education and paid employment during this period, women made up only 25 percent of applicants to the first OU courses.[16] The number of married women in the workforce, mostly in low-skilled positions, had increased rapidly from the 1950s, and by the early 1970s 49 percent of married women were already working outside the home.[17] But it was not until the 1980s that substantial growth in female participation in higher education was most marked.[18]

The new student that the OU captured was therefore not part of the constituency that had set the Robbins trend into motion and then dropped off in the 1970s, nor was this student the type that had been targeted by the British adult education movement

9
Committee on Higher Education, *Higher Education: Report of the Committee Appointed by the Prime Minister under the Chairmanship of Lord Robbins 1961–63* (London: HMSO, 1963), 8.

10
Peter Mandler, "Educating the Nation: II. Universities," *Transactions of the Royal Historical Society* 25 (December 2015): 1–26.

11
Mandler, "Educating the Nation," 13.

12
Daniel Weinbren, *The Open University: A History* (Manchester: Manchester University Press, 2015), 76.

13
Weinbren, *The Open University*, 122, 138. While 25,000 students enrolled in the OU in 1970, OU courses were of varying lengths, so the first students to complete their degrees by 1973 were likely a fairly small cohort who had taken shorter courses.

14
The Dearing Report, 20.

15
The Dearing Report, 21. While the small rise in the number of mature students in higher education between the 1960s and 1980s implies that the OU did not have much impact, it does suggest that the OU kept full-time enrolment figures stable, and even slightly increased them (as well as increasing the number of part-time students), in the 1970s, the period when overall participation in higher education otherwise stagnated.

16
"First students and first graduates," The Open University, http://www.open.ac.uk/researchprojects/historyofou/story/first-students-and-first-graduates.

17
Helen McCarthy, "Women, Marriage and Paid Work in Postwar Britain," *Women's History Review* 26, no. 1 (2017): 46–61, 47.

18
The Dearing Report, 21.

since the early twentieth century, which had focused on teaching political and economic topics to men employed in manual jobs.[19] OU students, typically full-time workers in a range of sectors independently pursuing their studies at home, were from the same broad public that had been courted through a range of new cultural policies since World War II. For example, in 1939 the Council for the Encouragement of Music and the Arts (CEMA) was created under the aegis of the Board of Education, signalling a break from the hands-off tradition of the British state towards national arts and culture. CEMA promoted cultural engagement during wartime, sponsoring amateur music and dance initiatives and travelling art exhibitions for museums nationwide.[20] In 1946, CEMA became the Arts Council of Great Britain, which was partly integrated into the Department of Education and Science in 1965.

By the mid-1960s the arts had become an official and legitimate policy concern, tightly bound up with educational development and broader debates over how to ensure that the best of culture was accessible to all people, across all regions.[21] These concerns were echoed in early OU programming, which functioned as a formal channel for disseminating arts education to the general public. This public, the OU's audience, was more likely to think of itself as a discerning group of citizen-consumers than as passive recipients of knowledge from the top down. The motivations of such an audience for learning were based on personal, intellectual, and cultural enrichment, an expression of the popular individualism that characterized new social identities in 1970s Britain. The OU therefore fulfilled a new and modernizing role in Britain's higher education landscape as British society shifted toward a post-industrial condition.

Pedagogical Debates and The Open University

The OU has been described as "the most pedagogically conscious university in the UK."[22] In fact, the question of what to teach and how to deliver it contained the same intrinsic challenge that had confronted educationists since the end of World War I: what should mass education for ordinary people look like?[23] On one hand, progressive educationists championed student-centric methods, which were guided by the notion that students were most successful when they followed their own interests within a topic. The curricula they developed were therefore fluid and adaptive to student needs. Conversely, traditional educationists advocated content-centric teaching methods, according to which bodies of knowledge were considered to be fixed and material was to be delivered using didactic techniques that ensured the highest level of comprehension. The struggle between these two positions underpinned most pedagogical debates in twentieth-century Britain.[24]

The content-centric approach was enshrined in older, traditional universities and the independent and grammar secondary schools that typically fed into them. After World War II, some reformers attempted to make vocational and technical secondary education in Britain mainstream because of the long-standing correlation they drew between economic competitiveness and vocational skills. But technical schools were never created on a significant scale, generating a paucity of demand for higher technical

19
Stephen Roberts, *A Ministry of Enthusiasm: Centenary Essays on the Workers' Educational Association* (London: Pluto Press, 2003).

20
F. M. Leventhal, "'The Best for the Most': CEMA and State Sponsorship of the Arts in Wartime, 1939–1945," *Twentieth Century British History* 1, no. 3 (1990): 289–317.

21
Lawrence Black, "'Making Britain a Gayer and More Cultivated Country': Wilson, Lee and the Creative Industries in the 1960s," *Contemporary British History* 20, no. 3 (2006): 323–42.

22
Weinbren, *The Open University*, 123.

23
See Gary McCulloch, *Failing the Ordinary Child?: The Theory and Practice of Working Class Secondary Education* (Buckingham: The Open University Press, 1998).

24
See Peter Cunningham, *Curriculum Change in the Primary School Since 1945: Dissemination of the Progressive Ideal* (London: Falmer, 1988).

education. In reality, between the 1940s and 1960s, the British secondary education system developed with a ratio of one secondary technical school pupil, to every seven grammar school pupils, to every seventeen secondary modern school pupils.[25] Secondary modern schools were therefore the primary site of mass education in postwar Britain. While progressive educationists strongly advocated for the integration of student-centric methods, these schools were severely under-resourced and often fell back on a mixture of vocational training, traditional methods, and progressive experiments.[26] Just as in these secondary modern schools, the OU's challenge in the 1970s was to communicate academic knowledge to a mixed-ability audience, without compromising the integrity of the material.

The OU academics poised to meet this challenge positioned themselves apart from their counterparts in traditional universities where content-centric methods prevailed.[27] An oral history study of the first generation of OU staff found that they remembered the OU of the early years as an unconventional organization with a familial atmosphere. The main campus at Milton Keynes was populated by "a large group of young, liberal, left of centre academics," and throughout the decade allegations of a left-wing bias at the OU echoed accusations routinely directed toward the BBC, and even some comprehensive schools.[28] These ideological tensions map onto the divide between progressive and traditional approaches to education, which became particularly marked in the polarized political context of the 1970s.

The OU tended to appeal to scholars who approached their discipline with flexibility. For example, course A100, Humanities: A Foundation Course, which ran from 1971 to 1977, included televised dramatic performances of stage plays wherein multiple interpretations of the production were presented; a quite revolutionary approach in the context of literary studies in the 1970s.[29] Moreover, the educational philosophy of Paulo Friere, which advocated active questioning and dialogue on the part of the student, was influential amongst OU staff.[30] This intellectual flexibility, whereby academics needed to be open to working with, and learning from, specialists in other fields, was essential to how new courses were designed at the OU.[31] The course teams were comprised of academics, BBC producers, and educational technologists who, together, implemented new models of teaching and learning along progressive lines, suited to the delivery of academic material to remote learners.

A Progressive Pedagogy for a Televisual Era

An OU course that exemplified the utilization of progressive pedagogy to make elite subject matter more accessible was A305, History of Architecture and Design 1890–1939. A305, which was first offered in 1975, was delivered through a combination of course unit booklets, broadcasting supplements, television broadcasts, radiovision programmes (radio broadcasts with accompanying booklets of reference illustrations), and anthologies of reproduced documents and images. The course presented both formal analysis and a substantial amount of empirical material to students—including architectural styles and biographies—endowing the broadcast material with academic authority.

25
Michael Sanderson, *Education and Economic Decline in Britain, 1870 to the 1990s* (Cambridge: Cambridge University Press, 1999), 80.

26
Simon, *Education and the Social Order,* 132; Laura Carter, "'Experimental' Secondary Modern Education in Britain, 1948–1958," *Cultural and Social History* 13, no. 1 (2016): 23–41.

27
Part of this change of culture was due to women entering academia and other high-skilled professions for the first time in the 1970s. At the OU, founding female members included Catherine King (Arts), Ruth Finnegan (Social Sciences), and Peggy Varley (Sciences).

28
Hilary Young, "Whose Story Counts? Constructing an Oral History of the Open University at 40," *Oral History* 39, no. 2 (2011): 104–5; Weinbren, *The Open University,* 104–5.

29
Amanda Wrigley, "Higher Education and Public Engagement in Open University and BBC Drama Co-Productions on BBC2 in the 1970s," *Journal of British Cinema and Television* 14, no. 3 (2017): 377–93, 382.

30
Weinbren, *The Open University,* 135–6.

31
Young, "Whose Story Counts?," 101.

Over the course of the twentieth century, the line between whether architectural knowledge was considered elite or everyday gradually blurred in Britain as the social and political significance of architecture was popularized. The BBC was influential in this transformation during the interwar period, when it began to prominently feature architecture on the radio. By 1939, 71 percent of households in England owned a radio.[32] Early broadcasters found that architecture contained inherently practical and familiar elements that translated effectively into factual and debate-based programming about housing, town planning, street design, and leisure.[33] These radio broadcasts were important foundations for the televisual and audio model of architectural education offered at the OU. From the 1930s onward, the BBC was pioneering more varied structures for educational programming, including dramatic readings with sound effects and musical interludes, intended to break up and enliven core narratives.[34] In turn, academics were guided on how to deliver their material slowly, clearly, and in a palatable tone.[35] These broadcasts were known as "illustrated talks," a format clearly built upon by the "television essay" which the OU used across its arts programming.[36]

Perhaps the most striking similarity between early OU practices and existing BBC structures was the parallel between the OU's course teams and the BBC's Central Council for Schools Broadcasting (CCSB). The CCSB was formed in 1929 and lasted in various forms until the 1960s, eventually covering educational broadcasting on both radio and television. The CCSB brought together educationists, teachers, and technological consultants into various subject committees and charged them with analyzing and approving the viability of programme ideas for delivery to schools.[37] This collaborative culture, which placed pedagogy and practicality alongside intellectual merit, prefigured the conversations and challenges that occurred within OU course teams as they attempted to distill complex ideas into multifaceted course material.[38] Many aspects of the pedagogy of A305 were a continuity of these foundations at the BBC and earlier pedagogical methods developed for mass education.

Visual education was a key tenet of progressive pedagogical methodologies. A305's highly illustrated print material and its television broadcasts were intuitive to a visual way of understanding and experiencing architectural space. But arguments

32
Ross McKibbin, *Classes and Cultures: England 1918–1951* (Oxford: Oxford University Press, 1998), 457.

33
Shundana Yusaf, *Broadcasting Buildings: Architecture on the Wireless, 1927–1945* (Cambridge, Mass: The MIT Press, 2014).

34
Kenneth Fawdry, *Everything but Alf Garnett. A Personal View of BBC School Broadcasting* (London: BBC, 1974), 45.

35
Asa Briggs, *The Golden Age of Wireless*, Volume II of *The History of Broadcasting in the United Kingdom* (Oxford: Oxford University Press, 1995), 117.

36
John Walker, *Arts TV: A History of Arts Television in Britain* (London: Libbey, 1993), 138.

37
David Crook, "School Broadcasting in the United Kingdom: An Exploratory History," *Journal of Educational Administration and History* 39, no. 3 (2007): 217–26.

38
Young, "Whose Story Counts?," 101.

for the incorporation of visual material into formal education challenged the strong academic and textual bias of traditional curricula.[39] Prior to this, Britain's Victorian tradition of richly illustrated, popular print culture had typically been associated with lowbrow, unedifying entertainment or with nursery school education because illustrations were regarded as "picturesque" rather than empirically informative.[40] Attempts to incorporate meaningful images into advanced educational material, such as school textbooks, were therefore met with opposition in the early twentieth century. Gradually, illustrations became accepted educational tools, bolstered by the advent of mass-produced photography, which endowed images with a sense of authoritative realism.[41]

A305's radiovision programmes embedded ample illustrations into aural teaching by structuring each lesson around a set of numbered figures—photographs, magazine images, and traditional illustrations—contained in an accompanying booklet.[42] In A305 course unit booklets, the text was very densely packed but it was wrapped around the images that were each referenced within the text, thereby encouraging readers to refer back and forth between the two. This method was standard by the mid-twentieth century, a sign that illustrations were not merely decorative but functioned reflexively in relation to text. In addition, A305's extensive deployment of architectural plans reflected the gradual acceptance of blending technical and academic knowledge.[43] Another notable visual device deployed in A305 material was the use of time charts, often at the beginning of course books.[44] Time charts were first developed as a pedagogical tool by educationists in the early 1920s, guided by the idea that the average person found it hard to comprehend chronologies in prose.[45]

The educational value of films was first discussed after World War I when cinema-going boomed in Britain, especially amongst the younger generation.[46] Detractors feared that films would allow the intrusion of cheap American melodrama and dangerous continental propaganda into the educational realm. On the contrary, advocates of both illustrations and films argued that mass education demanded different materials by drawing on nascent psychological ideas that less-academic pupils had primarily visual

39
Raphael Samuel, "History, the Nation and the Schools," *History Workshop Journal* 30 (Fall 1990): 75–80.

40
Rosemary Mitchell, *Picturing the Past: English History in Text and Image, 1830–1870* (Oxford: Oxford University Press, 2000).

41
Gerry Beegan, *The Mass Image: A Social History of Photomechanical Reproduction in Victorian London* (Basingstoke: Palgrave Macmillan, 2008); Historical Association, *A List of Illustrations for Use in History Teaching in Schools* (London: G. Bell & Sons, 1930).

42
Tim Benton, "Broadcasting the Modern Movement," *Architectural Association Quarterly* 7, no. 1 (1975): 45–55.

43
For example, Tim Benton, Charlotte Benton, and Dennis Sharp, *Expressionism*, course booklet for Units 9–10 of A305 (Milton Keynes: The Open University Press, 1975), 22–3.

44
For example, Charlotte Benton and Tim Benton, *The International Style*, course booklet for Units 13–14 of A305 (Milton Keynes: The Open University Press, 1975), 6–7.

45
Helen Madeley, "Time Charts," special issue, *Historical Association Leaflet*, no. 50 (1921): 1–3.

46
McKibbin, *Classes and Cultures*, 419.

capacities for processing information.[47] Predicated on these principles, the Council for Visual Education was formed in 1942 in order to promote the integration of "aesthetic appreciation" into all subjects, orientated around tasteful judgement of the built environment, natural landscapes, and commonplace objects.[48] After World War II, progressive educationists increasingly applied these arguments to the medium of television, which, by the 1970s, was a dominant feature of family life and leisure time in Britain.[49] Again, proponents of visual education argued against the cultural critics and suggested that television could be harnessed to promote active, rather than passive, viewing.

The twenty-four television broadcasts created for A305 were crafted precisely for such active consumption. Although styles varied between lecturers, the broadcasts subverted traditional "chalk and talk" didacticism to engage the viewer. The lecturer-presenters came across as authoritative but unpretentious, conveying a similar "intellectual modesty" to that of Melvyn Bragg, the popular presenter of the 1970s arts magazine programme *The South Bank Show*, aired on ITV, Britain's oldest commercial network.[50] Crucially, the lecturers neatly folded their critical analysis into the more mundane explorations and descriptions of the building at hand. In the first television broadcast of the course, "What is Architecture? An Architect at Work," Geoffrey Baker shows the viewer his initial sketch ideas for his house, laid out alongside sketches done in real time for the camera, while talking the viewer through the process.[51] In "The Universal International Exhibition, Paris, 1900," the camera scans a photographic panorama of the national architecture exhibitions, giving the viewer time to examine each one, before the lecturer's narration restarts.[52] The panorama was a popular early twentieth-century visual education device, particularly favoured for historical exhibitions in museums in the 1930s.[53]

Many of the television broadcasts featured the lecturer walking around famous buildings and houses, foregrounding the practical aspects of living in these houses and conveying the design rationale. For example, in "Le Corbusier: Villa Savoye," Tim Benton shows the viewer how the window mechanisms work; in "Charles Rennie Mackintosh: Hill House," Sandra Millikin is shown resting in one of Mackintosh's carefully placed seating areas; and in "What is Architecture? An Architect at Work," Baker's young son is shown playing with toys on the windowsill.[54] These examples of the everyday, lived facets of architecture and design show how A305's television broadcasts presented content in a varied and accessible way, interspersing academic content with practical and technical elements. The broadcasts transplanted many of the key devices of visual education into the televisual arena, offering a higher level of intellectual discussion than was available on general arts television programming during the 1970s in combination with slower and more detailed scans of buildings and objects. The programmes succeeded in conveying that art could contain complex ideological struggles highly relevant to society, just as the early BBC radio programmes on architecture had done.[55]

Another prominent aspect of A305's pedagogy was its consistent emphasis on primary sources, which was necessary to

47
A. M. Field, "The Educational Value of the Film," *History* 12 (1927): 142–43; G. T. Hankin, "The Decline of the Printed Word," *History* 15 (1930): 119–23.

48
W. F. Morris, *The Future Citizen & His Surroundings, Council for Visual Education Booklet No. 1* (London: B. T. Batsford, 1946), 12.

49
Joe Moran, *Armchair Nation: An Intimate History of Britain in Front of the TV* (London: Profile Books, 2013), 189–234.

50
Walker, *Arts TV*, 109.

51
"What is Architecture? An Architect at Work," television rogramme 1 of A305, presented by Geoffrey Baker, produced by Edward Hayward, BBC for The Open University, aired 15 February 1975.

52
"The Universal International Exhibition, Paris, 1900," television programme 2 of A305, presented by Tim Benton, produced by Nick Levinson, BBC for The Open University, aired 1 March 1975.

53
E. K. Milliken, "The Teaching of History by Means of Models," *History* 22 (1937): 139–48.

54
See "Le Corbusier: Villa Savoye," television programme 13 of A305, presented by Tim Benton, produced by Nick Levinson, BBC for The Open University, aired 14 June 1975, 13:07; "Charles Rennie Mackintosh: Hill House," television programme 3 of A305, produced by Nick Levinson, BBC for The Open University, aired 8 March 1975, 16:36; "What is Architecture? An Architect at Work," 22:40.

55
Walker, *Arts TV*, 139.

support one of the course's central tenets of developing a historic-ally situated assessment of the modern movement. This meant, in Tim Benton's words, placing "a great deal of emphasis on what the members of the Modern Movement really said and how they visual-ised their world."[56] The principle tool for conveying these historical references was *Form and Function*, an anthology that contained textual extracts to supplement the buildings and designs covered throughout the course.[57] The sources showed the active political and artistic dialogues occurring between contemporaries of the period, such as William Lethaby's vexed, patriotic commentary on German architecture from 1915 and Marcel Breuer's 1927 love letter to modernist furniture.[58]

The extracts in *Form and Function* were short (most were between one and three pages) and were accompanied by illustra-tions and photographs. Each chapter had a framing introduction, but otherwise the anthology offered up its texts as "raw material" to the student with minimal commentary overall.[59] A305 also reproduced original picture books of modern architecture from the 1920s, providing further unmediated primary source material for the students to engage with.[60] Working closely and critically on isolated textual extracts was an established literary technique for fiction, championed by literary critic F. R. Leavis in the 1930s as an educational tool for moral enhancement.[61] But non-fiction source books of this nature were relatively new in the 1970s. They had increasingly appeared on the school textbook market from the 1960s, buoyed by the growth in student-centric teaching methods that required resources which would enable students to follow their own interests.[62]

The television broadcasts also contained considerable pri-mary source material for the viewer to ponder. Focusing on significant, as well as a few more peripheral, buildings or architectural events from 1890 to 1939, the broadcasts offered both students and general viewers a rare and intimate glimpse into architectural spaces that they would be unlikely to visit on their own accord (this was especially true of the European and American examples).[63] In most cases these vis-ual tours were intercut with contemporary shots and historical photo-graphs of the building's construction and its original interiors. For

56
Benton, "Broadcasting the Modern Movement," 47.

57
Tim Benton, Charlotte Benton, and Denis Sharp, eds., *Form and Function: A Source Book for the History of Architecture and Design 1890–1939* (London: Crosby Lock-wood Staples in association with The Open University Press, 1975).

58
William Lethaby, "Modern German Architecture and What We May Learn from It," 55–6; Marcel Breuer, "Metal Furniture," 226–7; both in Benton, Benton, and Sharp, eds., *Form and Function*.

59
Benton, Benton, and Sharp, eds., *Form and Function*, foreword.

60
See Charlotte Benton and Tim Benton, eds., *Images* (Milton Keynes: The Open University Press, 1975).

61
Frank Raymond Leavis and Denys Thompson, *Culture and Envi-ronment: The Training of Critical Awareness* (London: Chatto & Windus, 1933).

62
For example, Peter Lane, *Documents on British Economic and Social History: Book 1. 1750–1870* (London: Macmillan, 1968).

63
Benton, "Broadcasting the Modern Movement," 48.

instance, in Geoffrey Baker's broadcast "The London Underground," interwar period posters advertising the transportation system are shown as an example of Frank Pick's unifying design vision, and in "R. M. Schindler: The Lovell Beach House," Sandra Millikin introduces the broadcast with photographs of the house under construction in 1922.[64]

Primary sources were also introduced into the broadcasts via contemporary readings by a narrator. For example, in "Charles Rennie Mackintosh: Hill House," an actor reads a letter written by Walter Blackie, the patron who commissioned Mackintosh to build the house; in "The Universal International Exhibition, Paris, 1900," Tim Benton uses excerpts from a popular guidebook from 1900 for the opening sequence; and in "The Semi-Detached House," Stephen Bayley features excerpts from a 1911 Ilford guidebook describing suburban development.[65] These source cameos provided an alternative perspective from that of the lecturer-presenter and added further contemporary context to the visual centrepieces of the films. The consistent emphasis on primary source material underscored the fact that the course did not aim to convey a fixed interpretation of the modern movement to its students; rather, it aimed to provide the tools for students to come to their own, albeit guided, judgment. This archetypical student-centric pedagogy culminated with A305 students defining their own project as the conclusion of the course.

This final assignment for A305 was a five-thousand word essay, researched over a period of eight weeks, on a building of each student's choosing, provided the student could visit the building and access original documents. As Tim Benton explained in 1975, "The underlying philosophy of the project is that the essential nature of a period can be best understood through a detailed analysis of one work."[66] Mirroring the approach of the television broadcasts, students were asked for a formal analysis and historical contextualization of a work of architecture, supplemented with primary source material. The project method was designed for educational environments with student groups of mixed ability as an alternative to fixed curricula and examinations that bred uniformity in teaching and learning. In a 1947 Ministry of Education pamphlet outlining the aims of the new secondary modern schools, projects were strongly recommended as a "stimulus of curiosity."[67] The project method was particularly popular between the 1920s and 1940s for teaching geography, a subject that had a strong tradition of fieldwork and investigative learning.[68]

A305 built on these foundations, adapting the student project method for distance-learning and higher education by blending it with the more traditional academic demands of essay writing. By asking students to base broader claims on a specific work chosen according to preference and accessibility, A305 aimed to elicit evidence-based judgements arrived at through individual critical exploration. The course material was peppered with advice along these lines: in A305's introduction booklet students are warned that "The most obvious trap to fall into in this course is to argue from the critical to the historical, especially drawing historical conclusions from your own likes and dislikes," and in the course unit booklet *The International Style,* students are advised that "Although we will

64
See "The London Underground," television programme 19 of *History of Architecture and Design 1890–1939*, presented by Geoffrey Baker, produced by Edward Hayward, BBC for The Open University, aired 30 August 1975; "R. M. Schindler: The Lovell Beach House," television programme 6 of A305, presented by Sandra Millikin, produced by Edward Hayward, BBC for The Open University, aired 12 April 1975.

65
"Charles Rennie Mackintosh: Hill House"; "The Universal International Exhibition, Paris, 1900"; "The Semi-Detached House," television programme 23 of A305, presented by Stephen Bayley, produced by Patricia Hodgson, BBC for The Open University, aired 11 October 1975.

66
Benton, "Broadcasting the Modern Movement," 48.

67
Ministry of Education, *The New Secondary Education* (London: HMSO, 1947), 38.

68
Rex Walford, *Geography in British Schools, 1850–2000: Making a World of Difference* (London: Woburn Press, 2001).

discuss these style labels... we will insist that you try to see through them to the complexities of individual architects' work and ideas, while grasping the overall pattern of events." [69]

When historical topics were being addressed, debates about objectivity, subjectivity, and empathy were extremely heated in pedagogical circles in the 1970s. Traditionalists were committed to the notion that history was a series of events and actions to be understood and explained in a detached manner, while progressives explored the idea that subjective responses to historical episodes might be usefully cultivated in order to enhance "soft" skills such as empathy. [70] Therefore, a measured and critical awareness of past actions and aesthetic decisions was perhaps the most advanced skill that A305 ingrained in its students, and was an ambition shared across many of the other early OU arts courses. [71]

The teaching methods deployed through A305 were embedded in a pedagogical discourse framed by both progressive and traditional approaches to academic subject matter. And most of these methods can be traced back to other experiments in mass education that occurred earlier in the twentieth century. Seen in this light, the pedagogy of A305 appears less radical. However, A305 transported these approaches into the context of higher education, a formidable feat in 1970s Britain. As the reassessment of this decade of British history develops beyond the idea of a nation in decline, the advent of The Open University and its early courses should be understood as one of the decade's most remarkable and enduring innovations.

69
Tim Benton and Geoffrey Baker, Introduction, course booklet for Units 1–2 of A305 (Milton Keynes: The Open University Press, 1975), 9; Benton and Benton, The International Style, 4.

70
David Cannadine, Jenny Keating, and Nicola Sheldon, The Right Kind of History: Teaching the Past in Twentieth-Century England (Basingstoke; New York: Palgrave Macmillan, 2011), 10.

71
Wrigley, "Higher Education and Public Engagement," 383.

13

Classroom of Solitudes

Joaquim Moreno

The operation of television is based on a combination of centralized broadcasting and individualized
reception. This relationship,
> rather than being the default condition
> of television technology,
> is a result of the commercial nature
> of the broadcasting industry,
which determines both the production of content
and of the domestic receivers through which that
content is disseminated.
> Through the proliferation of receivers
> in every house,
> television was being domesticated,
inventing de facto a new domesticity centred
around a new window onto the world. This mass
media network bypassed the shared public forum
and was received privately at home, giving shape
to a new type of mass audience:
> an endless multiplication of solitudes
> and household collectives.

When higher education began mobilizing the apparatus of mass media, it was inevitable that both the transmission of knowledge and the spatial and social organization of its reception would be heavily reorganized. For the masses receiving education through radio and television, the learning process was still synchronized,
> but it was no longer collective,
> as was the typical gathering of students
> within the conventional classroom.
This dispersal of teaching through broadcasting created a new classroom of solitudes.

[A]

Toward the end of his 1936 book, *Radio*, German theorist and psychologist Rudolf Arnheim fore-shadows televisual education by making the case for the pedagogical advantages of distinguishing the concern for broadcasting content that is important for everyone, from the solitary reception of that content.

What is meant for all must not on that account be always taken as a communal experience. In many cases the individual can absorb it more conveniently and in a more undistracted and concentrated way if he is alone.

The conventional experience of education was bound to be communal and its messages specific,
but mass education through mass media could turn the spectator or the listener into an active learner.
Each student would tune in to a particular portion of the flow of information or entertainment, and interact with it in a different way than a general audience would;
such differentiated viewer interactions could only be achieved in solitude, not within a collective.

Radio and television,
though both received at home and both essential to the dissemination strategy of The Open University, were structurally different and therefore each required different modes of interaction, different voices, and different ways of addressing the audience.
Radio—a blind media—required a type of attention that could be sustained while performing

other tasks,
but television demanded
more interpretation of content
and therefore total attentiveness,
often focusing the attention of
an entire household on a single screen.
Arnheim suggests that radio proposed a new way
of presenting reality,
while television offered new ways
to engage with multiple realities
at once. As Arnheim writes in *Radio*:

Television... proves to be a relative of the car and the
aeroplane. It is merely a means of transmission,
containing no such elements of a new mode of presenting
reality as the film and non-pictorial wireless, but like the
machines of locomotion that the last century gave us,
it alters our relation to reality itself, teaches us to know it
better, and lets us sense the multiplicity of what is
happening everywhere at one moment.

For Arnheim, television is thus better suited to
"facts" and the "individual" than radio,
because radio is
"abstract and non-figurative"
in its presentation of content.
Furthermore, television is "more the means of
instruction than the instruction itself." Following
Arnheim's arguments, television could therefore
sustain a distributed classroom because it was,
like the conventional classroom, a means of
social synchronization, albeit an ephemeral one,
because each student knew
that others were attending
simultaneously over the airwaves.

When this distributed classroom was inserted into the general flow of BBC programming, it generated for the audience a sense of being simultaneously part of a multiplicity and of receiving a private broadcast. Students could leave class early, or not attend at all, and no one would know.

> But despite such anonymity,
> simply watching or listening
> to broadcasts provided students
> a certain sense of belonging.

Marshall McLuhan later proposed a parallel vision of these other spatial arrangements of education in his essay "Classroom Without Walls," the opening text of the 1960 anthology, *Explorations in Communication*. As opposed to the idea of a classroom of solitudes in which media reached through domestic walls to synchronize learning, McLuhan tears down the walls of the classroom altogether by arguing that most learning already happens outside it, through mass media. He also notes that mass-produced, printed books were the precursors to broadcasting

> —they enabled different people in
> faraway places to read the same text,
> proposing a multiplicity of interpreta-
> tions moving across time and space.

The novelty of conventional television broadcasting was that the multiplicity it sustained was also explicitly synchronized.

The Varied Scene
Aspects of Drama Today

Episode Four

For McLuhan, the distinction between education and entertainment is a false one, and in "Classroom Without Walls" he argues there is indeed little difference between the two, because "it's always been true that whatever pleases teaches more effectively." If educational content—itself a central mandate of the BBC charter, together with information and entertainment—was reaching a shared audience through the domestic television screen, effectively being imposed upon many more spectators than solely those enrolled in Open University courses, then education should also entertain and, therefore, conform to general expectations for the media. McLuhan insists that

the more something entertained,
the more it pleased the audience,
and therefore the more effectively
it could educate.

The pedagogical space of The Open University was thus also engendered through the theoretical demolition of assumed limits and separations between learning and leisure.

The new type of classroom invented by the OU reconfigured models for teaching and learning, as well as personal and interpersonal dynamics. But when reflecting on these implications, it is important to note that the entire constituency of this domesticated education was not limited to the home.

This was a disembodied university,
open to many localized places
other than a typical home.
For example, from the very first year of teaching in
1971, the OU accepted enrolment
from institutionalized persons,
from military personnel
stationed abroad,
from workers on offshore platforms, and
—particularly significant as a case
of alternative domesticities—
from prisoners.
In this case, openness was complicated by safety
regulations that required the removal of dangerous
chemicals or tools from experimental kits, and by
difficulties in ensuring access to radio and television broadcasts or to recordings of them.

A more typical example of the challenges of the
classroom of solitudes as a model for accessing
higher education was central to the plot of
Educating Rita, a 1983 film adapted from the 1980
play by Willy Russell. Through an almost cliché
narrative, the film depicts higher education as a
"luxury," far removed from the everyday, working-
class life; so much so that the film's protagonist,
a hairdresser named Susan, feels compelled
to reinvent herself through the persona of Rita,
a twenty-seven-year-old woman who wants to
become a learned person by studying literature.

Against the expectations
of both society and her husband,
Susan chooses to enrol in the OU
in order to gain an education,
in a stereotypically bourgeois subject,
before having children.

[C]

-Are you coming to bed?
-I'll be up in a minute.

But unlike Susan, Rita actually has the courage
to cross the threshold into a conventional university campus, where OU tutorials were being hosted,
and rather than going to a classroom full of other
students, to go to the office of Dr. Frank Bryant,
a tired professor and part-time OU tutor, with whom
she has one-to-one sessions.
Allowing education to cross
the threshold of the home

is, however, the greater challenge,
because Susan must keep her studies
a secret from her husband,
hiding her books in the floorboards
—her husband eventually discovers her secret,
burns her books, and expels her from their home.
Though dated, the depiction of Susan's lonely
and redemptive path to self-improvement through
learning remains a powerful rendition of the
challenges many OU students faced in realizing
their ambitions. Though fictional, Rita was such
a clear student stereotype that the OU had developed marketing material for the original play with
the slogan, "You Could Be a Rita Too!"
For those forced to study
in solitary or confined circumstances,
the classroom of solitudes opened up
many of the walls around them.
By broadcasting education to students instead
of making students converge on a central place
of learning,
The Open University was building
bridges and breaching walls.

On the other hand, the entire range of The Open
University's teaching instruments
—from the mediation of real-life
experiences through television
and radio to domestic chemistry
experiments sent through the mail—

was inflected by the cycle of obsolescence intrinsic to the classroom of solitudes. A conventional classroom setting is continuously renewed through a cyclical flow of students,

> but when this cycle intersects
> the general flow of communication,
> as it did at the OU,
> it ages very quickly.

One of the limits of the classroom defined by broadcasting was thus that it shared the rate of obsolescence of mass media.

> Information,
> or the content of broadcasting,
> is replaced every day,
> and when education
> is combined with media,
> educational content inevitably ages
> at an accelerated rate.

Furthermore, because the OU assembled new technological resources and cultural innovations that were well adapted to the conditions of their time, its teaching and learning materials were highly vulnerable to obsolescence in the face of continuous technological change. Each classroom of solitudes thus receded into the distance as its content became out of date at an even faster rate than its media environment.

The complexities of technological obsolescence were also explored by McLuhan in his essay

"The Invisible Environment: The Future of an Erosion," published in 1967 in the student-edited journal *Perspecta*.

> McLuhan proposes that
> while immersive media environments
> are mostly invisible, they render
> earlier technological environments
> all the more visible.

Indeed, we can see in hindsight how, in the forty years since A305 was first broadcast, television has been progressively replaced by new technology, and its contents proliferated across the screens of the contemporary electronic environment—computers, tablets, and cell phones. This multiplication has made television visible

> as a medium
> and a discourse,
> signalling its obsolescence
> and transformation into an art form,

as per McLuhan's argument. For McLuhan, even print media became a space for artistic invention once it was no longer the most current media of its time: obsolescence is a form of liberation.

> Our ability to *see* television
> therefore means
> that we *are* after television,

and that we can finally perceive the vestiges of the domesticity it invented and the afterimage of the classroom of solitudes it engendered. Different media organize different political bodies

—new modes of spectatorship and new aggrega-
tions—through how they are received. As McLuhan
argues in "The Invisible Environment,"while printing created "the Public" in the sixteenth century,
"electric circuitry... created the mass, meaning an
environment of information that involved everybody in everybody."

In the same article, McLuhan also takes note of
wider transformations in print culture, particularly
the invention of Xerox photocopiers,
> which had a direct effect
> in the material configuration
> of the classroom:

> [Xerography] decentralizes the long-centralized publish-
> ing process. Authorship and readership alike can become
> production-oriented under xerography. Anybody can take
> any book apart, insert parts of other books and other
> materials of his own interest, and make his own book in
> a relatively fast time. Any teacher can take any ten
> textbooks on any subject and custom-make a different
> one by simply Xeroxing a chapter from this one and
> a chapter from that one.

More than representing a threat to the print
industry,
> Xeroxing,
> or the dissemination of
> private and partial reproduction
> of texts and images,
> provided the intellectual model
> for reference anthologies.

Xeroxes made in the early 1970s have already
faded, but the printed anthologies that were

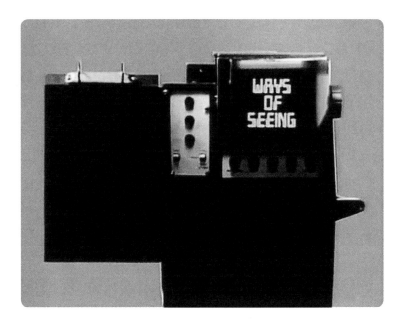

The Listener

Thursday 13 January 1972   Volume 87 No 2233   9p

Anatol Goldberg: cold wars. Keith Kyle: a Palestine plan 39,57
Paisley, Blaney, Devlin & Devlin...Raymond Williams 40,60
When 'God save great Thomas Paine' was the radical anthem 41
Alan Pryce-Jones visits Russia. A pair of Graves poems 44
Seamus Heaney and Ronald Blythe on a pair of Irish poets 55

'The face of a pretty girl': John Berger
discusses what happens when Botticelli's
Venus is taken from her context (her context appears on page 35)

Ways of Seeing —the first of four essays by John Berger concerns the work of art

I want to question some of the assumptions usually made about the tradition of
European oil-painting, that tradition which
was born about 1400 and died about 1900.
On this occasion it isn't so much the paintings themselves which I want to consider as the way we now see them, in the
second half of the 20th century. We see
these paintings as nobody saw them before. If we discover why this is so, we shall
also discover something about ourselves
and about the situation in which we are
living.

The process of seeing paintings or seeing anything else is less spontaneous and
natural than we tend to believe. A large
part of seeing depends upon habit and convention. All the paintings of the tradition of oil-painting used the convention of
perspective which is unique to European
art. Perspective centres everything on the
eye of the beholder. It is like a beam from
a lighthouse—only instead of light travelling outwards, appearances travel inwards.
And our tradition of art called those
appearances 'reality'. Perspective makes
the eye the centre of the visible world.
Yet the human eye can only be in one
place at one time. It takes its visible world
with it as it walks. With the invention of
the camera everything changed. We could
see things which were not there in front
of us. Appearances could travel across the
world. It was no longer so easy to think

a Pelican ⬤ Original

WAYS OF SEEING

Based on the BBC television series with

JOHN BERGER

Seeing comes before words. The child looks
and recognizes before it can speak.
But there is also another sense in which seeing
comes before words. It is seeing which establishes our place
in the surrounding world; we explain that world with words,
but words can never undo the fact that we are surrounded by
it. The relation between what we see and what we know is
never settled.

The Surrealist painter Magritte commented
on this always-present gap between words and seeing in
a painting called The Key of Dreams
The way we see things is affected by what we

utilizing its logic still persist, as immediate as books have been for centuries. This transformative vector both redefined notions of authorship and reconfigured traditional sequences of the production of knowledge. By organizing a different form of intermediation, television could thus utilize books, in the same way as books were utilizing Xeroxes, to capture its own memory and not simply adapt books to a televisual format. Education and cultural programmes could therefore also move

> from airwaves to print,
> from the screen to the page,
> not just the other way around.

Early examples of this were *Civilisation*, by Lord Kenneth Cark, first aired and published in 1969, followed by contrarian John Berger's *Ways of Seeing* in 1972, Aaron Scharf's *Pioneers of Photography* in 1976, and Robert Hugues' *Shock of the New in 1980*—or, across the Atlantic, by William H. White's *The Social Life of Small Urban Spaces* in 1980, which also coupled a film and a book. Perhaps the best example, in architectural culture at least, of this complex writing of history across multiple media is Reyner Banham's fascination with Los Angeles,

> spanning his four 1968 BBC
> radio talks, which were
> transcribed in *The Listener*,

his 1971 article "LA: The Structure Behind the Scene," published in *Architectural Design*,

> his 1971 book,
> *Los Angeles: The Architecture of Four Ecologies*,
> and the script for the 1972 BBC documentary,
> *Reyner Banham Loves Los Angeles*.

But McLuhan's theoretical distinction between

> hot media, such as radio,
> and cool media, such as television,
> provided the clearest modus operandi
> for effectively merging
> education and entertainment.

It was in his 1964 publication *Understanding Media: the Extensions of Man*, that McLuhan made the argument for how an audience relates to different media:

> A hot medium is one that extends one single sense in "high definition." High definition is the state of being well filled with data.... And speech is a cool medium of low definition, because so little is given and so much has to be filled in by the listener. On the other hand, hot media do not leave so much to be filled in or completed by the audience. Hot media are, therefore, low in participation, and cool media are high in participation or completion by the audience.

The A305 Course Team combined these ideas from McLuhan with Arnheim's ideas on the solitary and collective reception of broadcast content to develop different pedagogical strategies for radio and for television.

Episode Four

The hot medium of radio
was used for exposés of precise ideas
and more general topics,
as a new way of observing reality
in high definition,
and the cool medium of television
was used to present facts
and case studies,
as a way of enabling the audience
to inhabit distant, iconic examples
of modern architecture.
The Course Team thus appropriated both hot and
cool media for its purposes and made sure that
no combinations of hot and cool would hamper
student interactions across various media formats.

In its own way, A305 was bridging this emergent
mediascape, the classroom of solitudes, and the
bibliographic requirements of a university syllabus
—especially one that coordinated the delivery of
education through mass media. While the object
lessons of A305 were transported through the
waves to be received at home,
in an environment
of concentrated solitude,
the course's other study materials
had to pass through the narrow slit
of the mailbox,
in the humble paperback format.

The use of print as a way to intermediate radio and television programmes allowed students to interface with different media in different ways. The images printed in *Radiovision Booklet* that accompanied select radio programmes offered students a learning experience that combined the high aural definition of radio with the high visual definition of the photographic image.
And *Broadcasting Supplement*, *Part 1* and *Part 2* were structured according to a set pedagogical sequence which guided the analysis of each television and radio programme:

1.0 Outline
2.0 Aims
3.0 Before watching/listening the programme
4.0 (a note directing students to consider a series of questions)
5.0 After watching/listening the programme
6.0 Footnotes.

The logic of the broadcasting was thus used to organize the course's printed study materials according to different levels of autonomy,
or rather
different forms of engagement
with a wider audience,
in order to examine the topics at hand from various perspectives.

A305 Plan-reading guide

Walls

1 Load-bearing, usually brick or masonry
2 Partition wall
3 Cavity wall of brick or breeze block usually marked as **1**
4 Low wall or garden wall outside main building
5 Wooden partition
6 Movable wooden screen
7 Wooden or metal balustrade

Apertures

8 Glass framed by wood and metal from floor up
9 Door
10 Window set in a wall
11 Niche in wall
12 Fireplace

Overhead

13 Indicates a change in ceiling level or overhang of upper floors
14 Indicates an important structural beam overhead

Entrances

15 Main entrance
16 Alternative entrance for servants or to garden
17 Fitted furniture – seat, dresser
18 Fitted cupboard with double doors

Roofs

19 Projecting roof seen from above (sloping roof)
20 As above but flat roof

Stairs

21a Spiral stair (ascending in direction of arrow)
21b Straight stairs ascending in direction of arrow
22 Stairs down to basement

Circulation

23 Indicating areas of circulation in a house (corridors, passages etc.)
24 Paved areas on verandas and terraces

Supports

25 Wood, stone or concrete pillar
26 Steel stanchion
27 Flue for fire or boiler
28 North point

HALL OR H	–	Hall
LIVING OR LR	–	Living or sitting room or parlour
DINING OR DR	–	Dining room
BED OR BR	–	Bedroom
DRESSING OR D	–	Dressing room
NURSERY OR N	–	Nursery
BATH OR B	–	Bathroom
WASH OR W	–	Wash house (clothes)
KIT OR K	–	Kitchen
SC	–	Scullery
WC OR	–	Lavatory
STORE OR S	–	All forms of storage – coals, pantry, linen cupboard
SPACE	–	An empty space over a room below

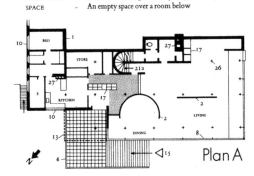

Plan A

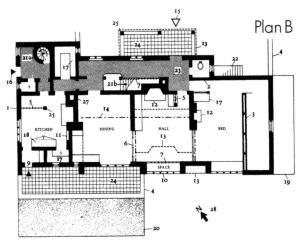

Plan B

The most autonomous among these printed works was *Form and Function: A Source Book for the History of Architecture and Design 1890–1939*, the anthology compiled by Tim Benton, Charlotte Benton, and Dennis Sharp. Like *Documents* and *Images*, A305's other reference collections,
> this encapsulated library
> gathered fragments
> and assembled them
> in a similar manner
> to a low-resolution Xeroxed copy

in an effort to map other discourses not represented in other anthologies from the contemporary field of postmodern debate. For example, Ulrich Conrads' 1970 book *Programmes and Manifestoes on 20th-Century Architecture*, one of A305's recommended readings, served as a matrix of existing discourses on the avant-garde from which the Course Team could diverge, in an effort to expand the range of perspectives represented in *Form and Function* and make a more inclusive outline for the course.

> One part of the course materials
> was therefore addressing
> the specific content of A305 courses,
> while another was addressing an
> overall moment in architecture culture
> through a broader set of perspectives.

Form and Function remains a relevant resource

today and an enduring legacy of the printed memory of the course's intermediation of education, media, and space.
A305 was not simply broadcasting modern architecture:

it was opening up this other,
distributed classroom
across a wide mediascape
and to far-reaching audiences,
utilizing new and old
means of presentation
to produce new ways
of perceiving and interacting
with modern architecture.

[A]
Still of staged Open University course materials from "Open University – BBC Continuity – 1981," https://www.youtube.com/watch?v=ZiQuEZaPOfO. The Open University.

[B]
An Open University student reading course material while on the bus. Reproduced from *The Open University: A History*, written by Daniel Weinbren, 2015: 154.

[C]
Student, Rita, studying for an Open University course at home. Stills from *Educating Rita*, directed by Lewis Gilbert, 1983.

[D]
Ways of Seeing, by John Berger, 1972, published concurrently through television, radio, and print.

(top) Still of title card from television programme 1. © BBC; (left) Transript of radio programme 1, published in *The Listener*. © Immediate Media; (right) Book cover. © Penguin Books

[E]
Film set of *Reyner Banham Loves Los Angeles*. Billboard designed by Deborah Sussman. Photograph by Charles Schwartz, Los Angeles, USA, ca. 1972. © Sussman/Prejza.

[F]
"Plan Reading Guide."Reproduced from Units 1–2 course booklet, *Introduction*, 1975. The Open University.

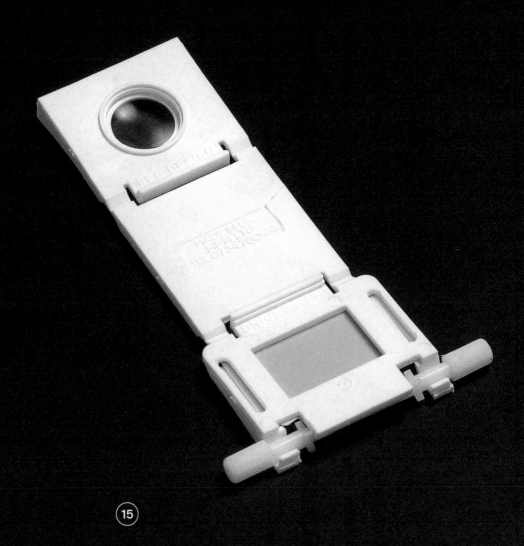

Televarsity:
At Home with The Open University
—Ben Highmore

In December 1961, *The Economist* ran a speculative feature about the future existence of "televarsities"—communities of learners serviced by an educational television channel dedicated to transporting lectures and science demonstrations "into people's own fireside."[1] The article warned that "if an ETV (education television) network does get set up, its worst enemy might well be the conservatism of educationalists themselves. Many of them are likely to be outraged by the prospect of standardized mechanical or electronic teaching."[2] Two years later, Harold Wilson, the leader of the Labour party and soon to be Prime Minister, announced the intention to create a "university of the air" during his speech, "Labour's Plan for Science." In Wilson's words this university was "designed to provide an opportunity for those who, for one reason or another, have not been able to take advantage of higher education."[3] By catering to what were often called non-traditional students, and by using mass-media formats to disseminate knowledge, the university would enrich the development of scientific and cultural fields and disciplines far beyond the bounds of the classical academy. This university of the air materialized as The Open University, and was ushered in by Wilson's government in the second half of the 1960s. It received its charter in 1969 and immediately began to produce course materials for the first intake of students in 1971.

Unlike the dedicated ETV imagined by *The Economist*, The Open University (OU) did not have its own television or radio channel; instead its courses jostled for space in the regular BBC broadcasting schedules, finding pockets of airtime amongst (very) late-night or early-morning programming. These schedules demonstrate the understandable unwillingness of the BBC to give up precious prime-time hours—seven to ten in the evening—and the fact that the ability of OU students to tune in was often constrained by the conventions of nine-to-five working days. Nor need *The Economist* have worried too much about the conservatism of the educationists because the OU attracted precisely those academics who saw the format of its courses—radio and television programmes, published anthologies of sources, course-specific

1
"Televarsities?," *The Economist*, 16 December 1961, 1105.

2
"Televarsities?," 1106.

3
Harold Wilson, *Labour's Plan for Science* (London: Victoria House Printing Company, 1963), 4. This document is a reprint of the annual Labour Party conference speech delivered 1 October 1963, in Scarborough, United Kingdom.

booklets, intensive summer schools, telephone tutorials, and written assignments and feedback circulated by mail—as an educational opportunity rather than as a limiting condition to overcome. Through these unorthodox formats, the OU pioneered an approach to teaching that had (and still has) technology and design at the heart of its operations and of many of its most innovative courses.[4] The development and use of communication technologies (from television to the internet, by way of VHS tapes, CD-ROMs, and DVDs) was central to its growth and to the way it treated pedagogy itself as a technology that could be tested, refined, and reconfigured. Indeed, the OU's Institute of Educational Technology (IET), formed in 1970, remains at the centre of curricular development: each course team includes a member of IET who considers every element of teaching material in terms of its pedagogic efficacy, from the length of sentences and the use of jargon, to the layout of booklets and the visualization of content for television.[5]

The OU was integral to a revitalized Britain that would be, in Harold Wilson's words, "forged in the white heat of [a scientific] revolution."[6] This was part of a soft revolution that was simultaneously technological, social, and cultural.[7] For instance, the *necessary* enabling conditions for the birth of The Open University included technological networks, such as a semi-automated postal service, a national broadcasting company, and a ubiquity of televisions and radios in people's homes, as well as a political and social will to extend the provision of higher education to those who had suffered from an "educational apartheid."[8] Indeed, as a cultural project, the OU was entangled in a set of forces and changes that were reaching into both the academy and the home. Mass communication, particularly in the shape of the domestic television, was not simply a vehicle for conveying OU course information, but also a social agent that was active in making and unmaking academic discourse, family life, and the imaginative possibilities for democratic culture.

At Home with Technology

When the OU rolled out its first year of teaching, half of Britain's housing stock was council houses, built to accommodate predominantly working and lower-middle-class families.[9] By then, British homes were already humming with technological devices designed to make modern life more hygienic, less labour-intensive, and more

4
The first courses offered by The OU in 1971 were four foundation courses. T100, the technology foundation course, was called The Man-Made World and was introduced by the then Minister for Technology, Anthony Wedgwood Benn.

5
For the work of the IET, see Janet Gale "Proteus in a Kaleidoscope: The Educational Technologist in Open University Course Production," *Journal of Educational Television* 6, no. 1 (1980): 4–7.

6
Wilson, *Labour's Plan for Science*, 7.

7
For a general account of Britain's soft revolutions, see Paul Addison, *No Turning Back: The Peacetime Revolutions of Postwar Britain* (Oxford: Oxford University Press, 2010).

8
Wilson, *Labour's Plan for Science*, 3.

9
Matthew Hollow, "The Age of Affluence Revisited: Council Estates and Consumer Society in Britain, 1950–1970," *Journal of Consumer Culture* 16, no. 1 (2016): 282.

conducive to leisure and entertainment. The idea of the labour-saving device took off in the early twentieth century alongside the expansion of middle-class, servant-less households. But of course, the diffusion of technology was never even, either in terms of its distribution amongst social groups or in terms of the type of technology in general. A 1958 survey of an estate of 120 council houses in Liverpool revealed that many such devices were, by then, almost ubiquitous. The survey, conducted to find out how people were using their electrical sockets in the newly-built estate, concluded that:

> Every house had an electric iron; 106 had a vacuum cleaner; 101 had a television; and 96 a radio. On top of this, a significant number of kettles, hair-dryers, sewing-machines, toasters and razors were also found, along with a handful of tropical fish tanks. In fact, the only area in which the council estate homes examined in this study could be said to be slightly lagging behind the rest of the housing market was in the kitchen, where the BRS [Building Research Station] only found 50 washing machines and a comparatively paltry 19 refrigerators.[10]

It would be a mistake to see class—and income—as the only guide to understanding patterns of diffusion of technology amongst households.[11] The most modernized houses in postwar Britain were often the mass of council houses, designed with the specific idea of working-class families enjoying the latest modern conveniences.

It is also worth looking at diffusion patterns of domestic technology from the perspective of individual devices. Across the twentieth century, patterns suggest that some kinds of domestic technology reached levels of market saturation much more quickly than others. The work of economic historians Sue Bowden and Avner Offer shows that, for instance, within the first half of the twentieth century, it took roughly forty years for the vacuum cleaner to become a fixture in half of British households while it took only ten years for the radio to be so widely circulated.[12] Following the practice of the retail market, Bowden and Offer distinguished between those devices promoted as time-saving, such as vacuum cleaners and washing machines, and those promoted as time-consuming, primarily radios and televisions. In short, time-saving technologies were adopted more slowly by the average household than time-consuming ones. This pattern of diffusion reflected a patriarchal model of households where men managed the finances for buying (often by paying in instalments) or renting large domestic appliances, and women were seen as responsible for daily housework.[13] Time-saving domestic devices save women time; time-consuming devices, to be enjoyed by all family members, were often controlled by men. A common scene for many children was their mother ironing while watching television and their father making an executive decision to change the channel over to "his" programme, even though others were right in the middle of watching something else.

The Open University made a significant intervention into the image and reality of the technological household and it did it in two ways: by recruiting large numbers of women, especially housewives,

10
Hollow, 283.

11
In the case of refrigerators, for instance, the primary factor guiding their diffusion may well have been cost, given that in the 1950s they were still inordinately expensive, but it may also have been that refrigerators were, in principle, less useful in an urban setting where local shops were plentiful.

12
Sue Bowden and Avner Offer, "Household Appliances and the Use of Time: The United States and Britain Since the 1920s," *Economic History Review* 47, no. 4 (November 1994): 725–48.

13
Sue Bowden and Avner Offer, "The Technological Revolution That Never Was: Gender, Class, and the Diffusion of Household Appliances in Interwar England," in *The Sex of Things: Gender and Consumption in Historical Perspective*, ed. Victoria de Grazia (Berkeley: University of California Press, 1996), 244–74. Few people could buy expensive appliances outright so hire-purchase agreements (referred to as buying on the "never, never") significantly increased the diffusion of items such as washing machines or three-piece sofas. By the 1960s, the majority of households rented their televisions rather than owned them.

for courses that required the use of time-consuming technologies, and by changing the use and experience of watching television and listening to the radio.

Learning at Your (In)Convenience

It is ironic that the education offered by the OU is often referred to as distance learning, when in fact that learning is usually being conducted at kitchen tables, in living rooms, and in bedrooms. It is the teaching that is at a distance, not the learning. The form of education that the OU student received could be described as both mediated and intimate. If the traditional university student received a one-to-one tutorial in a professor's book-lined office, then the OU student received a one-to-one tutorial via telephone while sitting amongst their own furnishings, free to indulge in biscuits and coffee (today, of course, such communication is an online affair).[14] While a student attending a traditional university lecture often had to find a seat amongst a barrage of other students, sometimes to be distracted by their commentary, an OU student usually watched a televised lecture alone.

But if watching television was usually a sociable experience, in which a household (or part of one) gathered together, then that of watching an OU programme as a student was entirely different. Here the sociability of the experience was virtual and remote. Indeed, the entire student experience could be understood as a peculiar state of being solitary, but with a sense of collective solidarity. One female student described: "[As I] sat alone each night at my kitchen table I was buoyed by the knowledge that thousands like me were also sitting with a cold cup of coffee at 1:30 a.m.!! I felt a shared isolation! I loved it."[15] This collective solitude was most powerful when, through television and radio, students were addressed as a collective body rather than as an anonymous abstraction known as an audience. And if non-student viewers and listeners found themselves, late at night, watching an explanation of how a particle accelerator functioned, then they too were addressed as part of this collective body.

In an era of one set per household, television had the power to draw a family together, but it was also the source of endless negotiations and conflicts.[16] Before the possibility of videotaping, when you had to watch a broadcast live, scheduling clashes were inevitable: a news programme versus *Top of the Pops* (a chart show, during which pop groups mimed to their latest single); a Saturday afternoon film versus *Match of the Day* (a football programme, recapping highlights and analysis from recent matches). In some ways, these conflicts were mollified by the introduction of colour television at the end of the 1960s, which was then widely adopted in the 1970s. Getting a new colour television (usually by renting one) meant that there was now a spare black-and-white set that could live in the kitchen or in a draughty back bedroom. The diaries compiled by Mass-Observation in the 1980s offer endless examples of women, usually with school-aged children, relegated to an upstairs room to watch their OU programme on the old black-and-white television.[17] For many women, studying at home was studying in their workplace. For one such OU student, living in a large three-storey

14
Cambridge and Oxford, although exceptional, primarily taught through one-to-one tutorials. Most universities would use one-to-one tutorials as part of an array of techniques.

15
Daniel Weinbren, *The Open University: A History* (Manchester: Manchester University Press in association with The Open University, 2015), 202.

16
For an account of television watching habits in the British context, see Joe Moran, *Armchair Nation: An intimate history of Britain in front of the TV* (London: Profile Books, 2014). For an account of the ambivalent role of television in relation to the family in the North American context, see Lynn Spigel, *Make Room for TV: Television and the Family Ideal in Postwar America* (Chicago: University of Chicago Press, 1992).

17
Mass-Observation was a project that began in 1937 as a form of "anthropology at home." It recruited volunteer observers who answered various questions (often about everyday life) as well as recorded diaries. After World War II it became a form of market research, before dissolving in the mid-1960s. The project was resuscitated in the early 1980s as a project to collect material about everyday life in Britain with the purpose of providing evidence for future social historians.

house, the choice of turning an attic room into a makeshift study, with a black-and-white television, was a strategic way of finding space as far away from the kitchen as possible. That way, if her teenagers wanted her, at least they had to make a bit of effort to find her.[18] Many, of course, did not have the luxury of a large house.

The OU degree was often a gruelling test of endurance, undertaken in isolating circumstances and during odd hours, which required a student to produce more written work and complete more exams than was common for a degree at a traditional university or polytechnic. As the OU Chancellor put it: "We came up with what is undoubtedly the most difficult way of obtaining a degree yet devised by the wit of man."[19] Television and radio, as disseminators of academic content, were both symptomatic of this experience, and a way of compensating for it. In other words, OU television posited a virtual community, but it also operated as a platform for mediating the specific social and educational circumstances that characterized the student experience. The OU's first broadcast, in January 1971, was *Open Forum*, during which the secretary of the University used television to welcome the 25,000 new students as well as hundreds of thousands of the general public. *Open Forum* was a magazine programme that presented the OU's plans for future expansion, explained the educational structure, discussed student retention, and relayed important events, such as degree awarding ceremonies. Its format usually involved a variety of components: it might start, for instance, with a tour of Walton Hall, the OU headquarters in Milton Keynes; then cut to a studio showing a discussion between students and tutors about the marking criteria for assignments; followed by students talking amongst themselves about their experiences and how they overcame various difficulties. Importantly, then, it was the broadcasting space where students participated *publicly* in the life of the university. On *Open Forum* students discussed issues both amongst themselves and with tutors, such as what it was like to be a mature female student with a husband who disapproved of studying, or how to write an essay having never written one before because of leaving school at fourteen to get a job. In directly addressing a collective body in this way, OU television was not simply part of a supply chain, it had developed a sophisticated feedback loop. Through *Open Forum*, power relationships between students and tutors were often reversed: the students would teach the tutors about the reality of life as an OU student, or cross-examine them about the way that they made judgements. In this way it revealed other possibilities for television that were closer to ideas about community television —television made by and disseminated within a local community—as a democratic space of grounded, public engagement in which knowledge flowed in multilateral directions.

18
James Hinton, *Seven Lives from Mass Observation: Britain in the Late Twentieth Century* (Oxford: Oxford University Press, 2016), 25–40.

19
Gerald Gardiner, quoted in Michael Richardson, *Countdown to the Open University*, produced by the BBC for The Open University, aired 8 January 1978, http://www.open.ac.uk/library/digital-archive/pdf/script/script:03ab4128fd5060485e81ccd-cc4c193b78b4d7d35.

20
Raymond Williams, *Marxism and Literature* (Oxford: Oxford University Press, 1977), 115.

21
Kenneth Clark, cited in the viewing notes accompanying the DVD set *Civilisation: A Personal View by Lord Clark*, presented by Kenneth Clark, BBC Worldwide, 2005. *Civilisation*, directed by Michael Gill and Peter Montagnon, aired 23 February 1969 to 18 May 1969.

The age of television coincided with an assault on a hierarchical ranking of culture. The flow of television offers seamless segues from a Mozart opera to a soap opera, from a documentary about malnutrition to an advertisement for frozen television dinners. If universities and museums have traditionally been given the job of establishing and maintaining what Raymond Williams called "the selective tradition" of so-called high culture (according to which Shakespeare is inherently superior to Agatha Christie), then television became one of the most powerful technologies for questioning the unassailable consecration of the masterpiece and the genius.[20] A television-based university was therefore caught in an ambivalent position between forces that sought to maintain a hierarchy of cultural production and those for whom culture was everywhere and ordinary. To make matters more complicated, the BBC, the OU's media partner, was, in the 1960s and 1970s, undecided about what kind of role non-commercial television would play in this struggle. The BBC was caught between a social mission to educate the population and to act as a guardian of "serious" culture, and a need to capture a popular audience that was, since the end of the BBC's monopoly of service as of the Television Act of 1954, being seduced by the pleasures of independent, commercial broadcasting. A partial settlement was reached in 1964 when the BBC launched BBC2, a second non-commercial channel dedicated to minority programming such as snooker and more challenging drama series (rather than football and variety shows), as well as eventually to the OU's academic programming. BBC2 allowed the BBC to create a space where broadcasting was not overly concerned with viewing figures and the competing (though sometimes overlapping) demands of entertainment and quality.

As the OU was being established, the BBC set about filming its most ambitious television series to date, *Civilisation*, which was written and presented by the art historian Kenneth Clark. Production of the series began in 1966 and it aired in 1969. *Civilisation* was a tribute to "the God-given genius ... of the great men that Western Europe has produced during the last thousand years."[21] It was also a vivid demonstration that such a civilization was often the property of a patrician class. In shot after shot, Clark was portrayed as the affable aristocrat guiding the television audience through "his" Europe; eminently at ease in the grounds of castles and palaces, or in pointing out stained-glass cathedral windows. In 1972, the Marxist critic John Berger produced *Ways of Seeing*, a four-part riposte to Clark's odyssey, in which he refused to separate old masters from advertising agents, both of whom depicted women as objects of the male gaze. Clark's televisual character wore a bespoke Savile Row suit and had short, slicked-back hair, while Berger had thick, slightly-unkempt hair that reached his collar, and he wore a casual, patterned shirt without (noticeably) a jacket and tie.

It soon became clear that the OU's cultural politics were closer to those of Berger than of Clark (even if neck ties and sports jackets were often the default attire of the predominantly male lecturers). Clark's civilization looked back on one thousand years of grand technological and cultural achievements; Berger's looked back on five centuries of other technological innovations such as the printing press, photo-chemical processes, and magnetic tape recording, as well as on a history of patriarchal relationships and property ownership. In line with Berger, the OU was born from an insistence that technology mattered, that technology shaped our perception of the world. As an institution, it shared Berger's sense of seriousness as well as his desire to question the assumptions that presumed the natural superiority of one mode of cultural production over another. The OU's cultural inquisitiveness was never going to be content with assuming that the selective tradition, as defined by Williams, was the only model of cultural study worth investigating.

The cultural values of the OU took seriously the critical challenges posed by writers in the 1960s, such as Reyner Banham and Lawrence Alloway, who argued that the modern world was no longer characterized by a dichotomy between an exclusive "high culture," appreciated by those with sensitivity and time, and a popular "low culture," beloved by the masses. Instead it was characterized by a cultural continuum, a so-called long front, that could include Elvis Presley *and* Bach, General Motors *and* Botticelli. The connoisseur's familiarity with the details of a style was no longer the preserve of those who loved oil painting and wine, but was also demonstrated by those who loved Hollywood musicals or detective novels and could draw nuanced distinctions between sub-genres. In the 1960s, Banham noticed that to be a pop-connoisseur (an amateur expert in popular culture, or simply a rock and roll fan) required the same training as to be a traditional connoisseur. The popular culture fan was, according to Banham, "trained to extract every subtlety, marginal meaning, overtone or technical nicety from any of the mass media. A Pop Art connoisseur, as opposed to a fine art connoisseur. The opposition, however, is only one of taste, otherwise the training required to become a connoisseur is the same." [22] The OU offered a space for new critical connoisseurs, like Banham, who were more interested in Detroit's latest offerings than in rhapsodizing about Raphael's greatest paintings. And television was the perfect training ground for new cultural production, whether through the self-conscious seriousness of an OU programme or through the greater access to movies, music, and comedy. In the wake of radical cultural theorists such as John Berger, Stuart Hall, and later Germaine Greer, the OU nurtured those connoisseurs who recognized that the selective tradition of high culture, far from being explained as the dispassionate evaluation of those born into it, was (to some degree at least) determined by the powerful forces of colonial, patriarchal, and economic elitism.

22
Reyner Banham, "Who is this 'Pop'?" in *Design by Choice*, ed. Penny Sparke (London: Academy Editions, 1981), 94. Essay first published in 1963. When Banham names something as "Pop art," he is not referring to the artworks associated with artists such as Andy Warhol, but with the commercial culture associated with Hollywood, Coca-Cola, and comics.

The Open University was always imagined as a public institution that included an audience beyond its specific student body. As a technical resource the BBC allowed the OU to be public in a way that was unprecedented for a university. The overlap between a broadcasting platform and a sense of public good were written into the OU's charter which stated that its objective was "to promote the educational well-being of the community generally." [23] Broadcast media was the perfect vehicle for extending the reach of the university to a national population because it brought education into the home, to nestle amongst the material environment of domestic life.

Television and radio, as live broadcast media, brought the world into the home in a way that newspapers never could, while also bringing in a new world of professional entertainment. The limits of private and public space continued to be fundamentally altered as television became both the public face of private life (through soap operas and *Play for Today* dramas that offered endless dissections of private lives),[24] and the private realm for witnessing public life (through news that showed the endless bombardment of a war-torn world every evening at six, and again at nine). As an alternative to these forms of entertainment, OU television created a different public sphere within the home, one that encouraged critical deliberation and that invited the viewer to talk back, albeit within the confines of an essay or an *Open Forum* programme. The OU, especially in its early years, gave an idea of how innovative research and pedagogical methods could imagine and produce a community of adult learners, and how television could be used to further the aims of democratic culture by embedding it in the day-to-day lives of a public that both watched and learned. In 2006, the OU broadcast its last televised course and, from that point on, turned to the less-than-public realm of online education, where communication might be via email, or restricted-access forums. If the Internet and social media encourage everyone to have their say, OU television fostered a space where feedback was combined with an ethics of listening (of spending time with the thoughts of others) that could open up new ways of seeing the world.

23
The Open University, Charter and Statutes, 23 April 1969, as amended to 2005. http://www.open.ac.uk/about/documents/about-university-charter.pdf.

24
Play for Today was an anthology drama series, aired from 1970 to 1984 on BBC1, that often showcased young writers and plays that dealt with families and their private lives. The show was sometimes controversial because of the way writers dealt with sensitive social themes such as unemployment and homelessness.

Adrian Forty
A305 Course Team member

Alexandra Palace, London, UK
24 July 2017

Adrian Forty [AF]
Joaquim Moreno [JM]

JM   I remember you telling me that what is still current about A305 is the possible futures it elicited. How did you become an instructor in the course?

AF   I was initially an outsider to The Open University. When I was invited by Tim Benton to contribute, the course was already well underway and they had already made quite a lot of it. I had nothing, really, to contribute to the original development of the course and the way in which it was set out, but there was some gap they wanted to fill. I was invited through Reyner Banham because I was working with him at the time. He had been involved in the A305 course and knew what I was doing, or what I was interested in, and he suggested that I might be a useful contributor. That's really how I met Tim Benton. I didn't know Tim before that. But he picked up on Banham's suggestion and that drew me into the course.

My first published piece of work, which precedes The Open University course, was about designed objects—radio cabinets —and was an attempt to make sense of the design of everyday things and to put together some kind of account of the social relations that lay behind the things that were familiar within everyone's houses. That provided some material for the OU unit that I wrote.

JM   Going now to your later work, "Lorenzo of the Underground," it leads us to the radio programmes Nikolaus Pevsner did about Frank Pick and the London Underground. How much of a presence did Pevsner have in the course?

AF   Pevsner was sort of the grandfather of the history of modern architecture and design in Britain. Pevsner's books from the 1930s, *Pioneers of the Modern Movement* and *An Enquiry into Industrial Art in England*, made him the key figure. There was a sense of deference to Pevsner. When he came to Britain from Germany, Pevsner was drawing attention to a whole new body of work which could be seen as coherent, and to the fact that you could think about modern architecture and design as being something that could be studied in its own way.

The historical study of architecture and design in England in the 1960s was built upon the foundation of Pevsner's *Pioneers of the Modern Movement*. It was what everybody referred to, even though it actually had rather little in it about modern design—but it seemed to be the main source, the point of reference. In a way, it was probably Pevsner's radio programmes that were more significant in focusing attention on modern architecture. Pevsner did a lot of broadcasting; he was very active in promoting modern architecture and design on the radio, particularly after the Second World War. In a sense, he's a progenitor both of that interest in modern architecture and design, but also of using the medium of radio to disseminate knowledge about it.

When I contributed to the course, I had also been an enthusiastic reader of Sigfried Giedion's *Mechanization Takes Command* and was particularly struck by the fact that he had found a way of writing about anonymous objects and anonymous history. This is one of those books that, when I first discovered it, I was astonished that somebody could have put together such an extraordinary collection of objects and produced a narrative about them. This was such a revelation; it completely blew my mind away. It was this kind of revelation: that we have a world of objects that are all to do with their impact on the human body, and that the way in which the human body and deportment are presented is something which you can read through design material—advertising materials, patents, illustrations from all sorts of sources. Giedion's book is fantastic and it has all these chapters about seating, the chair, and then stuff about water, bathing, and the mechanization of the bath. It is an absolutely fantastic piece of research, completely fascinating, and so diverse. I think this is one of the great classics of design history—or not even of design history: of social history.

That was really what I was interested in: how you could say things about objects where there was no known designer. In a way, this put me opposite to most of the people involved with the course, because the whole emphasis of the course was on the work of known or well-known designers and, to me, at the time, that wasn't particularly interesting. I did not want to pursue that line which followed through from the authorship of individuals. I was much more interested in the anonymous history.

In a way, my position in the course as a whole was anomalous. I was an oddity, a stranger, because the focus of the course was, in a way, a quite conventional architectural history. It was taking the work of canonical architects and designers, and presenting the material through the names of individual architects and authors, effectively through a largely biographical mode, and I—I really didn't have much sympathy with that.

It was a surprise that they wanted to have me on the team, but I think Banham had encouraged them to do so, to try and adopt a way of looking at history and architectural

history that wasn't focused on individuals and authors. This was an approach that Banham had become interested in at the time. He had become keen on the pursuit of history where there were no known authors. He had done this work on Los Angeles, *Los Angeles: The Architecture of Four Ecologies,* dealing with the history of Los Angeles as a city that was made by all sorts of people, many of whose names were unknown.

Reyner Banham was quite critical of Tim Benton's approach to the course, I think. He was very supportive but, at the same time, he was critical of it for being a quite conventional model of approaching history.

JM And you came and you just electrified it, literally.

AF [Chuckles] Well, *British Design* was one of the units in the A305 course, to which I contributed a section on the electric home. I can't remember exactly how this idea of a unit on the electric home came up, but it coincided with what I was interested in at that time and what I had been looking at.

I got interested in design history for a number of reasons, and the challenge was to see what you could say about objects even when we knew rather little about where they came from. How do you address something when you can't find any documents, or necessarily come to any obvious explanations of why it's there? How, then, do you approach it? That question was connected with the early origins of design history as well; there were other people interested in similar kinds of questions.

The interest in electricity, however, was something quite specific. At that time, there was a history of the electricity industry in Britain being worked on by an economic historian called Leslie Hannah. After meeting him and talking to him, I became interested in the question of how, essentially, the electricity industry promoted itself and looked to the home for new markets that could be assimilated but didn't exacerbate the peaks of demand created by industrial use of electricity, which had been the main market for electricity originally.

There was a pressure to find ways of bringing this new material, this new energy source, into houses, because the home is always reluctant to accept things from the outside world. Nowadays, this seems absurd, you know? Nobody would question electricity being a source of energy in the home, but a hundred years ago this was not so easy to accept. There were limited things that you could do with it, apart from lighting. There was uneasiness about it, a reluctance to accept electricity.

JM   You also illustrated this point through advertising, another form of design.

AF   A lot of the research I did at that time and subsequently was through looking at advertising, because that seemed to be a way of understanding how these products were being marketed and the world in which they were being promoted. In the early 1970s, there was a series of strikes in the mining industry which caused power shortages across the UK. There were periodic blackouts when electricity supply was cut off and, effectively, electricity was being rationed because of problems in the industrial relations between the government and the National Union of Mineworkers. We had a three-day work week when energy was not available. As a result there were also a lot of periodically inoperative electrical appliances sitting around in people's houses. Things that should be active but were defunct, non-functioning.

I was teaching in a design school at that time and I suggested that we put together an exhibition of appliances that were inoperative—and it became historical. We did two exhibitions of inert objects: one about vacuum cleaners and one about electric fireplaces. People brought in things they found or had lying around their homes, and we put them together in an exhibition. Electric fires were particularly embarrassing because during a three-day week and periodical electricity blackouts, there's nothing more useless than an electric fire. We put together a history of electric fires through this very simple process of just getting people to look in their attics, pick out stuff that was sitting around in their homes, stuff that was rubbish out on the streets, and bringing them together.

JM   You were examining the everyday, and those were the means through which the course was actually reaching people.

AF   One of the problems about the A305 course was that most of the materials it dealt with were things that people had never seen. Many of these iconic modernist buildings were not in Britain. Some of them were in fairly inaccessible parts of Eastern Europe. There was this difficulty of engaging people with the experience of materials that they would only ever see second-hand, through photographs or film. The programme was so successful, in a way, because it used film effectively and intelligently to introduce people to buildings.

My contribution to the course was to deal with the everyday, to deal with the material that people might actually have around them in their own homes and to think of it as designed material; to think about the processes through which they might have come into being and the part these processes might have played in people's lives. My contribution was a study of ordinary things in ordinary houses, which set out to do something that was rather different from most of the A305 course. There was significant value, I think, in shifting the course's attention away from distant objects to nearby ones, to things that might have some resonance with the students and elicit their curiosity in the process of taking the course. The students would recognize some of the things that were being illustrated and that they might not previously have thought about as being objects of design. I suppose I was able introduce a framework within which students might examine them.

JM   You also made a point similar to that Raymond Williams was making about television. There's nothing built into television technology that makes it domestic.

AF   No.

JM   Was Williams's work, *Technology and Cultural Form*, an important influence on the course, too?

AF   I don't think I was ever particularly interested in Williams's work on television, but I was certainly interested in how cultural forms and technology come together. Williams was a very powerful influence on the development of cultural studies in Britain and he was certainly on my horizon, but I couldn't see a way to use it in what I was doing.

I had been thinking about the question of radio as an invisible medium that reached into people's homes, and I had read Asa Briggs' history of the BBC in which he had some things to say about the kind of mismatch between what the BBC was broadcasting and what people might have wanted to listen to and accept.

JM   On a side note, Asa Briggs, in the last volume of his history of the BBC, has a chapter called "Pirates and Educators," where he brings together The Open University and pirate radio.

AF   They all come out of the same box, don't they? They go together in a way, and I mean, that was one of the wonders—and still is one of the wonders—of radio: you can switch between channels and get some utterly different things. I suppose that it was Briggs' cleverness to realize that the medium actually consisted of these juxtapositions, that this was what was going on. The BBC was always on the back foot in relation to pirate radio, they could never quite keep up, but I don't think The Open University was in open competition with pirate radio.

JM   A305 was mostly received at home, through radio and television programmes, but there were also the summer sessions. Do you recall those sessions and the role they played in the course overall?

AF   Well, I think I only did one or two summer schools. But certainly, within The Open University, the summer schools were major events because they were the opportunity for the students, first, to meet each other and to meet tutors and, secondly—my goodness—they were really intensive. A305 students were voracious in their appetite for studying. They were fun. I can't remember very much about what we were taught during the summer sessions exactly, but I do remember the kind of atmosphere, and the conversation, and that sense of enthusiasm and curiosity. The summer schools were really fantastic. People wanted to study, but they also wanted to live the student life because most of them were working, had

everyday occupations, or perhaps were housewives. They came to a university campus and they wanted to be students and, in every sense, this became a release and a kind of discovery of new life for them.

JM   Another strand of your contribution to The Open University is radiovision.

AF   Yes. Radiovision programmes were radio broadcasts that were accompanied by photographs. There was a text that came over the radio and related to the photographs. The programme I did was about the labour-saving home, using a case study of electricity in the home based around this exhibition house built in Battersea in the 1930s. Reyner Banham also did one, on mechanical services.

JM   Today, you can find the *Radiovision Booklet* and other course supplements in second-hand shops or online, some were properly rebound by a library then offloaded. It might say something about the life of these books.

AF   I am surprised that they've survived. Certainly when we were doing them, we saw them mainly as having the lifespan of the course, and there wasn't any expectation that they were going to go any further than that. I don't think we thought very much about what the future life of the course was going to be. As far as I was concerned, my involvement was very much in the moment, it wasn't something where we had an eye to posterity, to what might happen later.

JM   I read a lot of correspondence about trying to make something out of A305 when it was being discontinued. The audiences of The Open University, the audience for television, changed at different rates than the particular programming of the course, which made them obsolete at a different rate.

AF   I think, in my experience, that the course might have been whole for students of The Open University, who might have taken it, read everything, seen all the programmes, and studied it in its entirety, but that most of us took from it the bits that were useful to us, for example recordings of some of the television programs and maybe bits of texts from the booklets, and used those for teaching.

Outside the A305 course itself, I think it survived by being plundered for its best bits, so to speak. The programs, books and supplements had things that you couldn't get anywhere else, and some of the television programs—I remember there was one which Tim Benton had done about the Frankfurt housing program in the late 1920s, early 1930s—were really useful, you know? You couldn't find that anywhere else, a half-hour television program about a part of the history of modern architecture. I was certainly still using material from A305 with my students in the mid 1980s, showing some of the films. Eventually, the clothes that people were wearing in the films, and Tim's ties, became too much of a distraction. The whole late 1960s, early 1970s dress code and sense that was apparent in the films became off-putting, students stopped listening to what was being said or to what was being shown, and this made it difficult to watch the films.

I think that the course as a whole eventually ran out of steam. The way in which scholarship about modern architecture had developed, the rivalry of postmodernism and so on, which called into question so much of what was being presented in the programs, meant that A305 was no longer really viable as a coherent course. There must have been a point when it was seen as being obsolete.

The course was like a battleship, in that it only had a limited life, and then you took the bits apart and you used them for other things. That's really what had happened with The Open University, with A305. I would say that the bits that survived, like *Form and Function,* were the most valuable because they were really useful anthologies of texts on modern architecture and design, which you couldn't get anywhere else. *Form and Function,* and *Documents* were some of the first anthologies of texts, though these sorts of anthologies have now become quite commonplace. The work was really exceptional. Some of the pieces were original translations as well, so it had lasting value. I think it's still valuable, actually. I still occasionally go back to it.

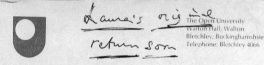

Laura's original

return soon

The Open University
Walton Hall, Walton
Bletchley, Buckinghamshire
Telephone: Bletchley 4066

THE OPEN UNIVERSITY

The BBC asked me to send you this material –

With the compliments of

Lindsay Gordon

---

of the casual adoption of new materials because they happened to
be available cheaply or free, of the small scale and hand
building of the most advanced furniture designs of the machine
age add fuel to the debunking of the myth about architecture
and design in the 20th century: that it was mass-produced with
the conscious use of the newest materials and methods.

2. Aims

a. To hear an outstanding designer and entrepreneur working
in a key area at a key time.

b. To look at some of the products of Isokon.

c. To examine the methods of production and design in a
key organisation in Britain in the 30s.

3. Before you Listen to the Programme
Parts ~~in Unit 18 and Four~~
Read ~~relevant set passages~~ ((- - -). Look at the pictures
in the Radio-Vision supplement.

4. After Listening to the Programme

a. List the parts of the design and production process that I
have described as "Ad hoc".

b. Jack Pritchard's education seems to be as surprising and
unusual for a proponent of new design in a different way: how
do I mean? How suitable was it for his career?

c. What were the other modern materials, and why did he reject
them?

d. How far do you think Isokon succeeded and in what ways?
How do you think its work compares with that of continental
designers? Use the illustrations to help you answer.

5. Discussion

a. The choice of design as a career, choice of materials, the
coming together of Isokon, the methods of production, testing,
marketing.

Radio-Vision Booklet for
The work of <u>Isokon</u>   A305/30

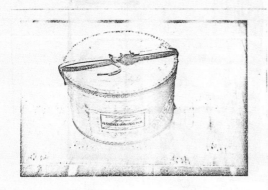

262A

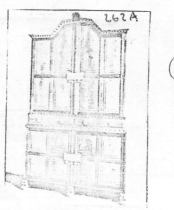

2662

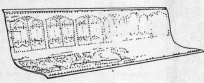

266a

⑩

⑪

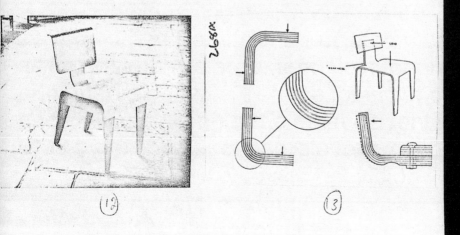

⑫

⑬

Episode Five

The Course
Was Listening

Joaquim Moreno

A305 was listening to the voices of surviving protagonists of the modern movement while also
giving voice to the otherwise anonymous students
of architectural history.
      Due to its use of media
      and its material outputs,
the course could both teach through the eyes
and voices of the modernist architects and historians, as well as survey the impact of modern
architecture across Britain from the perspective
of its students, as presented in their project reports. A305 also created new historical materials
by adapting the course content to the production
requirements of mass media. The extensive
research needed to transpose history to a new
media embedded itself all the way through
the listening process. Research did not stop
with the establishment of the syllabus, but rather
became a continuous process
      of recording,
      editing,
      and surveying

—in other words, listening—
which added other vectors,
voices, and visions
to the history of the modern movement.
Such a highly empirical method of study and
pedagogy resulted in a complex and recursive
relationship between research and teaching.

Taking advantage of the localized yet distributed
character of The Open University student body,
supported by the territorial coverage of the BBC's
broadcasting infrastructure, the A305 Course
Team operated a two-way system of communication and content development that extended well
beyond mass-produced teaching materials.
Local perspectives,
presented in dutifully researched
case studies that drew
from reliable primary sources,
were gathered into an imagined map
of British architecture and design
that was much more extensive
than the work of well-known architects.
At the same time, A305 presented
the unique contributions
of the modern movement's protagonists
in varied ways.
Via its radio programmes in particular, the course
offered critical commentaries by theoreticians
such as Reyner Banham,

dialogues and interviews
with designers and architects
such as Colin Lucas, Basil Ward,
and Amyas Connell,
and monologues from notable historians
such as Sir John Summerson
and Nikolaus Pevsner.
Because it listened to its time and to its constituents, A305 course materials and student reports
have now become primary historical sources;
more than accidental documents
symptomatic of their time,
they gathered the voices
of the modern movement
and carried them to our present.

Gathering these voices was also one of Reyner
Banham's most well-known contributions to
architectural historiography, particularly evident
in *Theory and Design in the First Machine Age*.
In Radio 8,
the A305 programme titled simply
"Frank Lloyd Wright,"
Banham bridges the historical gap by presenting
the voice of Wright, excerpted from a talk first
aired by the BBC in 1946. There was no more direct
way to explain ideas about
"an architecture of democracy"
and "organic architecture"

than through the very voice of their proponent. As the narrator, Banham announces:

> What was this Organic Architecture that he advocated? You will hear him explain it as something close to democracy itself: he sees both as aspects of the same thing—the right to be oneself, which was the title he gave this talk.

But, fulfilling his pedagogical role, Banham also uses his own voice to complicate Wright's arguments. He reframes Wright's conception of democracy and architecture as both organic and inseparable within the context of the United Nations' headquarters in New York, describing the final design as the outcome of a "highly democratic process," albeit a nominal and bureaucratic one:

> The various nations sent their top architects, who were mostly the respected and elected heads of their professions (and therefore did not include Mr Wright!), and these worthy men sat down together as equal partners to thrash out a design. Finally, almost inevitably, they took over a project by Le Corbusier and burocratised [sic] it around a bit. The result, as you know, was a tall glass slab full of bureaucrats towering over a relatively insignificant block for the General Assembly to meet in. It was, I suppose, a fair, average symbol of the kind of 'democracy' practised by most of the United Nations, but it could not be the kind of building Wright admired.

Banham's delicate political irony is not simply a commentary on the bureaucratic democracy of the United Nations. Banham is aware of his own position within the narrative and deliberately sharpens the contours of Wright's idea of democracy and how it should be embodied in the built environment. Wright calls for the Assembly room to be "a place

of light as wide open to the sky as possible"
rather than a "screen to hide ignoble fears or
cherish native hypocrisy." But Banham points out
that the room is virtually inaccessible and argues
that Wright's organic democracy relies on the
idea of an "open democracy of the frontier, or of
the camp-meetings of that living religion."

       Through the use of radio,
       A305 could offer its listeners
       two distinct voices:
       both that
       of a great architect from the archives
       and that
       of his contemporary critic.

A historian who also established a very particular
way of setting the stage for a play between the
protagonists of modern architecture was Sir John
Summerson—his voice was already well-known
on BBC radio through his 1963 lectures *The Classical Language of Architecture*. In the programme he
prepared for A305,

       Radio 28
       "The MARS Group and the Thirties,"
Summerson provides a panorama of
       the "aims,
       the composition,
       and the achievements"
of the Modern Architectural Research (MARS)
Group in Britain, following its foundation in 1933.

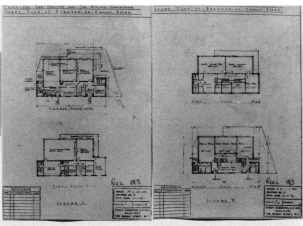

FIRST DESIGN : NOV. 1929

SECOND
DESIGN
FEB. 1930

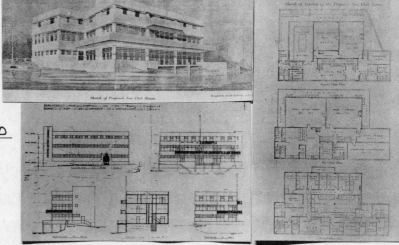

FINAL DESIGN

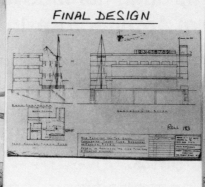

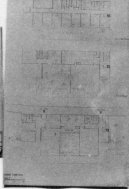

'At its best, modern architecture in England took care of client's needs and comforts and produced works of architecture of high formal quality which suggested vital alternatives to habitual patterns of life'.[1]   Yachting was a habitual, if unusual,pattern of life and Joseph Emberton A.R.I.B.A.,in his design for the Royal Corinthian Yacht Club, produced a vital alternative to previous designs of sailing club. The hotch-potch of the Royal Burnham Yacht Club (Fig.1) or, more specifically, the Essex boarded Georgian features of the Old Clubhouse (left of new building. Fig.2) illustrate traditional designs.

An outline for rebuilding a clubhouse on the site of the Old Clubhouse (Fig.3) was given at the Club's Annual Dinner (at the Connaught Rooms) in November, 1929. The earliest plans date from November, 1929, yet were it not for the dynamic Vice-Commodore at the time, Philip Benson, cheaper extensions to the Old Clubhouse may have been done instead. Impetus for a new building was given by the chance of acquisition of land next to the Old Clubhouse early in 1930. Decisive steps were taken at the Annual General Meeting of February 1930, following a change in Club Officers at this meeting. Benson became Commodore and a new flag officer, F.G. Mitchell,was elected as Vice-Commodore. He played a large part in the Club's history for the next 20 years. Two controversial issues were debated, that of admission of ladies as full club members and then the alternative Club-House Plans. After much discussion, a vote established a majority in favour of a new Club House, a 'large 3-storeyed ferro-concrete structure of advanced design',[2] costing £12-15,000. The minority favoured extension of the existing Club-House, at a cost of £2,500. We must judge the far-sightedness of the majority in the light of the economic depression at the time. Very little money was eventually borrowed. By November 1930, debentures and bonds for £6,000 had been received and increase in membership (at increased rates) was rapid even before the new building was ready.

The fortuitous association of Philip Benson with Joseph Emberton probably arose through advertising. Benson's father founded the advertising agency S.H. Benson which Philip directed from his father's death in 1914. During his partnership with Westwood, Emberton designed stands for the 1925 Wembley Exhibition and subsequently the stands for the Advertising Exhibition of 1927, steadily becoming more architectural in his approach, illustrated by the structure (not the newer internal design) at the base of the H.M.V. Oxford Street, staircase (Fig.4), where his connection with the selling world (see also Fig.5) continued after Simpsons of Piccadilly, 1936. (Fig.6)

(1) William Curtis. Open University History of Architecture and Design Course
            Units 17-18. Page 72.

(2) Cyril Goodman. 100 Years of Amateur Yachting. R.C.Y.C. Publication. Page 63.

Summerson opens the broadcast by describing the architectural climate of the period:

It was pretty flat. There was, as you know, a severe depression — the "great slump" — between about 1928 and 1932, and this had a devastating effect on architectural practice; in fact, it killed the old style of practice. But that style was flat anyway — there was a sense of inertia.

It was in this bleak context that the MARS Group emerged, its acronym encapsulating a vision of, according to Summerson,

"planetary exploration"
even more so than announcing
the formation of a "society
for modern architectural research."

The group was more "radical" than a society, and, as Summerson outlines, so were its aims.

Architecture was to be firmly linked with social consider-ations — social and technological. Housing, a major problem in the thirties as it is now, was to be lifted out of its despised and pedestrian obscurity and put in the glow of imaginative enterprise. Materials and methods of construction were to be studied in relation to industrial production. Urban planning was thought of in terms of liberating city centres by the creation of parkland and tower blocks.

Summerson's introduction positions the MARS Group as a bridge between

the more peripheral role
of modern architecture in the 1930s
and its acceptance into the mainstream
in the postwar period.

This created an invaluable map for following other traces of the MARS Group and the historical dis-continuity that followed. For example,

Summerson positions a selection of work by
MARS Group members in relation to each other,
such as:

Wells Coates's
Lawn Road Flats in Hampstead,
a 1934 housing block,
later called the Isokon building;
F.R.S. Yorke's
The Modern House and *The Modern Flat*,
1934 and 1939 compilations
of case studies;
or the engineering work of Ove Arup,
whose office, first established in 1938,
would latter consult
on the OU campus plan
designed by two other Group members,
Maxwell Fry and Jane Drew.

In Radio 14,
"Art, Ideology & Revolution,"
and Radio 27,
"A Commentary
on Western Architecture,"
Berthold Lubetkin, a student from the Russian
higher state art and technical studios
(VKhUTEMAS),
provides A305 students
with the perspective
of the itinerant architect.
Lubetkin emigrated to Germany in 1922,

where he stayed briefly before moving
to Paris and eventually relocating
to England in 1931.
He was a living connection to the Bolshevik
Revolution and the project of early Soviet modernity, before the Stalinist regime made crudely
evident the limits of the ideological mobilization
of architecture. Even though Lubetkin was a
practicing architect, he did not talk about notable
design works in his programmes, but instead
reminisced on a wider scope of discourse.

Because he was speaking as a witness
to a broader historical moment,
A305 listened to Lubetkin
like it listened to historians.
In "Art, Ideology & Revolution,"
he analyzes the ideological and
aesthetic debates that were unravelling
amidst the political upheaval
and the economic shortages
of the revolutionary period.
He describes how he decided to leave the Soviet
Union with the idea of returning (though he never
did) with "new competence" gained abroad, which
"was at the time not obtainable in Russia."

Lubetkin's second testimony,
"A Commentary
on Western Architecture,"
spoke to the present.

The programme begins with a synopsis of the
theoretical debates initiated by German art historian Wilhelm Worringer in the early 1900s, notably
with the publication of *Abstraction and Empathy*
in 1908, in which he set out a strict opposition
between rationalism (abstraction) and embodiment (empathy). Lubetkin relates Worringer's
framework to his own understanding of
> the opposition between
> expressionism and functionalism,
> based on his experience
> moving from Germany, to France,
> where he studied at
> the École des Beaux-Arts,
> to England, which he calls
> "the land of industrial revolution."

Lubetkin concludes his reflection with a critique
of what, without calling it postmodern, he sees as
a move away from rationalism into, as he calls it,
> an eclectic and "arbitrary pilling up
> of assorted,
> unrelated,
> fashionable elements."

And his criticism of the functionalization of
the image, applied retroactively and superficially,
is very stern:

> To think a building is nothing but a diagram of communication,
> an insulation chart, a time and progress schedule, a critical
> path analysis, or a bill of quantities, then they must inevitably
> call to their rescue a secret ingredient called beauty, to be
> spread over the surface in measured doses according to the
> budget. Thus, belief in functionism [*sic*] opens the door to
> raving irrationalism, and this is the real betrayal.

Episode Five

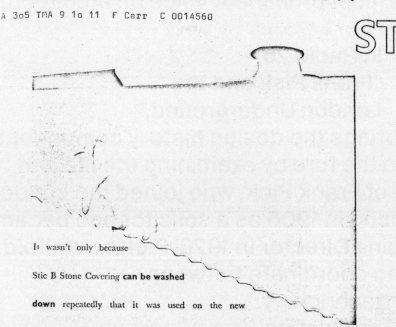
Architectural Review
July, 1934 opp. p. 38.   xxxvii

A305 was also listening to Nikolaus Pevsner, the BBC's most prominent voice on architecture history.

In Radio 25,
"Frank Pick and the
London Underground,"

Pevsner brings the design history component of A305 to the fore by examining the life and influence of Frank Pick, who joined the London Underground in 1906 as a solicitor and became its Managing Director in 1928. Pick's manifold capacity to coordinate between

technology,
production,
politics,
and design

was instrumental in the complex achievement of optimizing the architecture of London's transportation system, particularly when underground. Pevsner was fascinated with the complex array of

technological proficiency,
architectural clarity,
and efficient visual communication
that allowed the transportation system
to expand and operate
so precisely under Pick.

As Pevsner argues, Pick had relied on publicity to promote the Underground and attract more customers, and he had mobilized advertising to reach the public to a much greater extent than it had been used before. Pick's important contribution to the design discipline was thus

> to expand its role to include everything
> from commissioning new stations
> for the growing network
> to creating a new typeface
> for the entire London Underground.

Design could change the way people were transported around the city and the way they navigated the necessary complexity of that system —and this wide-reaching potential of design was what the A305 Course Team wanted to communicate to its students. Pevsner's method of focusing on the singular agency of a major actor was one way in which design history was told in the course, while other historians focused instead on anonymous objects and transformations of everyday life.

> Importantly,
> A305 was also listening to its students,
> or rather,
> to the collective voice of a student body
> which materialized in project reports.

These reports, developed through the local tutor-marked assignments established a feedback mechanism for assessing student engagement, while also building up a survey of roughly two thousand local examples of British architecture. In order to demonstrate to students how to develop an empirical report, the A305 course team used Radio 23 and 24 to establish

a model case study of a building
through primary sources
and recorded dialogue
between its designer and patron.
The team chose 66 Frognal,
a private house designed
by Connell, Ward & Lucas in 1936,

which had been a focus of debate between traditionalists and modernists during its planning stages, thereby giving the architects the opportunity to reflect on their work decades later. Amyas Connell had already appeared in

A305's TV 15,
"English Houses of the Thirties,"

in an interview with Geoffrey Baker about another one of the firm's earlier designs, the 1928 High & Over house in Amersham. Basil Ward was recorded in dialogue with Dennis Sharp in Radio 18, "Basil Ward on Connell, Ward & Lucas." And in Radio 24, Colin Lucas was given the turn to present 66 Frognal in a conversation with Mrs. Ursula Walford, whose husband had commissioned the house.

To accompany Radio 23,
"Project Case Study: 66 Frognal, Part I,"

the Course Team used *Documents*, A305's reference of primary source texts, to reprint two of

Project Case Study: 66 Frognal, Part1

Note: All these photographs were taken in 1972, while the house was unoccupied. We have tried to ensure that all the illustrations are of original installations, unless specified.

[C]

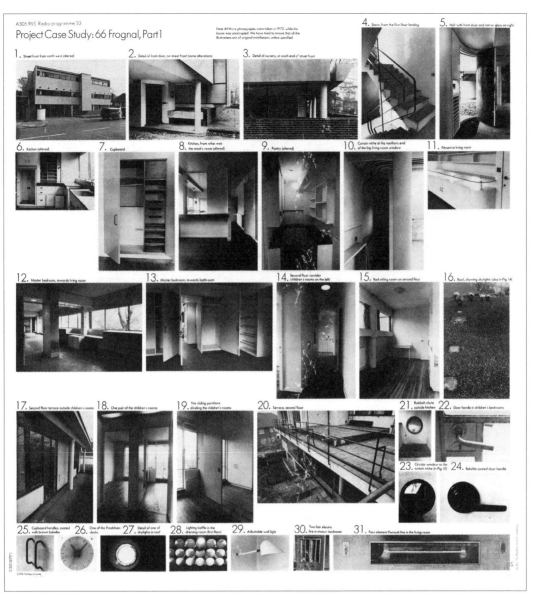

1. Street front from north west (altered)

2. Detail of front door, on street front (some alterations)

3. Detail of nursery, at south end of street front

4. Stairs, from the first floor landing

5. Hall with front door and mirror glass on right

6. Kitchen (altered)

7. Cupboard

8. Kitchen, from what was the maid's room (altered)

9. Pantry (altered)

10. Curtain niche at the northern end of the big living room window

11. Fitment in living room

12. Master bedroom, towards living room

13. Master bedroom, towards bathroom

14. Second floor corridor (children's rooms on the left)

15. Bed-sitting room on second floor

16. Roof, showing skylights (also in Fig.14)

17. Second floor terrace outside children's rooms

18. One pair of the children's rooms

19. The sliding partitions dividing the children's rooms

20. Terrace, second floor

21. Rubbish chute outside kitchen

22. Door handle in children's bedrooms

23. Circular window to the curtain niche (in Fig.10)

24. Bakelite coated door handle

25. Cupboard handles, coated with brown bakelite

26. One of the Frodsham clocks

27. Detail of one of skylights in roof

28. Lighting bottle in the dressing room (first floor)

29. Adjustable wall light

30. Two-bar electric fire in master bedroom

31. Four-element Ferranti fire in the living room

6.7a   A Client on his House by Geoffrey Walford

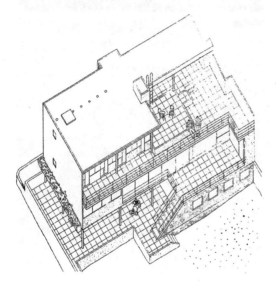

Above : Garden front

Left : Axonometric

The illustrations show the children's bedrooms on the top floor opening on to the roof terrace, the large horizontally sliding windows of the first floor living room, and the children's playroom and covered terrace on the ground floor

The building is of monolithic reinforced concrete, and is rendered externally with a scraped finish in varying tones of browns

Brickwork is used to enclose portions of the ground floor.   The terraces are paved with concrete slabs and the roof is surfaced with asphalt.   This side of the house receives sunshine until about 11 a.m.

the original 1938 publications of the project
—those in the *Journal of the Royal Institute of British Architects and The Architect & Building News*. In order to conduct a deep and extensive analysis of the house, the Course Team used a supplementary poster presenting a detailed photographic survey of the house, which *Radiovision Booklet* could not contain.

Tim Benton uses this survey as a script for Radio 23 to describe his "first impressions" of the house and to enunciate the kind of research questions the students should be asking in their own reports.

It's a "modern house," with a flat roof and long uninter-rupted windows. There are two long windows on the first and second floors, the lower ones are flush with the wall but the upper ones are recessed back into the wall a few inches. Now this is an interesting feature: it almost looks as if these windows were intended to be left unglazed and only glazed in later. Why in fact were they treated like this?

Following up on this question in Radio 24,
"Project Case Study: 66 Frognal, Part II,"
Tim Benton then moderates a discussion between Lucas and Walford, intended to offer to the students' consideration both the reasons behind the architect's design decisions and how they influenced the experience of the client.

Lucas: That was one reason, really, why we put this wall in front of the stairs, so that you could only see in side-ways and, after all, there's very little traffic up and down the stairs, and (that's) of a very private kind. Originally the glass of the staircase was clear, which enabled one to see right through and to see the landings behind the glass — which I think was much more interesting than to have obscure glass there.

Walford: The only thing that I minded about that was: you see the children were on the top floor and if somebody squeaked, say, in the early morning, or I had to go up and wake them up, I used to rather fly up the stairs for fear of being seen in my dressing gown nipping past the windows.

In short, Tim Benton demonstrates the project report methodology by first substantiating his initial impressions and early questions with further research into original articles and published evidence, and then verifying his findings by conversing with the protagonists of the project.

The rules of engagement for students were stringent: in a five-thousand word report a student had to
provide reliable visual evidence
of the lived experience of the building
on which they were reporting,
gather primary research materials
from local archives,
and assemble any published criticism
of the building.
Students would carefully bind
handmade drawings,
copies of blueprints,
annotated Xeroxes,
and ten by fifteen centimetre
colour photos

into a pre-established sequence that began with a title page including the research questions and an outline, accompanied by an optional evidentiary frontispiece, a detailed table of contents, followed by the body of the report itself, and concluded with a bibliography and a list of sources. With extraordinary personal testimony, some reports gave insight into the better-known protagonists of modern architecture and others into unattributed or forgotten buildings. After being returned to The Open University and processed by a central computer for grading and registration, many project reports accumulated at the RIBA library, thus becoming a resource for further research and building preservation.

Several reports still accessible at the RIBA library are eye-catching for how they demonstrate the way in which the course operated as a listening mechanism and the way it actively engaged with its contents. For example, after Berthold Lubetkin was given voice in the radio broadcasts, a student felt the urge to interview him again for his report on the Penguin Pool of the Regent's Park Zoo in London, designed by Lubetkin and Drake, of Tecton from 1933 to 1934. The report, almost 140 pages long, offers a carefully sourced analysis of the formal genesis of the pool and the ramps. It begins by

acknowledging Mr. and Mrs. Lubetkin;
moves on to quote Sir Christopher Wren
and Nikolaus Pevsner;
distributes Xeroxes
of references for the pool,
even hypothetical iconographic ones,
site photographs,
and drawings throughout the analysis;
and the report is so thorough that it closes by
presenting an edited version of an interview with
Ove Arup, the pool's engineer,
in which he contradicts the students'
own interpretation of the project.

Some student reports also echoed the course's
attention to particular issues such as environmental control in purpose-built cinemas, taking as
their object of study the Electric Cinema on Porto-
bello Road or the Odeon Cinema in Rochester,
for example. Others had tangible consequences:
Patricia Cusack's report on Weaver's Mill,
the oldest reinforced concrete building in England,
led to the building being listed
at the last minute before its scheduled
demolition,
and being preserved until 1984.
Cusack's report was then published
in *Concrete* in 1976.
And, in particular, many others greatly expanded
and elaborated on debates surrounding the

A reprieve for Weaver's Mill

by Patricia Cusack

After every appeal against the demolition of Weaver's Mill, Swansea, seemed to have failed, the Secretary of State for the Welsh Office has, in a last-minute reprieve, listed Britain's oldest reinforced concrete building for preservation. Marking the event, Patricia Cusack draws on exhaustive research to provide an article on the building.

Patricia Cusack has a First Class Honours Degree in Arts and Education, and became interested in Weaver's Mill while making an independent study of it as part of her Final Year Course at the Open University (History of Architecture and Design, 1890-1939).

WEAVER'S Provender Mill was the first building in the UK to be erected entirely of 'ferro-concrete'. It was constructed on the Hennebique System in 1897-8 for William Weaver Ltd., a Swansea flour-milling company. The working plans were executed in Hennebique's Nantes office and in fact number the mill as his fifth English commission; however, it is likely that the earlier ones, if carried out, were for ferro-concrete floors only.[1] The mill, rectangular in plan, measures 80 ft by 40 ft by 112 ft high, and the upper five of its seven storeys are cantilevered over space, the cantilever brackets extending 14 ft from the main vertical supports and carrying a load of 670 tons. The whole mill is of reinforced concrete (except for the basement walls which were faced in stone) including foundations, pillars and beams, staircase, floors and roof. The pillars are 'tapered' through the building as the load is reduced, and those placed over the cantilever on each floor are monolithic with a wedge-shaped concrete beam extending the 14 ft width of the cantilever. The roof was used as a reservoir to hold 100 tons of water.

The mill was designed by F. Hennebique (and possibly his agent, E. Le Brun) and H. C. Portsmouth, a Swansea architect. The circumstances of the mill's design were unusual in that it was the first large reinforced concrete building in the UK, and Mr. Portsmouth, the architect, would not have known anything about such construction. (Even at the end of the

first decade of the 20th century, hardly any consulting engineers or architects (in Britain) had yet studied or applied the theory of this material sufficiently to feel confident in issuing their own designs. . . .'[2]. Consequently the working drawings were prepared in Nantes, and probably the overall design for the mill too, which recalls Hennebique's other mills like the one in Fives, Lille (1896). No doubt Hennebique was personally involved in this, since although he had several hundred European contracts on hand at the time, only a few of these would have been for large and complete buildings, and this was the first British contract. H. C. Portsmouth

would have been responsible for facade details such as windows, stonework and ornamental motifs.

The new system and the mill

Hennebique's system of reinforced concrete construction, patented in France in 1892, had already been tried out in a number of projects in various countries. The system comprised: (1) An entirely new material, béton armé, or armoured concrete, for which L. G. Mouchel (the British agent) coined the term 'ferro-concrete' which unlike previous combinations of iron or steel, and concrete, made full use of the different physical properties of each, i.e., the compressive strength of concrete, and the tensile resilience of steel; and (2) the calculated and practical application of this material in the various structural elements, such as beams, columns, foundations.

Hennebique (who was also a master-carpenter) developed the shape of the elements of his system (for instance,

Weaver's Mill today stolidly awaits its future.

Concrete March 1976

PLATE 3

PLATE 5

Figure 6

PLATE 4

garden city, suburban living, and council flats. By analyzing a variety of projects such as Whitely Village in Hersham, a thriving retirement community founded in 1908, or the Kennet House in Manchester and Quarry Hill in Leeds, council estates both built in the mid-1930s and demolished in the late 1970s, the reports were surveying the current state of housing in Britain. Quarry Hill, one of the country's most contentious modernist housing projects, was filmed by the course after it had been designated for demolition and abandoned by residents, and one student later returned to Quarry Hill to document and analyze through photographs the demolition in progress. By asking questions about the ruination of mass housing and the simplification of the suburb into a ghostly and monotonous retirement community, the course was confronting key debates of its present. Through the student reports, A305 was therefore listening not only to the protagonists of modernity but also to the intense transformations of everyday life experienced by its student body at the time.

[A]
Excerpt from report on the Royal Corinthian Yacht Club (Joseph Emberton, Essex, England, 1931), written by A305 student J. A. Bunting. The Open University. © J. A. Bunting

[B]
Excerpt from report on The Penguin Pond (Lubetkin and Drake of Tecton, London, England, 1933–1934), written by A305 student Francis Carr. The Open University. © Francis Carr

[C]
Photographic sequence of House at 66 Frognal by Connell, Ward & Lucas, London, England, 1938. Supplement for Radiovision programme 23 of A305, "Project Case Study: 66 Frognal, Part 1," 1975. The Open University.

[D]
Title page of "A Client on his House," written by Geoffrey Walford, published in *Journal of the Royal Institute of British Architects*, 19 December 1938: 180. Reproduced from *Documents*, 1975: 97. The Open University. © RIBA

[E]
Title page of "A Reprieve for Weaver's Mill," written by A305 student Patricia Cusack. Reproduced from *Concrete: The Journal of the Concrete Society* 10, no. 3, 1976. © Concrete Society

[F]
Photographs from report on Quarry Hill (R. A. H. Livett, Leeds, England, 1938), written by A305 student D. Squire Jones. The Open University. © D. Squire Jones

Joseph Rykwert
A305 External Examiner

Hampstead, London, UK
24 July 2017

Joseph Rykwert [JR]
Joaquim Moreno [JM]

JM Thank you very much, professor Rykwert, for speaking with us. You were the external examiner of A305: how would you explain this particular role and its relationship to the course?

JR Well, it was normal in England for any university course to have an external examiner, so there was nothing unusual about my being appointed. I was then Professor of History of Art at the University of Essex, which was a new university at the time. I went to Essex in 1968 and it became the centre of student protests in England that year. It was a fraught time.

Tim Benton invited me to become External Examiner of A305 in 1975. I was a university professor already, so I was an appropriate person to become an external examiner. I was teaching the postgraduate course in history and theory of architecture, which was at that time becoming more widely known—not without some opposition from some of my colleagues at the University of Essex, who were afraid that I was going to start a school of architecture.

I had also begun to publish quite a lot, mostly on nineteenth- and twentieth-century architecture, but I was also interested in ancient architecture, particularly Roman and Greek, and the relationship between architecture and mythology. This was not something to do with the A305 course directly, but it was part of my general approach to the matter. I was at work building a kind of hermeneutics of architecture, which wasn't much thought about at the time. Although

Heidegger had done his lecture on building and thinking, unlike ancient philosophers, not very many twentieth-century philosophers were interested in architecture, and Hegel and Schopenhauer both were dismissive of it.

JM It is particular that you started the first postgraduate programme in architecture history and theory. The course was not part of an architecture degree, but it was the first moment in which architects could actually have a deeper scholarly understanding of theory. You were at the same time the External Examiner of A305, a course that was proposing to make modernity a topic of debate on public television. It appears that The Open University was reaching really far in getting you to be the examiner for this particular course, I assumed because it needed to be very stringent with its standards.

JR When I started offering my postgraduate course, I remember being summoned by the University of Essex Vice Chancellor one day—which always meant trouble—and he asked me what the RIBA had against me. I said I didn't think they knew I existed or thought I was of any interest, and he said that not only did they know about me, but that they knew I wanted to start a course in the history and theory of architecture. When I asked why that mattered, the Vice Chancellor said the RIBA had telephoned him to tell him to put a stop to it. His response to the RIBA was that, "Professors of this university teach what they think is fit. It's none of my business."

That protest passed by. The history and theory of architecture wasn't a popular subject at the time and it wasn't a popular matter to discuss. And this is why, of course, I was sympathetic to The Open University and to the way Tim Benton was seeing his A305 course. It had a much more interesting historical and theoretical basis than most teaching of history that I experienced in this country. In Essex, I was teaching Italian seventeenth-century architecture. One of the students asked me, after the third or fourth lecture, whether all these buildings we were talking about were Baroque. And I said, "If you like," and he said, "Well, you haven't used the word." I was very pleased, because I wasn't talking about style, I was talking about buildings.

JM   Yes. And how do you think your approach to teaching fit with the A305 course? I assume there was a bit of distance between how you established the Master of Architecture History at Essex with Dalibor Vesely and these very empirical strategies that The Open University was putting forward.

JR   Well, Dalibor had come from Prague and he'd been a student of Patočka before going to Munich, so he he had had a very different schooling from mine. I had gone through Wittkower's seminars at the Warburg Institute for two years, and then I discovered Sigfried Giedion. This was a view of history which I was curious and interested in, kind of differing from the Warburg's, but it was all so fascinating and dealt with the twentieth century. Then Benedict Nicolson had the bright idea of giving me *Mechanization Takes Command* to review for *Burlington Magazine*, when it came out. I was very worried about it, inevitably, and I fiddled with my review for many months. Finally, I went to Zurich and showed it to Giedion, who made me read it out aloud to him, like a seminar paper. But he was very nice about it, and then it was published—my first serious art historical publication.

JM   I assume that this is one of the moments in which *Mechanization Takes Command*

becomes an important book, and one that sets a whole different way of examining the everyday. It was also one of the reference books of A305.

JR   Yes.

JM   There were not many teaching materials like the ones The Open University was producing for this course.

JR   No, it was all much more hand to mouth. I was taught history at The Bartlett by Sir Albert Richardson, who later became President of the Royal Academy. He had on his desk a stack of six-by-six inch pieces of glass—that was the standard size of slides at the time—and a candlestick with a candle. He would hold the pieces of glass over the candle until they were quite covered in soot, and he would then draw on the slides with a needle, which he had ready at hand. And that's the way he made his slides. This sort of visual approach is, of course, very different from the one The Open University was cultivating.

JM   Do you have any perception of how the architecture world was reacting to The Open University and discussions on the modern movement?

JR   English architectural modernity is a subject which has been much explored, but when CIAM started in 1928, they didn't quite know who to invite from England. I don't know who suggested Howard Robertson, and then it was through Morton Shand, who was a very important figure at the time, not an architect, but he knew what was happening in Europe. It was Morton Shand who introduced young architects like Amyas Connell, Basil Ward, Colin Lucas, and Max Fry to CIAM.

JM   The A305 course was recovering all those voices. Connell, Ward, and Lucas were interviewed for the course, John Summerson was remembering the MARS Group, Berthold Lubetkin was talking about the Soviet Union. Why was a course from The Open University doing this historiographical work of recording all those voices that were so central to the history of English modernity? Were they being recorded somewhere else?

JR   Not that I know of. When I was twelve or thirteen, I was sent to University College School in Frognal, Hampstead, where I had an experience of modern architecture in England as a schoolboy. Just up the road, on Frognal Lane, I could see the work of Connell, Ward & Lucas, and the Sun House by Max Fry, designed before he associated with Jane Drew. There were also, across the road, two terraces by Ernst Freud.

And I was very lucky because in 1940, it was the Battle of Britain and my parents wanted me out of London. I was sent to public school, Charterhouse boarding school in Godalming, Surrey, which had a very intellectually ambitious headmaster who would invite, once a year, an intellectual nub of some kind to deliver a course of lectures for the sixth form. In my last year, when I was fifteen, the lecture was by Rudolf Wittkower.

Wittkower taught at The Warburg Institute, which had come to England in the 1930s. That story has been told over and over again, but there had been a very fraught withdrawal from Hamburg after the Nazis took over, and it took some time for the Institute to come to London and settle in the Imperial Institute, off Exhibition Road. The tower still exists, but the buildings of the Institute where the library was housed no longer do.

JM   And there was proximity with The Courtauld Institute of Art, which itself had a close connection with A305 through Reyner Banham or Adrian Forty.

JR   Well, Adrian came later to The Open University, but he was a graduate of The Courtauld and was then studying with Banham—who was himself also a Courtauld alum and a former student of Anthony Blunt. I did a year at The Courtauld as an external student, and I was taught by two tall, thin lecturers: Anthony Blunt and Benedict Nicolson. Nicolson was then also the editor of Burlington Magazine, and I got on terribly well with him so he started me reviewing for the Burlington Magazine.

JM   Did you know Tim Benton took the pictures for Blunt's early book Sicilian Baroque?

JR   I didn't know he had, but I'm not surprised.

JM   Somehow, the whole project seems to unfold through these connections. How do you recall your contribution to A305?

JR   I had the normal role of an examiner in any university course. I would receive the papers by mail, and I spent quite a lot of time over them. They were longer than most of my students' papers at Essex. It was very striking how Open University students were much more enthusiastic and much more committed to the course than students of the history of art in conventional university courses I had experienced. Coming from outside, I was struck by the high level both of the work produced and of the engagement of the students in the course. It was quite obvious from the work that Open University students were totally committed.

JM   Were you grading the papers or were they graded by the tutors?

JR   They were graded by the tutors, and I had to either agree or disagree with the grading but, on the whole, I had no quarrels with that. I would read the exams, the project reports, and the tutor assignments; I'd get the whole lot. Your role, as external examiner, is also to say whether the people who organized the course and the teachers were doing it right or doing it wrong. You're there as a kind of guarantee, to the whole body of universities and the educational system in general. It's also important for the applicants and people who are going to go to the university, to know they're going to a reputable institution. To me, the people involved with A305 seemed to be doing it absolutely right. Yet in the end, I think The Open University was being run-down, and that's always demoralizing.

JM   The Open University was constantly producing new courses and retiring older courses, which is not what one would do in a normal university.

JR   That's not always good. There's an old German joke about a professor getting ready to retire, he is visited by some young people and says to them, "I'm about to retire, and not many people come to my lectures nowadays. When I started here forty years ago, my lecture room used to be absolutely packed. And they're still the same lectures!"

JM   [Laughs] Precisely—and that was one of the very positive things about The Open University, that courses had sort of a time frame. But working through Tim Benton's personal archive, we came across several attempts to find a future for all these materials. A305 was not a lecture series, and it produced a lot of materials that, of course, couldn't go on playing because a television audience changes in a different way than a university audience. How could the course material from A305 produce other transformations?

JR   Well, in fact, I used to recommend the A305 booklets to my students at Essex because they were the best and most accessible account of modern architecture in England.

JM   The course anthology, *Form and Function* is one of the survivors. It was done in 1975 for the course with Dennis Sharp and it translated several sources of modernity.

JR   Yes. Very valuable, it was. I remember this book. And I remember going to see the Rietveld house in Utrecht.

JM   Ah! [Laughs]

JR   The first time I went to Utrecht, I tried to find the house, and nobody knew where it was. By chance, I walked past terrace houses obviously by Rietveld, looked through the windows of one of them, and I saw my edition of Alberti in the bookcase. I thought that gave me the freedom to ring the bell, which I did, and of course the resident was a teacher—art history at the university— and he knew exactly what I was looking for.

JM   There was a sustained debate to protect Weaver's Mill, the first Hennebique

building in the UK, that protracted somehow the demolition of the building for almost ten years, and that I think was based on an Open University student report. And there was another very sophisticated A305 project report on the Quarry Hill Flats, that made a case for how the poorly handled restoration of the structure had in fact condemned the building as much as the demonization of it by the Leeds City Council. And the producers of A305 filmed Quarry Hill before it was demolished. The Open University was paradoxically very local.

JR   Yes, it was. Most of the essays were about specific buildings and were detailed studies of those particular buildings. They were very catholic—with a small c—in their choices of objects of study. I think I have examined people in their forties and fifties, and even seventies. Three or four of those papers were publishable, I thought, which you can't say about many student papers. The standard was very high.

JM   So it was true, that The Open University was allowing a lot of people to learn and to become really proficient in academic topics.

JR   Absolutely. When I was approached to be an external examiner, I don't think I had met Tim yet, but they seemed to be doing very interesting things, and I was very glad to join in. In hindsight, I think there was no equivalent course in any British university that I know of.

THE OPEN UNIVERSITY

Arts: a third level course
History of architecture and design 1890-1939
Project guide

Project guide

A305/Reserve

 THE OPEN UNIVERSITY

Third Level Course Examination 1975

HISTORY OF ARCHITECTURE AND DESIGN 1890-1939

Time allowed: 3 hours

There are **THREE** Parts to this paper. Attempt **ALL THREE**. Each should take you about an hour and will receive equal credit. Follow carefully the instructions in each Part.

Make sure that you have the correct (A305/Reserve) EXAMINATION ILLUSTRATIONS SUPPLEMENT (8 pages) as well as this question paper.

If you wish to illustrate any of your answers with sketches or plans, do so; the examiners have been instructed not to take the artistic quality of any such drawings into account for assessment purposes.

Write your answers in the book provided. Remember to write your name, student number and examination number on your answer books – **failure to do so will mean that your paper cannot be identified.**

This question paper must not be taken away. It must be handed to the invigilator at the end of the examination.

1

Nik

Radio 32

Remarks

Scheduling

Internal Memorandum

From   Tim Benton

To   A305 Course Team

Subject   Date 6 August 1975

Looking carefully at the feedback information which Ellie
has been collecting (on TV 1-9 and Radio 1-12) and preparing
revised Broadcast Supplements for these programmes, it seems
to me that the following preliminary conclusions can be made:

1. Our television programmes are thought 'very useful' by
    60% of students answering CURF forms for the first half
    of the year (plus 30% 'fairly useful'), compared to 33%
    'very useful' for A302 and A303 (44% and 42% respectively
    'fairly useful'). Any criticisms of the programmes,
    therefore, must be set against this outstandingly good
    result. A305 radio programmes also emerge as most 'useful'
    among Arts Third Level courses: A305 - 47% 'very useful';
    A301 - 38% 'very useful'; A302 - 39% 'very useful'; A303 -
    42% - 'very useful'.

2. Where possible, I have tried to meet criticisms of both
    programmes _and_ supplements in the new supplements.

3. <u>Radio Programmes</u> criticised (on the basis of Ellie's verbal
    report to me):

    (i)   <u>Radio 1</u> (T.B. on design). Thought difficult.
          Students wanted more general introduction.
          Should be replaced in this slot for 1976 or
          1977. Replaced by what?

    (ii) <u>Radio 8</u> (Frank Lloyd Wright speaks). Thought
          'irrelevant' and confusing. Will write a proper
          supplement.

    (iii) <u>Radio 9</u> (Dennis Sharp regurgitating the Introduction
          to Glass Architecture). Found most of radio
          programmes should be remade. When? If not for
          1976, supplement needs complete re-write. Nick ?

    (iv) <u>Radio 10</u> (Charlotte on Futurism). Not liked by
          some students because students confused (also in
          Units) about how Futurism, Cubism and Expressionism
          fit together. Revised supplement should help.

    (v)   <u>Radio 11</u> (Franciscono on Werkbund). Thought
          'irrelevant' and confusing! I disagree. Any
          reactions? Supplement Outline being re-written.

Of these, I would opt for Radio 1 and Radio 9 to be remade
between 1976 and 1977.

O Bil

Outsides Remains the entire for me + author so

Nick

4./

—

CURF Units 9-10
Tv7 (ELLIE MACE, IET)
13.8.75
R9-10

CURF Data

BLOCK 5 (UNITS 9 and 10; TV7; R9 and R-V 10)

Total number of questionnaires returned so far: 65

Q.2 How do you feel about the amount of work you had to do on the pair of units?

Respondents: 64 out of possible 65 (i.e. 98.5%)

	No.	Percentage	Comments
Much too much	10	15.6%	)
			) too high
Rather too much	41	64.1	)
Just right	13	20.3	
Rather too little	-	-	
Much too little	-	-	
Didn't work on units	-	-	
	64	100	

Q.3 How interesting did you find the pair of units?

Respondents: 64 out of possible 65 (98.5%)

	No.	Percentage	Comments
Very interesting	31	48.4	
Fairly interesting	29	45.4	
Not very interesting	2	3.1	
Not interesting at all	2	3.1	
Didn't work on units	-	-	
	64	100	

Examining the Everyday

Joaquim Moreno

A305 examined, for the most part, notable but distant works of architecture and analyzed, through the lens of art history, the aesthetic decisions that shaped them.
But Units 19 through 22
—"A Survey of Design in Britain, 1915–1939,"
by Geoffrey Newman,
"The Electric Home,"
by Adrian Forty,
"Mechanical Services,"
by Reyner Banham,
and "The Modern Flat,"
by Stephen Bayley
—were presented
as corrective counterparts
to this distancing effect.
They focused on the transformation of daily life by addressing objects that were close and familiar to students and environmental technologies that permitted the implementation of a modern notion of domestic comfort. Units 19 through 22 examined

the everyday from the perspective of its common and largely anonymous objects, and through the flows of energy and information that regulated modern life. The audience of the course would have been all too familiar with the unsigned inventions,
made possible
by electrification and wired energy,
through which domestic labour
was being "mechanized"
and new ways of conceptualizing
and performing domesticity
were being given form.
Students were thus being encouraged to draw from their own experience in order to be able to think critically about the reasons for the shape and character of their immediate environment.

In the first part of Unit 21,
"The Background
to Environmental Control,"
Reyner Banham radically transforms the frame of reference for understanding the home by asking students to consider:

If you are a householder, how much of your weekly budget goes on environmental power (gas, electricity, coal, oil) and how much on environmental structure (rent or mortgage payments).

How much does a household spend
on running things
and how much does it spend
on building them?

This separation between energy and structure, which defined the limits of the power of architecture to control the interior, was one of Banham's fundamental contributions to architectural theory and history, which he had brought to the attention of a wider audience in the opening pages of his 1969 publication, *The Architecture of the Well-Tempered Environment.*

A suitable structure may keep a man cool in summer, but no structure will make him warmer in sub-zero temperatures. A suitable structure may defend him from the effects of glaring sunlight, but there is no structure that can help him to see after dark. Even while architectural theory, history, and teaching have proceeded on the apparent assumption that structure is sufficient for necessary environmental management, the human race at large, has always known from experience that unaided structure is inadequate. Power has always had to be consumed for some part of every year, some part of every day.

A structure would in itself not be particularly habitable without mechanical aids for heating and lighting; therefore, architecture must use energy—an energy that takes on a form and, therefore, transforms space. Banham's corrective take on a more formal and technical analysis of architecture, is staged in Unit 21 almost as a scene of situational comedy, in which the reliance on by then normative inventions serves to mock the so-called formal autonomy of iconic forms, like the skyscraper.

Without the telephone the elevators of the new office blocks would have been permanently jammed with junior staff bearing written messages by hand! And ... imagine what these buildings would have been like without flushing toilets and main drainage!

Just as a modern building cannot function without power and telecommunications, a modern house can be turned off with a switch. Banham's object lessons in environmental technology were thus making the case for electricity as the most modern form of energy, readily available at the flick of a switch and flowing through wires with enough intensity to power a mechanized domesticity. This electricity was no longer the low intensity current of telegraphs from the early days of the communications revolution. As Banham argues in Unit 21, Thomas Edison's major achievement was "to devise a safe and reliable system of switching, distributing, and metering the current between generator and bulb." Banham was thus less interested in singular inventions than in the forms of dissemination and control mechanisms that made a particular technology pervasive, and in the general social effects of an ensemble of technological changes.

> He preferred to focus
> on the overall process
> of modernization
> than on particular
> manifestations of modernity.

Banham's unique contribution to A305 was to suggest other perspectives and fields of interest that could bridge to the modernized environment of the students' everyday.

Unit 20
The Electric Home

Radiant Heat

The pervasive extent to which domestic life was being modernized is the subject of
> Unit 20,
> "The Electric Home,"

in which Adrian Forty builds on his own research in the new symbolic and cultural forms
> and ways of living
> engendered by the vast array
> of electric appliances
> invading the domestic sphere.

Unit 20 presents a case study on the domestic revolution of the interwar years, which considers
> "the relationship between products and
> buildings and the people who use them."

The variety of objects being considered in Forty's analysis extends beyond what Herbert Read

called, in his 1934 book *Art and Industry*,
   "well-designed" objects
   like microphones and table lamps,
to include those of general use, selected because
of their extensive social effects. While Banham
proposes a new balance between energy and
structure that still addressed architecture and
building standards, Forty argues that
   most of the domestic improvements
   of the twentieth century resulted from
   the mass-produced home equipment
   made available by industry.

   The argument is that it was electricity that made the
   mechanization of the home possible, but that it was the
   rapid growth of the household appliance industry and
   the very active house-building programme of the interwar years that created the conditions for the possibility
   to become a reality.

The first part of Unit 20, titled
   "Economic and Social Change
   in the Home Environment,"
together with Radio 20, titled
   "The Labour-Saving Home,"
addresses the complex ideological constructions
of what domestic labour actually was.
The second part,
   "Appliances in the Home,"
is a material history of the objects as actors
of these changes, namely
   "baths,
   water-heating equipment,
   cooking appliances,

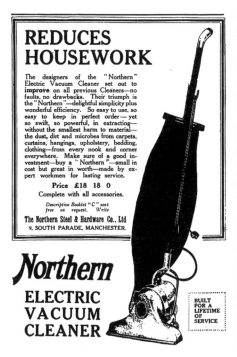

REDUCES HOUSEWORK

The designers of the "Northern" Electric Vacuum Cleaner set out to **improve** on all previous Cleaners—no faults, no drawbacks. Their triumph is the "Northern"—delightful simplicity plus wonderful efficiency. So easy to use, so easy to keep in perfect order—yet so swift, so powerful, in extracting—without the smallest harm to material—the dust, dirt and microbes from carpets, curtains, hangings, upholstery, bedding, clothing—from every nook and corner everywhere. Make sure of a good investment—buy a "Northern"—small in cost but great in worth—made by expert workmen for lasting service.

Price £18 18 0

Complete with all accessories.

Descriptive Booklet "C" sent free on request. Write

The Northern Steel & Hardware Co., Ltd
9, SOUTH PARADE, MANCHESTER.

Northern

ELECTRIC VACUUM CLEANER

BUILT FOR A LIFETIME OF SERVICE

Figure 36   Advertisement for labour-saving equipment, Northern vacuum cleaner (The Lady 14th July, 1921).

6 Household Efficiency

At the same time as the W.L.L. was active, other people had become interested in the organization of the efficient household. The movement for household efficiency originated in America, where, because domestic servants had always been scarce, there was a long history of rationalizing housework. The study of household efficiency began with Catherine Beecher in 1869, but there was a renewed interest in it when around 1910 the principles of Taylorism, now known as time and motion studies, were applied to housework in 1912 by Christine Frederick. Mrs Frederick's book, *Scientific Management in the Home*, which was published in the USA in 1915 and in England in 1920, gave advice about rationalizing the layout of kitchens to reduce distance walked, and about fitting standard height work surfaces. **Figure 35** is an illustration of the kind of motion study of household tasks that she carried out. She also studied at some length the effect of different household appliances on the work process, and made some evaluation

of the saving on time and effort they gave: for example she compared the relative time, effort and efficiency of cleaning by a vacuum cleaner and by broom.

Mrs Frederick's ideas were discussed in England among the class who could afford to buy labour-saving appliances. But it was manufacturers who seized most quickly on her arguments about the reduction of time and effort, and used them indiscriminately to advertise their products [**Fig. 36**].

In the popularized form in which her ideas reached the general public, the message was that any mechanical appliance would reduce housework. In fact her studies showed that the saving was often minimal and sometimes did not exist at all, but the subtleties of her arguments did not come through the advertising, and most people came to accept without question the idea that any appliance meant less work.

The lessons of Mrs Frederick's ideas about rationalization were slow to catch on in British design. By the 1930s, kitchen designers like Mrs Darcy Braddell (who designed the kitchen illustrated in Radiovision booklet, Programme 20, Fig. 14) were designing rationalized kitchens. The characteristics of the rationalized kitchen are continuous working surfaces, with a flow from food store to stove and sink (Mrs Frederick's efficient kitchen [**Fig. 35**] is less efficient than she tries to make it appear, because she does not allow for the need to go to the sink in the process of preparing food); shoulder-high cupboards to avoid bending down, and easy to clean surfaces. All these are familiar things in modern kitchens, but they were quite rare in the 1930s, except in the most progressive house designs. Radiovision booklet, Programme 20, Fig. 13 is another good example of a rationalized kitchen, but as the other photographs in the booklet show, that was by no means a typical inter-war kitchen; and yet another example is the minimal kitchen designed by Wells Coates shown in **Plate 62b**.

7 Hygiene

The idea that I want you to consider in this section is that the ordinary person became increasingly conscious of dirt and cleanliness in the early part of the century.

In the working hours of the average housewife, cleaning occupies about one-third of her time, and this proportion has remained roughly constant over many decades, although the standard of cleanliness now achieved is very much higher than it was sixty years ago. What we are considering is the improvement in results that people get when they clean, and the question is to understand why people should have wanted to achieve a higher standard of cleanliness. Robert Roberts in his book *The Classic Slum*, which is about life in a slum in Salford before 1914, gives the following description:

refrigerators,
washing machines,
irons,
vacuum cleaners,
space-heating equipment,
and finally radio sets."
Forty was interested in the history of anonymous
objects, or, paraphrasing Sigfried Giedion,
in the anonymous history
of the objects through which
mechanization took command,
especially of the home.

In fact, with respect to the impact of design in
everyday life, the Unit 20 booklet included in the
list of recommended readings the sixth section
of Giedion's 1948 publication, *Mechanization Takes
Command: A Contribution to Anonymous History,*
"Mechanization Encounters the Household."
The A305 Course Team also
viewed the development
of the commonplace appliances
that enabled the electric home
as a defining thread within
the history of modern architecture
—these anonymous fragments could also be
made to expose the guiding trends in the history
of modern architecture, like, as Giedion said, iron
filings revealing the forces of a magnetic field.
Giedion's anonymous history was a history of

inventions instead of authors. It displaced attention from singular works that did not have to justify their similarity to or difference from others, to inventions that were on the contrary compelled to give evidence of their distinctiveness. After having published *Space, Time and Architecture* in 1941 —a comprehensive overview of the world through the historical account of the "growth of a new tradition"—Giedion was now gathering a constellation of inventions and fragmentary changes to show the conditions of possibility for the world onto which this new tradition unfolded. As Giedion writes at the beginning of *Mechanization Takes Command*:

> History writing is ever tied to the fragment. The known facts are often scattered broadcast, like stars across the firmament. It should not be assumed that they form a coherent body in the historical night. ... Pictures and words are but auxiliaries; the decisive step must be taken by the reader. In his mind the fragments of meaning here displayed should become alive in new and manifold relations.

A305 students reading Giedion, as part of the course's suggested supplementary readings, could thus use their experience to establish these manifold relations, thereby becoming active learners. A student glancing diagonally through the section of Giedion's book titled "The Electrical Heat Source," would come across the following caption:

> The Electric Range Popularized: Mail-Order Catalogue, 1930. *The pattern of the cast iron cooking is still evident. The mail-order catalogue forms a yearly index to American civilization. Any article in its pages has entered large-scale production.*

Giedion was pointing out, in a nutshell, the inertia of formal characteristics and that the systems of distribution and production of a commodity were symptomatic of a wider transformation in social structures.

Simultaneously,
Giedion uses the regulatory
and operational controls that organize
the registration of an invention,
to illustrate the complexity
of technological systems.

The Patent Office files egg beaters in the same category as other rotating or oscillating mechanisms, such as cement mixers, kneading machines, or butter makers.

Such an exhaustive mode of historical inquiry into the mechanization of the household, through its
technological,
productive,
and social consequences,
provided a useful scaffold to support both Unit 20 and the development of Adrian Forty's research, which culminated in the 1986 publication of *Objects of Desire: Design and Society 1750–1980.*

In Unit 20,
building on Giedion's methodological structure, Forty organizes his analysis into two sections. The first details the regulatory transformations that culminated in the Housing Act of 1924, through which the separate bathroom and the

sanctity of hygiene became the standards of civilized life in Britain.

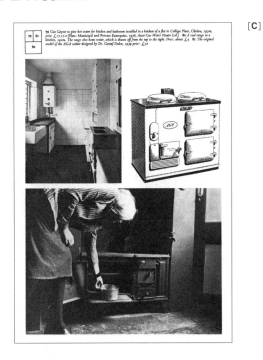

79 Gas Geyser to give hot water for kitchen and bathroom installed in a kitchen of a flat in College Place, Chelsea, 1930, price £17.17.0 (Flats: Municipal and Private Enterprise, 1938, Ascot Gas Water Heater Ltd.) 80 A coal range in a kitchen, 1920. The range also heats water, which is drawn off from the tap to the right. Price: about £4 81 The original model of the AGA cooker designed by Dr. Gustaf Dalen, 1939 price: £50

The second section is further divided into seven sub-headings—"Baths and hot water systems," "Kitchens," "Kitchen appliances," "Cooking," "Washing and cleaning," "Space heating," and "Entertainment"—under which Forty discusses the availability of domestic appliances and the ways in which they influenced people's lives as well as the design of homes. He presents these objects as contradictory cultural signs,

on one hand
separating the work they enabled,
particularly among women,
from the class construction
associated with that work;
and on the other hand,

97	98
99	100

97 *Daisy hand-operated vacuum cleaner, marketed 1908–1925* **98** *Hoover vacuum cleaner, 1919, price: about £20 (Science Museum)* **99** *Universal vacuum cleaner, 1926. This type had no brushes and operated by suction alone (Electrical Review, 22 October 1926)* **100** *Hotpoint vacuum cleaner, 1937. The streamlined cast aluminium casing conceals the motor and works, price: £10.17.6*

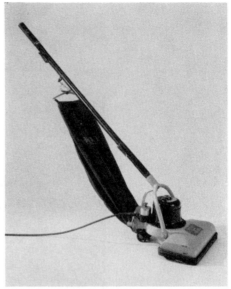

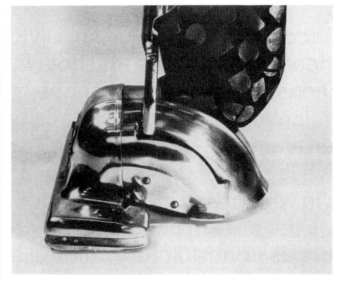

101 *Hoover vacuum cleaner, 1938. The casing is of aluminium and plastic. Price:* £16.16.0 102 *Hoover Model 160, 1938, light enough to be carried with ease* 103 *Gas fire with trivet burner by John Wright Ltd., 1900 (Science Museum)* 104 *Bratt–Colbran 'Portcullis' gas fire, 1935, price in 1939:* £5

transforming the design
of domestic appliances into a craft
subject to professional standards.
Appliances did not save any work:
they made it even more
demanding and crafty, erasing labour
more than they were saving it,
and exposing the domestic sphere
as the front line of some of
the most prominent political
and cultural battles of modernity.

In the section on kitchens, Forty analyzes spatial transformations in housing structure by asking students to imagine preparing and eating a meal in different examples of domestic plans. In doing so, Forty underscores the transformation of the kitchen and scullery combination into an isolated food laboratory and its separation from the dining room
—a necessary distance
for staging middle-class life
away from the work
taking place in the kitchen.
The kitchen appliances section—covering modes of cooking according to the type of fuel, auxiliary appliances, and food storage—could be summarized as an analysis of the effects on daily life of an active regulation of heating and cooling sources. Forty emphasizes the contradictions inherent in

the development of labour-saving devices.

> While the equipment simplified work, it also made the
> housewife able to attain higher standards, and if she did
> not want to, or could not do so, the effect of the equipment
> was to make her feel at fault.

He also clearly points out the far-reaching influence and dissemination of the refrigerator on the way people shop and eat, and on the rise of the suburb and the supermarket.

> The immediate effect of the refrigerator was therefore to
> remove the necessity to shop every day, and so increase
> the freedom of housewives, by making it more possible
> for them to go out to work. ... Another side effect of the
> refrigerator is that when people shop less often, they
> are prepared to go further to shop: this fact has, amongst
> other things, contributed to the decline of small local
> shops, and to the development of chain stores and
> supermarkets.

This elaboration on the nutritional, economic, and urban consequences of the domestic appliances clearly compelled students to conceptualize their everyday actions and the structure of their immediate environment in a new way.

The brief section on washing and cleaning is dedicated to irons and vacuum cleaners, the best-selling domestic appliances. These appliances greatly
transformed the domestic work
they purported to perform
and were the instruments,
especially the vacuum cleaner, of a fiction about domesticity and social class operating through the griminess of housekeeping. Forty then analyzes

space heaters from a symbolic perspective, refer-ring to them as "electric fires" that had established an adequately evocative image of its radiant function—an image that was evidence of function, not form.

In Forty's words, the space heater found a new form that reassured the user of its purpose and performance, which was to deploy heat where it was necessary, dislodging the fireplace from the central and symbolic position of the hearth. The symbolic centre of the room could now be anywhere it was needed, available at the turn of a switch, and limited in range only by the length of the cord that connected it to the wall.

The last section of Forty's unit, "Entertainment,"
is dedicated to the radio,
> a "useless" appliance that,
> paradoxically,
> absorbed the surplus income
> of even the most modest households.

By 1939, nine million sets were registered among
forty-six million residents in Britain, suggesting
that radio was widely accessible. The role of this
popular appliance, according to Forty,
> was not to save labour,
> but rather to enliven the home
> and transport the listener,
> even briefly, away from
> their sometimes bleak surroundings.

Broadcasting reached unknown listeners through
shared airwaves, and the voices of the BBC were
welcomed into homes everywhere via the radio
cabinet, without distinguishing between economic
circumstances. The last images in the Unit 20
booklet show two notable radio cabinet designs
from the 1930s:
> Serge Chermayeff's Ekco receiver
> and Wells Coates's Ekco AD-65.

These specific objects, however, were far from
"anonymous" objects:
> their formal qualities were not derived
> according to function or purpose,
> but instead originated from the need
> to make a magical piece of technology

118 *'Ekco' receiver designed by S. Chermayeff, 1934* (Architectural Review *Dec 1935*)   119 *'Ekco' AD-65, 1934,*
Bakelite cabinet designed by Wells Coates (Geffrye Museum)

amenable to the domestic interior. Adrian Forty had also elaborated on this point earlier in his 1972 article in *Architectural Association Quarterly*, "Wireless Style: Symbolic Design and the English Radio Cabinet, 1928–1933."

> Because the radio was responsible for diffusing the outside world into the home, the cabinet had to be assimilated into the furnishings of the home in such a way that the apparent unreality of broadcasting would seem natural.

A305's call to examine the everyday and its apparently un-authored environment, was reaching the audience through radio and television sets, likely the most modern pieces of design in many households. Unit 20 was thus examining the very tools through which it was being broadcast, intervening in the very everyday domesticity it was examining. This was the most performative unit of A305:

> a self-reflexive exercise,
> both in terms of the apparatus
> through which the course operated
> and in terms of the way
> students were asked to reflect
> on their own environment.

Developing his research further in Radio 20,
            "The Labour-Saving Home,"
Adrian Forty addresses the ways in which the middle class was constructed by establishing a distance between itself and the working class not only through education, but also through the acquisition of labour-saving electric appliances

　　　　　　　　—a substitute for servants and
　　　　　　　　a gesture to upper-class living.
As Forty points out, only the minority who could
afford to have servants could also afford the high
cost of a set of these appliances.
　　　　　　　　For those who couldn't afford servants,
　　　　　　　　appliances promised
　　　　　　　　to make daily routines more tolerable
　　　　　　　　and would project
　　　　　　　　an image of a household
　　　　　　　　with higher social standing.
But this aspiration would only be attainable to the
majority much later, in the 1950s, once owning
a combination of refrigerators, vacuum cleaners,
electric razors, and washing machines became
more affordable.

The accompanying images presented in *Radiovision Booklet* are mostly of a model home,
the 1927 Battersea Electric House, which
　　　　　　　　staged a new and alluring way of life
　　　　　　　　in order to incentivize
　　　　　　　　domestic consumption of electricity
—in spite of the common fear of electrocution
from appliances predating modern safety
regulations. The exhibition was yet another way
of thinking about the everyday: part of a complex
and regulated system of energy consumption in
which new forms of domesticity had a powerful
effect on the electrical grid at a national scale.

8 *Battersea Electric House, 1927, Bathroom*

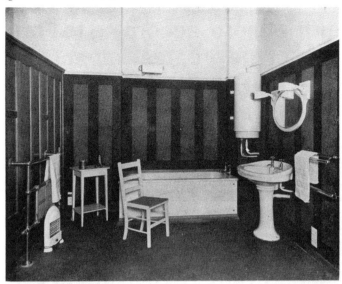

9 *Kitchen*

72

More widespread use of electricity in homes
would balance the supply grid, evening out the
peaks and valleys caused by heavy industrial
demand. Furthermore, according to Forty,
> one of the greatest impacts of electricity
> was that it allowed the possibility
> to "disperse the kitchen
> throughout the house"
—an electric kettle in the bedroom to make early
morning tea or a toaster on the living room table
for a dignified breakfast. The transfer of a function
from a designated space to a moveable appliance
resulted in the deconstruction of the established
rules according to which domesticity had been
organized. In particular, the introduction of the radio
and telephone into the kitchen,
> two objects which established
> new connections with the outside world,
represented a different symbolic construction
of the kitchen as something other than an isolated
space.

> Objects that embodied use,
> function,
> energy,
> and information
were changing forever the British way of life and
shaping the space of housing in which it played
out—the space at the core of modern architecture.
And so, studying largely anonymous objects as

part of design history demanded an examination of the everyday both as a technology and as a cultural form, an examination which A305 undertook by directing its attention to the manner in which common objects designed energy and information.

[A]–[B]
Title page of and excerpt from "The Electric Home," written by Adrian Forty, in Units 19–20 course booklet, *British Design*, 1975: 37 and 47. The Open University.

[C]–[F]
All images reproduced from "The Electric Home," written by Adrian Forty, in Units 19–20 course booklet, *British Design*, 1975. The Open University.

[C]
Gas Geyser, coal range, and AGA cooker: 85.

[D]
Vacuum cleaners and gas burners: 90–91.

[E]
Space heaters: 92.

[F]
Ekco receiver, designed by Serge Chermayeff, 1934 and Ekco AD-65 Bakelite Cabinet, designed by Wells Coates, 1934: 96.

[G]
Images of the bathroom and kitchen of the Electric House by Henry Hyams, Battersea, London, England, 1927: 72. Reproduced from "The Labour-Saving Home," by Adrian Forty, in *Radiovision Booklet*, 1975: 72.

THE INTERNATIONAL STYLE

HENRY-RUSSELL HITCHCOCK AND PHILIP JOHNSON
WITH A NEW FOREWORD AND APPENDIX BY HENRY-RUSSELL HITCHCOCK

The Pelican History of Art

Architecture:
Nineteenth and Twentieth
Centuries   Henry-Russell Hitchcock

TH
DE
IN THE
F
MA
AC

Nikolaus Pevsner

Pioneers of Modern Design

from William Morris
to Walter Gropius

A PELICAN BOOK 150 illustrations 5s

RY AND
GN
ST
INE
EYNER
ANHAM

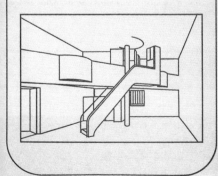

LE CORBUSIER

Towards
A New Architecture

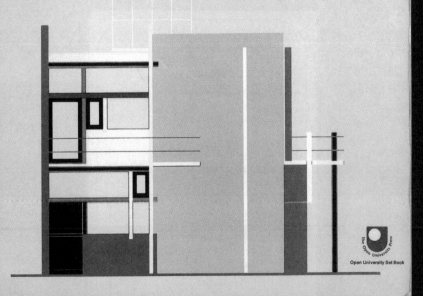

Tim & Charlotte Benton
with Dennis Sharp

form and function

A Source Book for the History of Architecture and Design 1890-1939

Writing and Teaching Architectural History in the Second Machine Age
— Joseph Bedford

In January 1975, Tim Benton announced his new course, A305, History of Architecture and Design 1890–1939, to the students at the Architectural Association (AA) in London in the pages of their school journal. In doing so, he positioned A305 within the tradition of architectural history addressed to future practicing architects.[1] In reality however, the course was quite removed from this tradition, situated within the art history department of the newly founded Open University (OU)—an innovative institution in which learning took place remotely, in the evening, through course materials sent by mail and lectures co-produced and broadcast on BBC radio and television. Most of Benton's OU students were part-time, adult learners, taking architectural history in conjunction with other courses across the university curricula, and few were training to become professional architects. Yet, when advertising A305 to students within a school of architecture such as the AA, Benton made the claim that the OU's use of television as a tool for writing and teaching architectural history could also benefit practicing architects.

In the frustrated atmosphere of the decade following the events of 1968, Benton's course sought to respond to the dissatisfaction of many art history students with the seemingly irrelevant and disengaged connoisseurship of their professors. The emerging field of design history, along with architectural history, promised to re-engage art history with the world, by focusing on objects, their use, and their social significance. It was clear what architecture could offer to art history in the context of the OU, but what did the OU, through A305, offer to architecture, its history, and its practice? Or more specifically what could A305 tell a student that they could not already read in the, by then, classic history books: Henry-Russell Hitchcock's *The International Style,* Nikolaus Pevsner's *Pioneers of the Modern Movement*, Siegfried Giedion's *Space, Time and Architecture*, and Reyner Banham's *Theory and Design in the First Machine Age?*[2]

Making his case to the AA students, Benton began by arguing that reading books alone was insufficient and that too many of these books had failed to fully communicate the experience and use of the buildings of the modern movement. As Benton put it: "Not enough architectural students went to see the buildings for themselves .... Many of them ... took on trust inaccurate descriptions ...."[3]

1
Architectural history has often been written by art historians, or by amateur local historians for a more general audience. However, it has predominantly been written by architects within schools of architecture, or by art historians closely associated with certain architects or schools, whose parallel duty has been to teach history to aspiring professional architects.

2
Henry-Russell Hitchcock, *The International Style: Architecture Since 1922* (New York: W. W. Norton & Co., 1932); Nikolaus Pevsner, *Pioneers of the Modern Movement* (London: Faber & Faber, 1936); Siegfried Giedion, *Space, Time and Architecture: The Growth of a New Tradition* (Cambridge, MA: Harvard University Press; London: H. Milford, Oxford University Press, 1941); Reyner Banham, *Theory and Design in the First Machine Age* (London: The Architectural Press, 1960).

3
Tim Benton, "Broadcasting the Modern Movement," *Architectural Association Quarterly* 7, no. 1 (1975): 46.

Books alone thus propagated rather than dispelled, what Benton called, the "myths of the Modern Movement ...: 'less is more,' 'the house is a machine for living in,' 'art and technics—a new unity,' [and] 'fitness for function.'" [4] Some blame for the failures of modern architecture and planning lay, as Benton explained, with the "idealism" of the first generation of the 1920s and 1930s, yet a significant portion of the blame lay with the next generation of architects who, distanced by history and geography, failed to properly understand the experience and use of their predecessors' work. [5] This distance might have produced a sophisticated second-order modernism, yet it had also reproduced many of the technical failings of modernist designs and construction details. [6]

If books failed to accurately describe modern architecture, then television, the innovative new teaching tool deployed by the OU, could remedy this failure and, by consequence, could create a "healthy architectural climate." [7] Benton argued that A305 cultivated a different method of writing and teaching architectural history because television collapsed the geographic distance between the architect (or the aspiring architect) and the actual experience of a building. By taking the camera inside the buildings, A305 promised to help overcome the problematic modernist myths of machine living. And to pique the interest of architecture students reading his article, Benton wrote: "Any of these [buildings] you haven't seen inside lately? Well, tune in to BBC2 at 8:55 on Saturdays." [8]

A History of Architectural History

If A305 is to be considered part of the field of architectural education and practice, then what precisely was its contribution to architectural history as it was approached in schools of architecture? More specifically, what kind of history of modern architecture did A305 offer in contrast to the histories already circulating in these schools—such as those of Hitchcock, Pevsner, Giedion, and Banham—or for that matter, in contrast to more contemporary architectural histories being developed within these schools in the 1970s—such as those of Manfredo Tafuri, Bruno Zevi, Kenneth Frampton, Colin Rowe, and Joseph Rykwert?

4
Benton, "Broadcasting the Modern Movement," 46.

5
Benton, 47.

6
A good example to illustrate Benton's case is James Stirling who, when first visiting Le Corbusier's Paris houses in 1955, wrote: "The Paris Corbs are disappointing, one knows them so well from the books, it is a sad shock to see them in their natural habitat." Mark Girouard, Big Jim: The Life and Work of James Stirling (London: Pimlico, 1998),

80–81. Stirling's knowledge of the modern movement was thus largely second-hand, mediated through books such as Alberto Sartoris's Encyclopédie de l'architecture nouvelle (Milan: Hoepli, 1948). And while distance produced its own creative misreadings, it also reproduced many of the technical problems of the work he was imitating. In the Engineering Building at the University of Leicester, for example, the second circulation stair does not reach the ground floor, creating daily bottlenecks around the main stair; plants grow in the cascade of glazing because there is no way

to clear them out; in the History Faculty Building at the University of Cambridge, the ventilation system is never used and staff offices overheat due to direct sunlight from skylights; and tiles also regularly fall off because of a poor bonding agent.

7
Benton, "Broadcasting the Modern Movement," 46.

8
Benton, 47.

Writing and scholarship on architectural history could be traced back to Vitruvius's reflections on the origins of architecture and its canonical orders in *De Architectura*, or perhaps to the consciousness of historical time emerging among Renaissance humanists and the commentaries on architecture by Latinists such as Leon Battista Alberti.[9] The practice of teaching architectural history, however, was first instituted in the French Academy of Architecture in the late seventeenth century, in which treatises from the fifteenth to seventeenth century were used to authorize and debate canons of proportion. One might consider François Blondel's and, later, Jacques-François Blondel's published courses as precursors of the first books on architecture with a historical emphasis.[10] Yet it was with the beginnings of archaeology, under a dawning romantic paradigm, that the first architectural history books properly emerged. Initially, they presented the past as a catalogue of building types and styles from which architects could choose.[11] Such books as those by Johann Bernhard Fischer von Erlach and Jean-Nicolas-Louis Durand, through to those of James Fergusson and Banister Fletcher, offered architects regional, periodic, or typological displays from which to select in accordance with a patron's desires.[12]

While these romantic histories focused upon surface attributes of style, the architectural history emerging in German universities in the nineteenth century, alongside the first histories of painting and sculpture, approached style on a deeper level; as a symptom of cultural spirit. German historians of architecture, such as Jacob Burckhardt, Heinrich Wölfflin, and Aby Warburg, developed a more analytic approach to form, in order to identify a cultural spirit beyond the specificity of different art forms and the intentions of particular authors, thereby bringing architectural history closer to history per se.[13] Their work set in motion a new consciousness of cultural historical unity and development that would deeply inform German modernist historians, especially Siegfried Giedion, a student of Wölfflin.

While these German developments challenged eclectic historicism, another proto-modernist challenge to historicism can also be traced to architecture educators in late nineteenth-century Britain who were inspired by the Arts and Crafts movement. William Lethaby—first principal of the Central School of Arts and Crafts from its foundation in 1896 until 1911—argued that architecture ultimately reflects the conditions of its production and function rather than surface characteristics. As Lethaby quipped, "It would be difficult to prove that the most superb castle was designed to look romantic, it was designed to be strong."[14] Good architecture would come from good building practices, and thus if history was to be taught in schools it was to be a history of experiments in construction methods and not a history of styles and ornament.

Yet, despite this challenge to historicism, the longevity of Beaux-Arts teaching methods—rooted in a command of the neoclassical style—was extended well into the 1930s as a result of the late nineteenth-century alliance between architectural education and the university. The Royal Institute of British Architects (RIBA) pushed to establish architecture schools within universities in order to control the identity of the architect and therefore licensure.

9
Vitruvius, *Vitruvius: Ten Books on Architecture*, trans. Ingrid D. Rowland and Thomas Noble Howe (New York: Cambridge University Press, 2001), 34, 55; Leon Battista Alberti, *On the Art of Building in Ten Books, 1443–1444*, trans. Joseph Rykwert, Neil Leach, and Robert Tavernor (Cambridge, MA: The MIT Press, 1991), 157–9.

10
François Blondel, *Cours d'architecture enseigné dans l'Academie Royale d'Architecture* (Paris, 1675); Jacques-François Blondel, *Cours d'architecture, ou traité de la décoration, distribution et construction des bâtiments...* (Paris, 1771–1777).

11
Initiated by Antoine Desgodetz in *Les Edifices Antiques de Rome...* (Paris, 1682).

12
Johann Bernhard Fischer von Erlach, *A Plan of Civil and Historical Architecture...*, trans. Thomas Lediard, (London: Thomas Lediard, 1730). First published in German (Vienna, 1721); Jean-Nicolas-Louis Durand, *Précis des leçons d'architecture...* (Paris, 1802–1805); James Fergusson, *History of Modern Styles in Architecture* (London, 1862); Banister Fletcher, *A History of Architecture on the Comparative Method* (London, 1896).

13
Jacob Burckhardt, *Die Kultur der Renaissance in Italien* (Basel, 1860); Heinrich Wölfflin, *Renaissance und Barock* (Munich, 1888).

14
William Lethaby, *Architecture: An Introduction to the History and Theory of the Art* (London: Williams and Norgate, 1912), 11.

As a result, history teaching in many of the new British schools of architecture, such as the University of Liverpool and The Bartlett at University College London, focused on the stylistic tropes of classical architecture. Despite fierce debates over the Beaux-Arts and Arts and Crafts methods, particularly between John Ruskin and Robert Kerr in the late nineteenth century, the Beaux-Arts method prevailed because of the testable nature of composition and styles.[15]

This approach was eventually replaced by a modernist one which, as a result of the success of modern architecture in practice from the 1920s to the 1940s, began to spread throughout schools of architecture in the 1930s. Yet ironically, while a first generation of modernist architectural historians were producing early histories of the modern movement—with German émigrés such as Giedion building upon the intellectual strengths of Wölfflin—the teaching of these histories diminished in the schools that emulated Gropius's demotion of architectural history in the Bauhaus curriculum. For Gropius, the historicist approaches to architecture that underpinned academic education stifled the imagination of students. By suppressing them, architecture would once again be free to be of its own time. After Gropius became Chair of Department of Architecture at the Harvard Graduate School of Design (GSD) in 1937, he only permitted history teaching in the upper-year curricula as a confirmation of principles previously studied in studio; "for older students who ha[d] already found self-expression."[16]

Thus, between 1930 and 1960, just as Hitchcock, Pevsner, Giedion, and Banham began to consolidate the first historical accounts of the modern movement, the proportion of history teaching included in many architecture curricula decreased.[17] Given that few other historians offered alternatives during this decline, the accounts of these modernist historians stood unchallenged well into the 1970s. Indeed, Tim Benton still listed their books as the required reading for A305 in 1975, even though his course aimed to challenge them. Their success as textbooks within schools of architecture was due to their ability to offer a coherent account of modern architecture and a shortcut to understanding its history in a simplified form. Yet this success came at the expense of turning history into myth, by selecting only those buildings which supported a unified view and removing anomalous evidence that belied a more plural or contradictory history.

Hitchcock, Pevsner, Giedion, and Banham can be grouped together as myth-making, modernist historians because of their shared view of modern architecture's principal myth; the Hegelian conception of spirit progressing. They viewed modern architecture as a movement that sought to express the unified spirit of the age, defined by industrial power (speed, electricity, and standardization), new materials (concrete, glass, and steel), and new conceptions of space (open, fluid, and dynamic).

Henry-Russell Hitchcock was the first to offer an account of modern architecture in Modern Architecture: Romanticism and Reintegration, published in 1929. Hitchcock's approach emphasized the unity, even the universal or "international" unity, of modern architecture as a style, though he did so largely in formalist terms—characteristic horizontal windows, flat roofs, and walls treated as planes that no longer met at the corner; all rendered in white.[18]

15
Mark Crinson and Jules Lubbock, Architecture, Art or Profession?: Three Hundred Years of Architectural Education in Britain (Manchester: Manchester University Press, 1994), 59.

16
Walter Gropius, "In Search of Better Architectural Education," in A Decade of Contemporary Architecture, ed. Siegfried Giedion (Zurich: Girsberger, 1951), 51, cited in Mark Swenarton, "The Role of Architectural History in Architectural Education," Architectural History, no. 30 (1987), 206.

17
J. A. Chewning estimates that time spent teaching architectural history in the United States declined from 10.8 percent in 1920 to 8.8 percent in 1960. J. A. Chewning, "The Teaching of Architectural History during the Advent of Modernism, 1920s–1950s," special issue, Studies in the History of Art 35, Symposium Papers XIX: The Architectural Historian in America (1990): 101–10.

18
Henry-Russell Hitchcock and Philip Johnson, The International Style: Architecture Since 1922, (New York: W. W. Norton & Co., 1932).

In contrast, Nikolaus Pevsner, who published *Pioneers of the Modern Movement* in 1936, argued that modern architecture should be understood in functionalist terms.[19] Pevsner's historical narrative traced the conditions for the emergence of modern architecture in a line from William Morris to Walter Gropius. He argued that Germany had inherited the historical line of development from England because, whereas the English had been held back by "intellectual ludditism" and a fear of the social promise of a machine aesthetic, Germany alone was able to fully embrace industrial machinery.[20] For Pevsner, this new architecture was defined by the embrace of the machine within society, not simply by the representation of the machine as a new style.

For Siegfried Giedion, in his 1938–1939 lectures that were published as *Space, Time and Architecture,* the task of the historian was to establish, in the student's eyes, the "true, if hidden, unity ... in our civilization."[21] That unity was the spirit of history in the Hegelian sense; an unfolding development that, while changing over time, has a unity in any one moment. As Giedion put it, "*history is ... an insight into a moving process of life.*"[22] If modern architecture was a style, it was so in the deeper sense of a unified and shared unconscious of a culture. Yet for Giedion, modern architecture was the simultaneous expression of both the material and ideal conditions of the spirit. On the one hand, industrialization had transformed the material condition of contemporary construction and, on the other hand, modern theoretical physics had transformed the idea of space. Giedion selected only those works of architecture in the twentieth century that he believed exemplified a civilizational unity of the age, leaving out expressionist and organicist architects, such as Antoni Gaudí, Erich Mendelson, and Alvar Aalto, in the first edition of his book.

Despite writing decades later, Reyner Banham also remained within the modernist approach to architectural history insofar as he continued to view modern architecture as a response to the (ultimately technological) spirit of the age. In *Theory and Design in the First Machine Age,* published in 1960, Banham offered the first critical reading of the modern movement for having created merely an *image* of its technical age, yet he did so only to urge architects to embody that age more radically than through representation alone. In Banham's view, the understanding of machine forms as "objet-types," by purists such as Le Corbusier, or the understanding of space as a symbol, by elementarists such as Gerrit Rietveld, had led modern architects to "cut themselves off" from "the world of technology," aborting their own revolution.[23] The rubric of a "second machine age" was intended as a means of "superseding," rather than "reversing" the modern movement.[24] Banham marked the continuing primacy of the machine in the history of modern architecture and a second chance at responding to its new conditions, those of "domestic electronics and synthetic chemistry."[25] He urged architects to stay clear of historical revivalism and nineteenth-century eclecticism, instead calling upon the contemporary architect of the early 1960s to "run with technology... to emulate the Futurists and discard his whole cultural load."[26]

The modernist approach to history, as it persisted in schools of architecture in the early 1960s, was given new impetus during these years by the promise of more specialized scientific research.

19
Pevsner, *Pioneers of the Modern Movement*, 38.

20
Pevsner, 26.

21
Giedion, *Space, Time and Architecture*, 1st ed., vi.

22
Giedion, vi (italics in the original).

23
Banham, *Theory and Design in the First Machine Age*, 12, 211, 326.

24
Banham, 12.

25
Banham, 10.

26
Banham, 329.

Under the spell of computation, modernist educators leading top schools in Britain at the time, such as Richard Llewelyn-Davies at The Bartlett, preferred that their students specialize in the social or natural sciences rather than follow a history survey course. And indeed Banham, then teaching at the Bartlett, abolished the chronological survey sequence, replacing "the formalist approach based on historical precedent" with an approach focused on architecture's responsiveness to the "present conditions of men."[27]

Yet by the late 1960s, semantic and populist critiques of modern architecture as well as methodological critiques of modernist history were developing in the hands of a younger generation of architect-historians such as Joseph Rykwert, Robert Venturi, Colin Rowe, and Manfredo Tafuri, and art historians and critics teaching in schools of architecture such as Vincent Scully and Charles Jencks. Banham may have continued to stand against these developments, but as early as the late 1950s Scully, for example, was already beginning to construct semantic analogies and references between modern architecture and a more ancient past, opening up modern architecture to a new plurality of meanings. Banham was critical, for example, of Scully's efforts to render modern architecture as deeply symbolic, arguing that Scully's approach overlooked modern architecture's "significance in terms of modern life."[28]

By the mid-1960s in the United States, the discourses of communication theory and psychology helped to focus the attention of architects on concepts of symbolism and meaning. This was especially evident in the work of Kevin Lynch and his influence upon members of the Philadelphia School, such as Denise Scott-Brown and Robert Venturi. In Britain, it was Rykwert who was one of the first to raise the concern for semantic meaning in his writings.[29] Rykwert developed his position into a pedagogical project, establishing a new program in architectural history and theory at the University of Essex dedicated to a hermeneutic analysis of architectural meaning. By 1965, Jencks, a doctoral student of Banham, had begun to rebel against his advisor's dismissal of architecture's cultural significance. In *Modern Movements in Architecture,* published in 1973, Jencks advocated for a pluralist approach to history which emphasized the significance of taste and consumer society in shaping the multivalence and ambiguity of architecture's semantic codes.

While the pluralization of historical narratives by postmodern historians of architecture led to a greater complexity of historical interpretation, it also led—in light of the political contestations of the late 1960s—to the emergence of a critical approach

27
As an alternative to the Beaux-Arts, history was to engage "the present interest in physiological conditions and environmental controls, in anthropometrics and perception studies, the gamut of what we now call human sciences." Reyner Banham, "Historical Studies and Architectural Criticism," *Bartlett Society Transactions* 1 (1962–1963): 45–7.

28
Banham, "Historical Studies and Architectural Criticism," 42.

29
Joseph Rykwert, "Meaning in Building," *Zodiac* 6 (1958): 193–6.

to architectural history that sought to delve deeper into the crisis that architecture was then perceived to be in. For historians such as Manfredo Tafuri, this crisis was far more extensive than the failures of modernist housing programs or of the cooption of modernism into corporate capitalism; the crisis was of a deeper intellectual character, involving architecture's own mode of thinking, dating back to at least the Renaissance.

Tafuri's more rigorous critical history challenged the "operativity" of the mid-century historians, such as Banham and Bruno Zevi, by arguing that, though well intentioned, their histories were too heavy-handed in editing the past. In foreclosing the complexities of the historical process, they precluded new insights from emerging out of the attempt to wrestle with history. For Tafuri, the forces of capitalist development would not be so easily surmounted by the will of the practicing architect. The architect had to engage in the long game of historical analysis, and this meant leaving history's own self-contradictory strands unresolved.[30] For Tafuri, teaching contradiction itself was the historian's contribution to the practice of architecture, because it gave students the depth of the problem rather than a shortcut to a false solution.

Tafuri's method was an inspiration to a younger generation of architect-historians in Britain and the United States who were seeking not only to pluralize architecture's historical references but also to engage in a quasi-psychoanalytic critique of the history of architectural practice. And this development in the writing of architectural history helped fuel the renewed emphasis on the production of architectural history within schools of architecture, rather than in the institutions of art history.

Art History or Architectural History

While the teaching of history had diminished in British architecture schools in the mid-twentieth century, it had correspondingly flourished in a number of institutions of art history. Due to emigration during World War II, many followers of the German tradition of art history—art history as a function of cultural history per se—settled in Britain at the Warburg Institute, established around Aby Warburg's private library for cultural studies which was relocated from Hamburg in 1933. Historians such as Rudolf Wittkower and Fritz Saxl, who wrote in *The Journal of the Warburg and Courtauld Institutes* and *The Art Bulletin*, established new standards for architectural history in terms of the interpretation of architecture's cultural significance. Young architects and scholars such as Joseph Rykwert and Colin Rowe, as well as young practitioners such as Alison and Peter Smithson, were attracted to the writing of these art historians for this reason. Yet, the discipline of art history in Britain in general still tended to study buildings in stylistic terms, in the manner defined by the Courtauld method. The Courtauld Institute of Art, a self-governing college within the University of London, was one of the few places in which one could study art history prior to the 1960s, and its approach was largely tied to the art market—to the need for skilled eyes that could attribute, date, and value works for the auction room. This tendency led to a visual and formal method of analysis that could apply to all the

30
On Tafuri's critique of Operative History, see Manfredo Tafuri, "Operative Criticism," in *Theories and History of Architecture*, trans. Giorgio Verrecchia (New York: Harper & Row, 1980), 141; see also Andrew Leach, "Instrumentality and Criticality," in *Manfredo Tafuri: Choosing History* (Ghent: A&S Books, 2007), 115.

arts, minimizing the specificity of architectural practice, and thus the economic, technical, urban, and political context of buildings. Up until the late 1960s, the historical analysis of architecture as a specific medium was rarely addressed in the way art history was practiced in Britain.[31] It was thus precisely inside schools of architecture that architects began to rescue architectural history from departments of art history, and introduce their own approach that implicitly challenged art historical methods.

Part of the critique of modern architecture taking place in schools of architecture in the late 1960s involved the reinvigoration of history by practicing architects. At Princeton University, for example, architectural history had been part of art history until 1964, after which Kenneth Frampton, Anthony Vidler, and later Alan Colquhoun, were hired, helping to establish the distinctly new figure of the architect-historian. The art historian writing architectural history was now increasingly seen, according to Rykwert, as "a eunuch in a brothel." That is, the art historian "knows who does it with whom, how many times, which way, and in which room; but what he can't understand is why they want to do it in the first place."[32] As Lawrence Anderson put it: "It is rare to find academic scholars who are truly sensitive to the art aspect of architecture, while also being responsive to its scientific, social, mathematical, and technical facets."[33]

Architectural schools thus sought to employ architects that could write their own histories from the perspective of the experience gained through architectural practice. In contrast to the art historian, the architect was expected to understand the nature of the design process, the architect-client relationship, and the rhetoric of practice. And the architect was as also expected to ask a broader range of questions that corresponded to the breadth of knowledge, and especially practical knowledge. This could include a wide range of knowledge about the performance of building types; organization of functions; implications of structural systems; patterns of circulation; sequences of construction; constraints of industry; relationship to city building and urban planning; and the business of winning projects.

At the same time, the practice of architecture was also seen as one of projecting new things into the world. The responsibility of the architect to manage a client's money and to assuage the criticism of a wide range of stakeholders also expanded the conviction that design must make the world better—that all the practical knowledge with which the architect grapples also has an

31
Alina A. Payne, "Architectural History and the History of Art: A Suspended Dialogue," *Journal of the Society of Architectural Historians* 58, no. 3 (September 1999): 292–9. Payne elaborates on the strength of the history of architecture within art history in the 1950s as well as on the schism that then emerged within the architectural history pursued in architecture schools.

32
Joseph Rykwert, "A Healthy Mind in a Healthy Body," in *History in, of, and for Architecture: Papers from a Symposium*, ed. John E. Hancock (Cincinnati: School of Architecture and Interior Design, University of Cincinnati, 1981), 45.

33
Lawrence B. Anderson, "History's History," in *The Education of the Architect: Historiography, Urbanism, and the Growth of Architectural Knowledge*, ed. Martha Pollak (Cambridge, MA: The MIT Press, 1997), 439.

ethical purpose; an orientation towards good outcomes. Architects thus differ fundamentally from art historians because their vocation requires them to take a view on what is good, what is right, what is better. It is for this reason that the history of architecture by architects often verges on myth, or "operativity," because the historical knowledge required for such a projective practice serves a normative as well as critical role. Thus even as architects searched for a critical history, critique was still bound by a vocational commitment to the possibility of making the world better.

By 1975, architectural history was seen as asking very different questions than art history and was housed in a very different institutional setting.[34] In its new home within the school of architecture, architectural history began to leave behind the language of visual description, aesthetic judgment, and genealogical influence. Instead, architectural history wrestled with its own relation to myth and operative history, manifested in architecture's increasingly uncritical servitude to corporate interests and its implication in the fate of urban renewal and social housing programs. Architectural historians were in search of a "critical history" aimed at the analysis of architectural practice and the intellectual universe of the architect as much as at the appreciation of buildings in their context.

The Historiographical Challenge of A305

Tim Benton's new course, History of Architecture and Design 1890–1939, appropriated the methodological apparatus of television and used its institutional setting within the Open University to contribute to the writing and teaching of architectural history. By the time A305 went on air in February 1975, the histories of Hitchcock, Pevsner, Giedion, and Banham were seen, by Benton at least, as complicit with the unlivable, inhumane, and non-symbolic nature of many modern buildings. These histories were semantically problematic for maintaining myths about living in the machine age, rather than addressing the meaning, use, and experience of modernist buildings. And they were historiographically problematic for excluding buildings of the period that did not exemplify the spirit of technology, that deployed ornament for symbolic effect, and that still approached architecture as a form of cultural expression. Counter to these failings, A305 promised that, by tuning in on Saturdays, students would better understand the experience of living in the buildings of the 1920s and 1930s; they would see how they worked as social and symbolic mechanisms; and they would be exposed to a much wider range of buildings than previous histories had included. A305 thus claimed to expand the canon of early twentieth-century architecture, as well as to open each building up to a more user-oriented and symbolic analysis.

Yet, the twenty-four television broadcasts framed modern architecture largely as a stylistic problem. They began by illustrating nineteenth-century revivalism through the 1900 Universal International Exhibition in Paris; then moved on to the Arts and Crafts movement by way of Charles Rennie Mackintosh's Hill House; and then progressed to examining the machine aesthetic in Peter Behren's AEG Turbine Hall. The film crew then travelled to the United States for two television broadcasts, first to the familiar ground

34
As Elizabeth McKeller points out, the pedagogical setting of the school itself—"the review article, the lecture hall, the crit and jury" —play a large role in shaping the architectural histories produced therein. Elizabeth McKellar, "Architectural History: The Invisible Subject," *The Journal of Architecture* 1, no. 2, (1996): 160.

of Frank Lloyd Wright's Robie House, and then to the previously overlooked projects of Rudolf Schindler's Lovell Beach House and Richard Neutra's Health House. Returning to Germany, the course included the expressionist work of Erich Mendelsohn before arriving at modern architecture's central paradigm of a rational way of living. A305 explored this paradigm both as myth, through the vision represented by Le Corbusier's Villa Savoye, and as reality, through the Berlin and Weissenhof Siedlung, before examining the British version of modern living at Quarry Hill in Leeds.[35]

A305 tried to draw a distinction between the admirable, but idealistic, intentions of modernist architects and the limits of the construction techniques available to realize their visions.[36] But the course nonetheless argued that, as one presenter, Stephen Bayley, put it, these visions and the myths they propagated "did contain the seeds of the future."[37] Modernist architects bore some of the responsibility for the purported unlivability of their buildings that resulted from their apparent rejection of taste and symbolism. As another presenter, George Baker, remarked, modern architecture was "rejected by the public at large because the forms … failed symbolically." And he went on, arguing that, "a sense of shelter, security, and happiness was often absent" from modern architecture and that, despite the architect's intentions, buildings "did not always coincide with the psychological and sometimes practical needs of their users." [38]

The course team then introduced a series of buildings previously excluded from historical accounts of the period, because they understood these examples to contain valuable lessons for architects in the mid-1970s who were considered more attuned to symbolic communication and livability. Hans Sharoun's Moorhouse was advanced as "the best living space," despite its retreat from the machine aesthetic into the Teutonic vernacular demanded in Hitler's Germany;[39] Edwin Lutyen's Deanery Gardens was praised for having a rich "domestic" quality that was "charged with meaning;"[40] and Wallis Gilbert & Partners' Hoover factory was celebrated for its good handling of decoration, thus "challenging" purist buildings by

35
"The Weissenhof Siedlung, Stuttgart, 1927," television programme 10 of A305, presented by Tim Benton, produced by Edward Hayward, BBC for The Open University, aired 17 May 1975, 10:05 – 15:30; and "Le Corbusier: Villa Savoye," television programme 13 of A305, presented by Tim Benton, produced by Nick Levinson, BBC for The Open University, aired 14 June 1975, 1:41. Benton challenged the myth of machine living by revealing a laundry list of mechanical failings when walking through the Oud House in the Stuttgart Siedlung, and by remarking on the way that Le Corbusier had "rather limit the freedom of his clients" when walking through Villa Savoye.

36
As Baker put it "they evolved too rapidly" with "inadequate … expertise." "English Houses of the Thirties," television programme 15 of A305, presented by Geoffrey Baker, produced by Edward Hayward, BBC for The Open University, aired 19 July 1975, 22:14.

37
"The Housing Question," television programme 24 of A305, presented by Stephen Bayley, produced by Miriam Rapp, BBC for The Open University, aired 18 October 1975, 3:30.

38
"English Houses of the Thirties," 22:14.

39
"Hans Scharoun," 1:34.

40
"Edwin Lutyens: Deanery Gardens," television programme 18 of A305, presented by Geoffrey Baker, produced by Edward Hayward, BBC for The Open University, aired 16 August 1975, 6:56.

acknowledging the need for "a more popular range of emotional content."[41] Finally, the course presented the typical semi-detached house in suburban London, about which the presenter, Stephen Bayley, posed the following question to the viewer: "Look at the Le Corbusier housing at Pessac, and look at a semi-detached house, or perhaps your own home. Which do you honestly think is the better machine for living?"[42] Yet given the damming critique of the livability of the Pessac houses by Philippe Boudon, in his widely read *Lived-in Architecture: Le Corbusier's Pessac Revisited*,[43] translated into English three years prior to A305's first broadcast, the framing of this seemingly neutral question was nonetheless a way of leading the viewer to a favourable view of the semi-detached house.

Thus, though the methodological inclusivity of A305 may have been informed by Tafuri—insofar as its treatment of the 1930s maintained the contradictory strands of functionalism and a residual classicism—its inclusivity and semiological concerns ended up resembling the populism of Charles Jencks, Philippe Boudon, and Denise Scott-Brown, which was part of the wider "elitist-populist debate" of the 1970s.[44] The buildings folded into the historical canon, through the sympathetic lens of the camera, did not in the end challenge previous operative histories in the rigorous negativity and analytic complexity modelled by Tafuri. Instead, they reformulated another operative approach along semantically populist lines. Ultimately, A305 had two main shortcomings that limited its capacity to analyze architecture through the lens of the camera. Firstly, its presenters continued to describe buildings primarily through art historical terminology, and thus kept returning to questions of sensation, affect, feeling, and impression, rather than analyzing deeper historical, institutional, economic, and practical layers of reality. Secondly, it failed to deploy the full spectrum of possible cinematographic techniques inherited from the twentieth century—such as montage—that could have reinforced the depth of analysis by drawing connections across time and space; an approach that might have made the medium itself critical.

As part of the post-1968 response to the perceived disengagement of art history, A305 *did,* however, have a critical position when it came to its account of public housing. For example, Benton's earlier television broadcasts on the Berlin Siedlung and the Quarry

41
"Moderne and Modernistic," television programme 20 of A305, presented by Geoffrey Baker, produced by Nick Levinson, BBC for The Open University, aired 13 September 1975, 23:28–24:40.

42
"The Semi-Detached House," television programme 23 of A305, presented by Stephen Bayley, produced by Patricia Hodgson, BBC for The Open University, aired 11 October 1975, 23:59.

43
Philippe Boudon, *Lived-in Architecture: Le Corbusier's Pessac Revisited* (London: Lund Humphries, 1972), first published as *Pessac de Le Corbusier* by Dunod, 1969.

44
By "populism" or "populist" I refer specifically to what Eisenman named the "elitist-populist debate" of the late 1960s and early 1970s. It was a debate both guided by academic appropriations of semiology, by figures such as Charles Jencks and George Baird, and by journalistic critiques of modern architecture, by figures such as Jane Jacobs and

Tom Wolfe. A classic illustration of the elite-populist debate was the 1971 dispute between Denise Scott-Brown and Kenneth Frampton, which unfolded in the pages of *Casabella*. See Peter Eisenman, "Building in Meaning," *Architectural Forum* (July/August 1970): 90; Denise Scott-Brown, "Learning from Pop," and Kenneth Frampton, "America 1960–1970: Notes on Urban Images and Theory," both in *Casabella* 35, no. 359–360 (December 1971); and Denise Scott-Brown, "Pop Off: Reply to Kenneth Frampton," *Casabella* 35, no. 359–360 (December 1971).

Hill estate praised the initial vision, community spaces, and public amenities, and blamed the eventual demolition of Quarry Hill on the council's failure to maintain it.[45] Stephen Bayley also came to a similar conclusion about Pruitt-Igoe, in the final television broadcast, "The Housing Question." Yet, as much as A305 displayed some common historiographical traits with the histories being recuperated inside schools of architecture again after 1968, its institutional distance from schools of architecture and closer tie to art history left it at odds with those histories in other ways. It might have used film to transport its students inside a wider range of buildings, but it was limited to the stylistic terminology of art history in the way that it asked students to look at those buildings.

While Tim Benton was educated at The Courtauld, he had prior training as a historian at Cambridge University and, in several of the units that he developed for A305, he engaged with the historical circumstances of early twentieth-century Germany. With Behrens's AEG Turbine Hall and Gropius' Fagus Factory, for example, Benton knit together a history of industrialization with a close reading of the treatment of construction details of iron and glass. Yet even Benton resorted to the stylistic categories common to the Courtauld method, emphasizing Behrens's debts to classicism.[46] Similarly, at Bruno Taut's Hufeisensiedlung, Benton tells the viewer that elements of the building "helped to guide the eye into" the central space,[47] and in the Schmidt Henner house he asks viewers to "notice how the pairing of the windows introduces a strong counter rhythm."[48] In addition to such visual description, aided by adjectives to convey aesthetic assessment—such as "exquisite," "masterly," "cubistic," "vigorous," "exciting," "ethereal," and "bold"—the viewer is given frequent references to genealogical influences between works.

Benton's polemic to the AA students insisted that television, the technology that epitomized the second machine age, could help the historian escape the impoverishing distance from which history writing and teaching suffered when limited to printed words and pictures and to lecture slides. In this respect, one of the targets of Benton's historiographical critique could be seen as traditional historians such as Hitchcock. Yet Hitchcock once argued in a different context that the distance between the lecture hall and

45
"It is clear that there is a feeling of community in the estate. ... The main faults resulted from a loss of will on behalf of the Leeds corporation to finish the job properly. All over the estate, communal facilities have been allowed to decay. This play shelter is now used for rubbish, and this space, intended as a playground, has been asphalted over. Although 80 percent of the site is not built on, little of it is really usable in any way by the community." "English Flats of the Thirties," television programme 14 of A305, presented by Tim Benton, produced by Edward Hayward, BBC for The Open University, aired 12 July 1975, 14:01, 13:20–13:40.

46
As Benton remarked, "notice the way that he suggests a classical entablature merely with a row of bricks end on ... Behrens even provided skeletal capitals." "Industrial Architecture AEG and Fagus Factories," television programme 4 of A305, presented by Tim Benton, produced by Nick Levinson, BBC for The Open University, aired 15 March 1975, 11:42.

47
"Berlin Siedlungen," television programme 9 of A305, presented by Tim Benton, produced by Nick Levinson, BBC for The Open University, aired 10 May 1975, 9:06.

48
"Berlin Siedlungen," 09:06, 1:05.

the actual building did not necessarily impoverish historical understanding, and rather through "skillful selection and juxtaposition" the historian, removed from real experience outside the lecture hall, could actually give a *more* detailed account of the building than one could get by visiting it.[49] In doing so, Hitchcock defended the work of the historian against the populist and realist idea that one knows the building better by being there. Another example of selection and juxtaposition was Tafuri's method of historical analysis, evident in his 1968 book *Theories and History of Architecture*.[50] Written in fragments, with texts and passages moved around in a historical montage, Tafuri's writing often jumped across widely different intellectual spaces, historical periods, and geographies, precisely to create a more penetrating account of the complex terrain of architectural thought.

For A305 students enrolled in the course, the use of television as a proxy for physical experience was accompanied by a wider range of print material for analytical study—from source books of primary documents and images to course unit booklets that guided study while watching the broadcasts. Something of both the juxtaposition which Hitchcock felt he could achieve in the lecture hall and the more penetrating account that Tafuri had achieved in his writing, can be found in these course unit booklets.[51] And students of A305 were asked to read through these materials in advance such that, it was hoped, they would carry word and image together in their mind as they watched the television. Yet for students and educators in schools of architecture such as the AA (or for that matter, the general public), A305's television broadcasts were offered as a standalone history. Without an analytical or cinematographic juxtaposition of past events, contexts, and ideas, these students were left with the argument that televisual proximity surpassed textual distance as a means of understanding the history of the modern movement.

However, what Hitchcock described as the procedure of selection and juxtaposition in the lecture hall could be understood as a parallel to the capacity of the cut in film, and especially of the technique of montage, to give critical meaning through the radical displacement of the camera's lens in a fraction of a second. If film language, just like the historian's tool kit, contained the potential to move far beyond the experiential limits of bodily perception, in order to construct a higher order of knowledge of reality that combined abstract and concrete phenomena, then A305 rarely used the potentials of film to this end. Only in one or two broadcasts did the film crew cut between a building and its images in a way that would tie together its historical, technical, sociopolitical, and economic context, such as in the sequential juxtaposition of several early Wright buildings—conveying an abstract image of formal development that would never be visible by simply being inside the Robie house—and in the simultaneous juxtaposition of Mendelsohn's words and sketches with music and archival footage of World War I trenches.

More often than not, television was used primarily as a means of simulating presence and narrative action. The camera typically followed the presenter around the building: walking down corridors, describing and appreciating the experience of details

49
Henry-Russell Hitchcock, "Introduction," in *World Architecture: An Illustrated History*, eds. Seton Lloyd et al. (London: The Hamlyn Publishing Group, 1963), 11.

50
Manfredo Tafuri, *Teorie e storia dell'architettura* (Bari: Laterza, 1968), translated into English by Giorgio Verrecchia as Manfredo Tafuri, *Theories and History of Architecture* (New York: Harper & Row, 1980).

51
For example, William Curtis gives the A305 students a vivid montage sequence of the historical fate of the Villa Savoye: lived in for only a moment; then occupied only during the summer months; then left unoccupied; then used by the Nazis for storing hay during World War II; then restored at the behest of Andre Malraux; and finally turned into a monument to Le Corbusier's own architecture—though sadly devoid of the pastoral setting to which it was once tied. Such historical images race in rapid succession within the written space of one paragraph, giving an insight into the building's temporal, social, and political circumstances that was deeper than filming the actual building could offer. William Curtis, *Le Corbusier: English Architecture 1930s*, course booklet for Units 17–18 of A305 (Milton Keynes: Open University Press, 1975): 9.

and features, turning door handles, and opening drawers.[52] For example, when Benton walks through the Villa Savoye, the camera cuts from Benton's hand reaching towards the main patio door handle to a downward shot from the roof terrace as Benton enters the space, as if the presenter had become the protagonist of a television drama—a space of fantasy and desire more than a space of critique.

One could argue that the use of such techniques in the case of the Villa Savoye were at least a means of highlighting Le Corbusier's cinematic conception of movement through space, yet the film crew adopts similar tropes in other buildings—at times the camera zooms from inside a building towards the window pane, viewing the presenter outside on the grass, and then cuts to view of the presenter sitting on the grass, looking back at the building while speaking about it. Such techniques no doubt enriched the production values by which architecture was presented to a broader audience, but the language of the cut and the montage was rarely used for its broader critical effect, as a tool of abstraction that could raise new ideas from the juxtaposition of concrete facts.[53] Instead it remained within the typical set of techniques often deployed by the BBC in its television dramas.

Benton had claimed that the televisual apparatus used by A305 would convey the livability and use of modern buildings and therefore dispel the myths of the modern movement. Yet the older apparatus of writing, as a medium of history, arguably remained better equipped to delve into the partly concrete and partly abstract space of architectural practice. Thus, as much as the televisual apparatus deployed by A305 advanced the writing and teaching of architecture by taking a historiographical step forward with respect to the use and experience of modern architecture, the same apparatus also led A305 to take a historiographical step sideways with respect to critical advances of history writing being developed inside schools of architecture by a new generation of architect-historians.

Tafuri, Frampton, Vidler, and Colquhoun were once again developing new architectural histories within architecture schools, as well as confronting the myth-making histories of a prior generation by analyzing the complex technical and ideological forces at play in the development of architectural practice. At the same time,

52
See for example, the sequence in television programme 3 on Mackintosh's Hill House in which the camera tracks forward along the corridor to the sound of Sandra Millikin's description: "along the corridor are typically well-designed linen cupboards warmed by hot water pipes which run through them. Then a surprising alcove, a confiding window seat." And as the camera comes upon the window seat and turns its gaze to the left, Millikin describes the first-person perspective saying, "again Mackintosh offers us a chance to pause, to rest with a book or some sewing, or just sit and relax by the window." "Charles Rennie Mackintosh: Hill House," television programme 3 of A305, presented by Sandra Millikin, produced by Nick Levinson, BBC for The Open University, aired 8 March 1975, 8:35–9:20.

53
As Sergei Eisenstein wrote in a series of essays written between 1928 and 1945, "montage is an idea that arises from the collision of independent shots—shots even opposite to one another." Sergei Eisenstein, Film Form: Essays in Film Theory (London: Harcourt, 1949), 49.

A305 was addressing the popularization of architectural history beyond not just architecture schools, but also the entire academy. In the process of adopting such a popular medium as television, A305 took the risk of, in turn, being controlled by that medium and presenting architecture in the terms of livability, use, symbolism, and experience. It thus ran in parallel to the development of critical histories of architecture by architects, but it did not intersect them.

Thus, as a case in the history of writing and teaching through new media, A305 sounds a cautionary note, reminding us that innovating with media in order to reach larger audiences does not necessarily lead to innovation in the development of historical analysis itself. Although A305 is unlikely to take its place in the long line of historical analyses that have grappled with writing a history *for* architecture, rather than a history *of* architecture, it will likely take its place as an episode in the elitist-populist debate surrounding the critique of modern architecture, as well as an important media experiment and an exercise in the democratization of education.

A305 DATE CHART

You may like to use this chart to pinpoint useful information and to compare the dates of buildings, publication of periodicals and design movements in different countries.

History of Architecture and Design 1890–1939

the War years

1900 1 2 3 4 5 6 7 8 9 1910 1 2 3 4 5 6 7 8 9 1920 1 2 3 4 5 6 7 8 9 1930 1 2 3 4 5 6 7 8 9 1940

SPAIN
Gaudí b. 1852 — Gaudí d. 1926

SWITZ‑ERLAND
Hannes Meyer b. 1889 — Hannes Meyer d. 1954
Le Corbusier b. 1887 — LC goes to Mexico

HOLLAND
H.P. Berlage b. 1856 — H.P. Berlage d. 1934
Gerrit Rietveld b. 1888 — Gerrit Rietveld d. 1964
J.J.P. Oud b. 1890 — J.J.P. Oud d. 1963
Theo van Doesburg b. 1883

U.S.S.R.
Leonid Vesnin b. 1880 — Leonid Vesnin d. 1933
Viktor Vesnin b. 1882 — Viktor Vesnin d. 1950
Alexander Vesnin b. 1883 — Alexander Vesnin d. 1959
Vladimir Tatlin b. 1885 — Vladimir Tatlin d. 1953
Moisei Ginzburg b. 1892 — Moisei Ginzburg d. 1946
Konstantin Melnikov b. 1890 — Konstantin Melnikov l.
Berthold Lubetkin b. 1901
Serge Chermayeff b. 1900
El Lissitzky b. 1890 — El Lissitzky d. 1941
Bruno Taut d. 1938

1933 to 1936 Bauhaus opens/1936 Jobs in Istanbul
1934 NAAF goes to Africa

UNITED KINGDOM
C.R. Mackintosh b. 1868 — C.R. Mackintosh d. 1928
C.F.A. Voysey b. 1857 — C.F.A. Voysey d. 1941
Wells Coates b. 1895 — Wells Coates d. 1958
Sir Edwin Lutyens b. 1869 — Sir Edwin Lutyens d. 1944
Amyas Connell b. 1901 — Amyas Connell l.
Basil Ward b. 1901 — Basil Ward l.
Colin Lucas b. 1906 — Colin Lucas l.
E. Maxwell Fry b. 1899 — E. Maxwell Fry d. 1962
F.R.S. Yorke b. 1906 — F.R.S. Yorke d. 1962

Berthold Lubetkin l.

Hermann Muthesius b. 1861

Theo van Doesburg d. 1931

in Japan 1895 to 1922
in New Zealand 1921 to 1926

1934 MOLLISON goes to Palestine

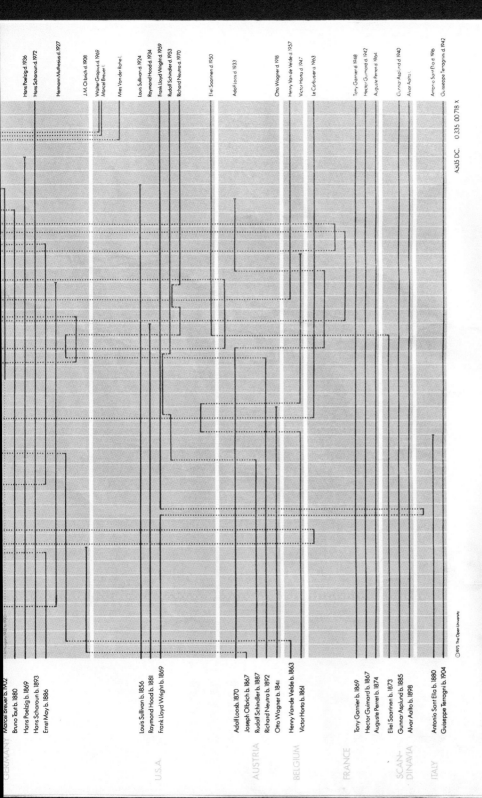

Would You Like to Live in Villa Savoye?

Joaquim Moreno

Unit 17 of A305, "Le Corbusier," mobilized the extensive material and media production resources of the course to dissect the Villa Savoye, an iconic example of modern architecture.

        The course unit booklet began
        by asking students to consider
        a matrix of twenty questions,
        the fourteenth of which was,
        "Would you like to live in such a house?"

[A]

This direct question, a test of taste and lifestyle, compelled an immediate response to one of the most evident embodiments of modernist design principles and strategies. Unit 17's narrow focus on a single object produced a tight web of references across the range of materials available to students enrolled in the course:

the unit booklet,
the photographic film strip,
the radio and television programmes,
the *Broadcasting Supplement, Part 2,*
and the *Radiovision Booklet*, coupled
with a supplementary poster
of drawings of the Villa's design
development.
Each of these components played a specific role
in analyzing the Villa Savoye:
the Unit 17–18 course booklet,
Le Corbusier, English Architecture 1930s,
confronted the project in a critical way with
questions about its occupation, the theoretical
principles underlying its design, and different
historical visions of the modern movement;
the television programme,
TV 13 "Le Corbusier: Villa Savoye,"
enacted the experience of visiting the house and
questioned representations of it in other moving
images, from which the film crew had taken
inspiration;
the radio programme,
Radio 17 "Villa Savoye:
Preliminary Drawings,"
discussed how the early design drawings of the
Villa Savoye, assembled on the *Radiovision* poster,
illustrated apparently conflicting iterations
of the project's design; the film strip showcased

photographs of the house in high-definition and full colour;

and the *Broadcasting Supplement, Part 2* threaded together all the lines of investigation into a multifaceted dissection of the modern icon.

How then to dissect this symbolic embodiment of theoretical principles, compounded with material and technological constraints and conflicting cultural values?

To enable a deeper learning process, the course unit booklet provided questions and answers that encouraged reacting and relating to an object, rather than absorbing textbook knowledge through periodization or formal analysis. Even if the phrasing of the questions was

lengthy,

sometimes rhetorical,

and pointed to an expected answer,

the underlying structures of inquiry were very straightforward. The questions prompted the students to reflect on

formal,

material,

and spatial composition,

as well as on the broader context of stylistic taste and reception, and of the role of the Villa in Le Corbusier's work:

- Is what we are seeing still the same as when it was built?
- What is its physical setting?
- How do we arrive at the building?
- How does it look?
- How does it compare to other buildings?
- How does it stand up?
- What is it made of?
- Where is the door?
- Can the exterior tell you how the interior is organized?
- How is the interior laid out and what feelings does it elicit?
- Does the layout look familiar to you?
- How do you move around?
- Is the person who lives here rich or poor?
- What do you see from the windows?
- Do you recognize the style?
- What do you think was the architect's main idea?
- And how do you imagine the architect's other work?
- Would you like to live here?

The architectural historian Williams Curtis was responsible for setting up the course unit booklet as a probe into architectural language. The first section of the text quickly demonstrates the symbolic complexity of the Villa Savoye by contrasting the building's inhabitation and its status as a cultural icon. As Curtis writes:

> Today it is not lived in and effectively serves as a demonstration of Le Corbusier's architectural elements. Yet, despite its bleak private history, the Villa Savoye has had a glowing public life in the photographs and the texts of the history books of the Modern Movement.

[C]

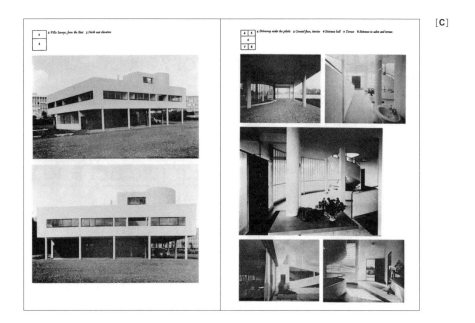

The object of analysis is a private house that survived not because it was lived in, but because it had a public life, due to its cultural value. A house with such a rich history

cannot be interpreted in a singular way, and so the course team preferred to summarize the different symbolic, and almost mythical, appropriations of the house over time.

Under the heading "Historians of Le Corbusier and the Villa Savoye," Curtis provides a guide to the small library of references assembled in the complementary course books (set books and anthologies), summarizing and annotating each recommended reading in order to conjure up a multifaceted vision of the Villa's history. Curtis's survey creates a play of historical voices, the first of which is Henry-Russell Hitchcock. His analytical method is described by Curtis as a safe historical approach that groups together stylistically similar buildings based on formal analysis and categorization, leaving out any symbolic interpretation. Curtis contrasts Hitchcock's formalist reading of the modern movement, most evident in *The International Style: Architecture Since 1922*, with Reyner Banham's more technological and mechanical framework for analysis, developed in *Theory and Design in the First Machine Age*:

> Banham certainly has an axe to grind, and a very valuable one: he seems determined to knock the purely "functionalist" explanation of modern architecture on the head for good. He succeeds by showing the influence of such diverse sources as Cubist painting, filtered Beaux-Arts ideas, and mathematical idealism on the architecture of the twenties. Unlike Hitchcock, Banham is not satisfied simply to discuss the Villa Savoye and its sources in exclusively formalistic terms; he wishes also to reveal some of the many levels of underlying meaning.

Banham's method of confronting modern buildings with the public statements of their creators,
bringing to light entirely different historical perspectives,
is evidently closer to A305's overall ambition of refuting a single narrative about the Villa Savoye.

But the most authoritative voice on Le Corbusier at the time was Sigfried Giedion, who, in *Space, Time and Architecture*, describes the Villa Savoye as the embodiment of a new conception of space.

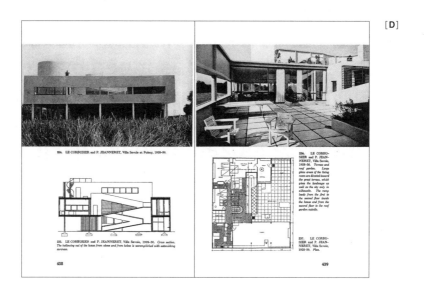

[D]

For Giedion, architecture was a construction in space-time;

> impossible to comprehend
> from a single vantage point,
> a continuous interpenetration
> of inside and outside.

The Villa, hollowed out in every direction as it was, was thus an emblematic convergence of Einstein's theory of relativity and analytical cubism, according to which the totality of space was not jeopardized by transparency and the simultaneity of multiple points of view.

> Curtis completes the montage
> of historical voices with
> Nikolaus Pevsner and Leonardo

Benevolo, arguing that, together,
these five perspectives
"make a useful frame of reference:
the purely stylistic,
the symbolic,
the spatial,
the rational,
[and] the socialist."

Following the questionnaire and the play of historical interpretations, Curtis directs the student to leave the printed page and move to the television set, in order to continue developing the analysis by experiencing the house through a different medium.

TV 13 and Radio 17 were presented by Tim Benton, and in developing these components he positioned himself as a scholar of Le Corbusier. Benton undertook substantial primary research in order to avoid making a redundant television programme about a building that was already made famous in film and print publications.

His research references included
Pierre Chenal's 1930 film
L'Architecture d'aujourd'hui,
co-written with Le Corbusier;
sketches from Le Corbusier's
lectures in Argentina
published in *Précisions*
sur un état présent de l'architecture
et de l'urbanisme, also in 1930;

Une auto...

Un avion...

Une maison...

...est une machine pour rouler.

...est une machine pour voler.

...est une machine à habiter !

and the statements Le Corbusier put forward in his 1923 manifesto *Vers une architecture*. Through television, the course was able to offer a clear analysis of the Villa that was also intelligible to a wide audience. In TV 13, Tim Benton visits the Villa, entering through the main door and moving from room to room,

> presenting the internal distribution
> and relationship between interior and
> exterior, and suggesting to the viewer
> the experience of inhabitation.

In parallel, the overall sequence of material
presented in Unit 17 had to both
> demonstrate the difficulty
> of identifying
> a singular interpretation
> of the Villa Savoye,
> and answer
> the impossible question
> of what it was like to live
> in an iconic house;

as if the everyday experience of the audience
and the importance of the Villa as an emblem of
modern architecture could ever overlap.

[F]

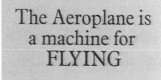 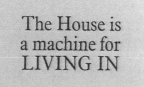

The Motorcar is
a machine for
TRAVELLING

The Aeroplane is
a machine for
FLYING

The House is
a machine for
LIVING IN

The opening sequence of TV 13 replicates that of Chenal's film, translating the original captions into English. This prologue sets up a triple line of inquiry:
> Why did Le Corbusier design the house as a machine for living in?
> What were the technical, social, and symbolic implications of this machine?
> And what was the experience of living in such a machine?

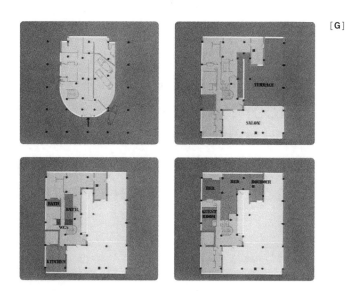

[G]

Benton simplifies theoretical concepts into slogans and contrasts them with
> moving images,
> redrawn schemes,
> and construction photographs.

In doing so he shows the complexities and com-promises that resulted from the collision between,
> on one hand,
> the intention to use industrial processes

and mass-produced materials
to create the object
and, on the other,
to maintain that object's singularity
—a conflict between standardization
and iconicity.

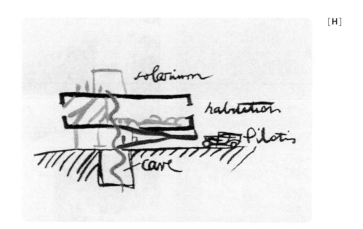

[H]

Le Corbusier's five principles of architecture are
rendered with the sketches from his lectures in
Argentina, mobilizing the low resolution (limited
provision of information) of a cool media (television)
to help the audience sense the contradiction
between abstract principles and their concrete
manifestation.

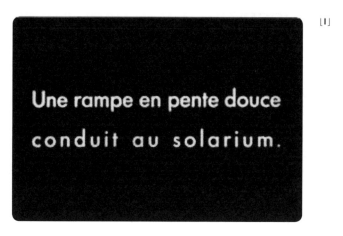

[I]

To enact key spatial concepts that share a close affinity with the moving image, such as the *promenade architecturale*, Nick Levinson, the producer, separates the movement of the camera from the movement of the user.

For example, Tim Benton walks up the stairs while the camera moves up the ramp, and he strolls from the inside to the outside ramp and up to the terrace, replicating one of Chenal's most recognizable sequences.

Benton's narrative reaches a high point when an English narrator voices over one of Le Corbusier's well-known sentences from *Vers une architecture*, displayed in French on the screen: "Architecture is the masterly, correct, and magnificent play of masses brought together in light."

Benton then moves through the solarium to illustrate the play of masses in light, before progressing back down into the house, building the narrative around the topic of materialization which, again, is highlighted by the narrator as he speaks another of Le Corbusier's statements,
> "The business of architecture
> is to establish emotional relationships
> by means of raw materials."

Industrial materials—glass, steel, and concrete—are animated with emotion, and pure forms are dramatized in the light, directing the narrative back to form and space. The last theme explored in TV 13, the intimacy of living in the Villa Savoye, is illustrated with photographs of the kitchen and the private quarters in use, mostly as a summer retreat. What was conceived of as a machine for a simple and idyllic, but bracketed, life, was, in turn, publicized through staged photographs of its interior.

Having experienced the building through media, Unit 17 moves from general discourse to deeper study, by asking students to return to the scholarly material provided by Curtis in the unit booklet. Building on the historical interpretations surveyed in the first part of the booklet,
the second part,
"The Early Years of Charles
Edouard Jeanneret,"
details the origins of Le Corbusier as a character along with his own technical and formal innovations, namely the Dom-Ino frame and the adaptation of Purist paintings to architectural form.
Part three,
"Towards an Architecture,"
illustrates Le Corbusier's adherence to the Esprit Nouveau, formulated first in the magazine *L'Esprit nouveau* and later in *Vers une architecture*, which redefined modern architecture's relationship with the classical past, exemplified in the pairing of automobiles and classical temples as works of selection based on established standards.
Finally, part four,
"Elements of Le Corbusier's
Architectural Language,"

sets out the broad landscape of Le Corbusier's references, theoretical principles, built work, and utopic urban ambitions, all of which were represented in the Villa Savoye.

> Curtis concludes his complex synthesis
> by saying that the Villa Savoye
> is "drenched in symbolic meanings
> which express attitudes
> to technique, to life, to the past,
> to the machine, etc."

The inquiry into Le Corbusier's architectural language thus culminates with a description of the Villa as an abstraction of a modern machine and a symbolic temple of modernity—in Curtis's words, a "machine age temple"—extraordinarily rich in interpretations and mythical in its genesis.

At this point the dissection of the Villa Savoye appears to be complete, the experiment having addressed its initial questions and produced a new synthesis capable of moving scholarship forward and communicating to a broad audience. But any understanding of the design process as linear is complicated by the back cover of the course unit booklet, which portrays two sets of plans for the Villa Savoye, one captioned as

> "Project A 1096–8 October 6 1928,"
> and another as
> "Final scheme April 12 1929."

Villa Savoye

0 335 00708 2

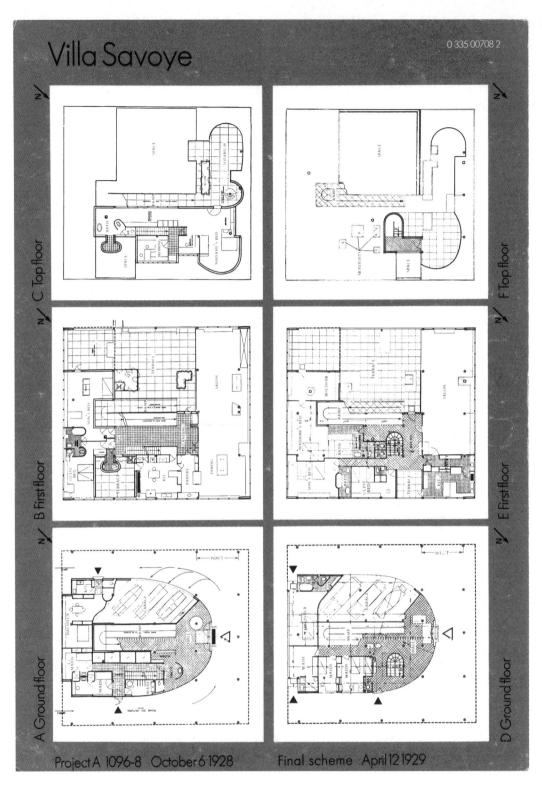

C Top floor

F Top floor

B First floor

E First floor

A Ground floor

D Ground floor

Project A 1096-8   October 6 1928

Final scheme   April 12 1929

The drawings look almost identical,
                    however, upon close inspection,
                    it becomes clear that they have
                    the same proportions
                    but different scales,
obscured by the fact that they are reproduced at the same size. Grasping this difference of scale requires closely reading the fine print and the dimensions of the structural module—5 metres in Project A (Le Corbusier's standard) and 4.75 metres in the final scheme. The optical illusion of this printed image hides the missing metre from the building's overall footprint (absorbed by 0.25 metres in each of the four bays of the structural grid) and opens up a line of inquiry into the complex development of the project's design.

In order to explore this history in adequate detail, Tim Benton used radiovision rather than television or print. The scale at which Benton wished to present the Villa Savoye's preliminary drawings did not fit the standard A4 format of *Radiovision Booklet*, and instead required a much larger format, a twenty-four by twenty-four inch poster that was sent to students through the post, rolled into a tube.
                    The poster effectively disseminated en masse primary research gathered from the then newly established Fondation Le Corbusier.

This final product of the detective story was entering uncharted scholarly territory, where there were no guidelines or protocols for making primary research accessible through complementary radio broadcasts and posters.

As Tim Benton put it in Radio 17, the research he was modelling was "an obstacle course in Le Corbusier's thought processes and creative imagination." The note on the side of the radio-vision supplementary poster, "Villa Savoye Preliminary Drawings," explains that the primary source material presented is organized according to dates found in the entries of Le Corbusier's studio logbook. Between the very similar first and last design schemes, Benton discovered that there were two other versions of the design,
> which he called
> Project B and Project C,
> that at first glance follow
> no sequential logic.

For Benton, it was difficult to rationalize that the genesis of such an apparently absolute design could have, in fact, occurred through such a non-linear process. In the poster notes, Tim Benton does point out that the studio logbook dates could be wrong and therefore may not correspond to the dates of completion of the drawings,
> meaning that Projects B and C
> could have been earlier proposals,

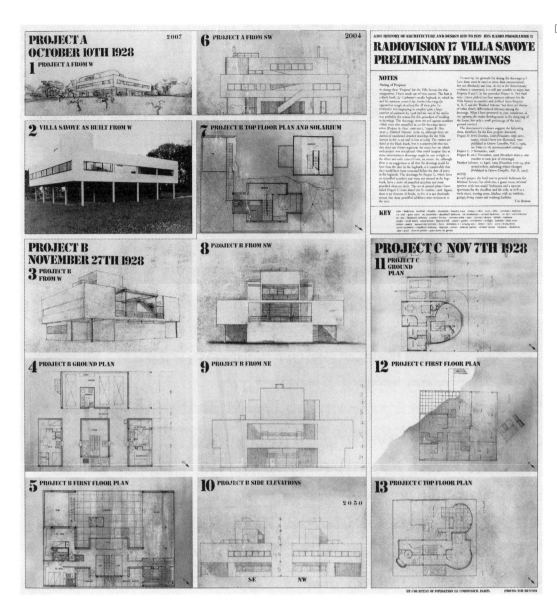

PROJECT A
OCTOBER 10TH 1928 2007

1 PROJECT A FROM W

6 PROJECT A FROM SW 2004

2 VILLA SAVOYE AS BUILT FROM W

7 PROJECT B TOP FLOOR PLAN AND SOLARIUM

A305 HISTORY OF ARCHITECTURE AND DESIGN 1870 TO 1939 BYS RADIO PROGRAMME 17

RADIOVISION 17 VILLA SAVOYE
PRELIMINARY DRAWINGS

NOTES

PROJECT B
NOVEMBER 27TH 1928

3 PROJECT B FROM W

8 PROJECT B FROM SW

PROJECT C NOV 7TH 1928

11 PROJECT C GROUND PLAN

4 PROJECT B GROUND PLAN

9 PROJECT B FROM NE

12 PROJECT C FIRST FLOOR PLAN

5 PROJECT B FIRST FLOOR PLAN

10 PROJECT B SIDE ELEVATIONS 2050

SE NW

13 PROJECT C TOP FLOOR PLAN

BY COURTESY OF FONDATION LE CORBUSIER, PARIS. PHOTO: TIM BENTON

295

and Project A could have led directly to the Final Scheme.

Tim Benton thus writes an entire detective story to defy the rationalist narrative according to which the Villa was the inevitable monumental outcome of a strictly functionalist design process.
His contribution to the history
of the Villa Savoye is ultimately
to demystify the genesis of an icon
of modern architecture
and challenge dominant narratives
about its design by presenting
a series of conflicting
and sometimes banal iterations.
However, the way Tim Benton plots his research is paradoxical. Despite framing his approach as purely empirical, following traces and verifying incongruencies, Benton also relies on interpretation and conjecture. Indeed, Benton concludes Radio 17 with an ambiguous probability:

What I am suggesting, therefore, is that there was a critical minimum size beyond which Project A could not be reduced without intolerable compromises. But why reduce the scale of Project A in the first place? What probably happened was that Madame Savoye, on being shown Project A and the estimated of cost for building it, was horrified and stipulated an overall reduction in built volume. Corbusier's first reaction was to try to reduce the area but he got stuck, with Projects C and B which he recognised as unsatisfactory. So how was the cost problem resolved? Well, you know the answer, he scrapped the top floor in Project A putting Madame Savoye's bedroom on the first floor which meant that the kitchen had to go in part of the space originally occupied by the salon in Project A.

The unique achievement of Tim Benton's dissection of the Villa Savoye was thus to decipher an icon by transforming it into an open work. Ironically, this was performed with the pedagogical tools of The Open University, which often had to make interpretations converge in order to fit into specific diffusion formats (booklets, posters, radio, and television). And if television was cool, requiring extensive interpretation on the part of the viewer, then radio and the printed image were hot, the ideal media to convey Tim Benton's detailed detective story. Unit 17 ultimately proposes a way to combine research and mass media and an opportunity to reframe the discourse around a piece of architecture already transformed by mass media.

[A]
Villa Savoye, by Le Corbusier, Poissy, France, 1928–1931. Still of Tim Benton standing on terrace from television programme 13 of A305, "Le Corbusier: Villa Savoye," presented by Tim Benton, 1975. The Open University. 00525_3042 © Fondation Le Corbusier/Sodrac 2018

[B]
Detail of film strip accompanying Units 17–18 course booklet, Le Corbusier, English Architecture 1930s, 1975. The Open University. © Fondation Le Corbusier/Sodrac 2018

[C]
Photographs of Villa Savoye. Reproduced from Units 17–18 course booklet, Le Corbusier, English Architecture 1930s, 1975: 78–79. The Open University. © Fondation Le Corbusier/Sodrac 2018

[D]
Photographs, section, and plan of Villa Savoye. Reproduced from Space, Time and Architecture: The Growth of a New Tradition, written by Sigfried Giedion, 1949: 438–439. © Harvard University Press. © Fondation Le Corbusier/Sodrac 2018

[E]
Stills from L'Architecture d'aujourd'hui, directed by Pierre Chenal, written with Le Corbusier, 1931. © Fondation Le Corbusier/Sodrac 2018

[F]–[H]
All stills from television programme 13 of A305, "Le Corbusier: Villa Savoye," presented by Tim Benton, 1975. The Open University. 00525_3042. © Fondation Le Corbusier/Sodrac 2018

[F]
Caption cards, a motorcar, aeroplane, and Villa Savoye.

[G]
Redrawn and annotated plans of Villa Savoye.

[H]
Sketch of Villa Savoye by Le Corbusier.

[I]
Still of title card from L'Architecture d'aujourd'hui, directed by Pierre Chenal, written with Le Corbusier, 1931. © Fondation Le Corbusier/Sodrac 2018

[J]–[L]
(left) Stills from L'Architecture d'aujourd'hui, directed by Pierre Chenal, written with Le Corbusier, 1931; (right) Stills from television programme 13 of A305, "Le Corbusier: Villa Savoye," presented by Tim Benton, 1975. The Open University. 00525_3042. © Fondation Le Corbusier/ Sodrac 2018

[M]
Iterations of floorplans of Villa Savoye. Reproduced from Units 17–18 course booklet, Le Corbusier, English Architecture 1930s, 1975: back cover. The Open University.

[N]
Drawings of the design development of Villa Savoye. Supplement for Radio programme 17 of A305, "Villa Savoye: Preliminary Drawings," 1975. The Open University.

The Architectural Association

T.J. Benton, Esq.,
Open University,
18, Larkhall Lane,
London, S.W.4.

Patron: Her Majesty the Queen
Constituted 1847
Incorporated 1920

~~36, Bedford Square, London, WC1B 3ES. Telephone 01-636 0974~~

Secretary: Edouard Le Maistre

No.1, Sloane Street, London, S.W.1.   01-235 8877

RA/JS   7th January, 1976

Dear Mr. Benton,

I understand that you have been the author and organiser of Open University Course 305, "Architecture and Design" and I would like to offer my congratulations on an absolutely splendid contribution to architecture and the environment.

I have watched and listened to the programmes, seen all the course units, assignments and summer school programme. I would hope the 'project material' could be housed somewhere that is available to architects and architectural students as a resource for future use.

If I could be of any help, I should be pleased if you could join me for lunch one day to discuss your future plans.

Again many congratulations,

Yours sincerely,

RAYMOND ANDREWS
President

cc: Eric Lyons, O.B.E., P.R.I.B.A.
    Alvin Boyarsky, Chairman AA.
    David Dean, Librarian R.I.B.A.

L'architettura

CRONACHE E STORIA

direttore Bruno Zevi   redazione : via Nomentana 150
ETAS - KOMPASS editrice   00162 Roma - telefono 83.80.481

February 22, 1976

Mrs. Charlotte Benton
Research Assistant in Art History
Arts Faculty
THE OPEN UNIVERSITY
<u>Milton Keynes</u>

Dear Mrs. Benton,

   I am sorry to answer with much delay your kind letter.
The reason of this delay is simple and sad: my father was very sick and
finally died. He was living abroad, so that during the past months I was
ofter out of Italy to assist him...

   I have the greatest interest for the work you are doing
in the architectural field. I judge it to be of very high standard: the
best in the world, and I wonder how it could be distributed in Italy. I
heard rumours that Mondadori was planning an Italian editions of your
texts. Is it true? If not, can I do something to help to find some other
publishers? There is now a boom in architectural books in Italy, in spite
of the economic crisis. I suppose that it would not be difficult to organize
a collaboration with you.

   Of course, I would need to know: a) how many architectural
texts you have produced, and perhaps get a copy of them; b) what are your
conditions for the translation in Italian.

   In other words, I am at your full disposal, to enlarge the
audience of the magnificent work you are doing.

   With the best wishes,

Stephen Bayley
A305 Course Team member

Soho, London, UK
20 July 2017

Stephen Bayley [SB]
Joaquim Moreno [JM]

JM You are nowadays known as a design guru, but could you tell us about what your role was in the A305 course? How did you get involved with The Open University?

SB I've accepted the term "design guru" with what I like to think of as self-deprecating irony. It's not something one would take seriously. I was responsible for creating London's International Design Museum, but before that I worked at the Victoria & Albert Museum, putting on exhibitions about design. But crucially, before that, I was of course working for The Open University. It was, in fact, virtually my first job. I was plucked from the obscurity of my postgraduate course in the Liverpool University School of Architecture and given this opportunity, by Tim Benton, to participate in A305.

I had always been interested in the history of modern architecture, but I was not an expert—I was in fact writing a thesis about an aspect of nineteenth-century architecture. But The Open University course A305 had extraordinary expertise and ambition, and it was a privilege for me to take part in it as a young, inexperienced person. I don't know how much the students learned from the experience, but I learned from it an enormous amount. It gave me a sense of authority in the matters of modern architecture and design, which I've kept with me ever since, for the past forty years.

JM You worked during the last stretch of the course, having to make sense of a lot of things as the programme was drawing to a close.

SB I worked with A305 for two years. I was always excited by the idea of modern architecture and design, but before A305, the topic wasn't particularly well-researched in the UK. Tim Benton had this vision, a mixture of absolute genius and mischief, and being able to participate in it was marvellous.

Tim Benton had understandably marshalled all The Open University's resources—media, print, and editorial—and he wanted to make a true and compelling record of classic modern architecture. I think the people running The Open University had no idea what Tim was doing, no idea of his scope or ambition, or of the fact that film crews were going to America and all over Europe. It just shows that one man in possession of a very particular vision can achieve a lot, even in the most bureaucratic circumstances.

Tim did the programmes about Le Corbusier, Frank Lloyd Wright, and all the glorious masterpieces of high-modern architecture. It sort of fell to me to cover more humble things, like cinemas in Finsbury Park in North London, or the Letchworth Garden City, Hartfordshire, or something interesting but frankly a bit mundane, like mechanical services. I was probably less competent in doing historical topics, but writing about mechanical services, the modern flat, the garden city—these were ways in which I could elevate my own growing enthusiasm for modern architecture and design.

By doing A305, I was learning about media and architectural design history. Now that we have online courses and teaching through computers, it is difficult to remember how radical and how exciting England's Open

University was, using old-fashioned, clunky televisions and radios to reach a very large audience. For a young person like me to be given the scope of educating tens, possibly hundreds, of thousands of people was an extraordinary experience—and it still amazes me. It's better quality work than I am capable of today.

JM   When you were teaching A305, you somehow had to deal with all the reservations against modern architecture. Did you think of your role in A305 as also being that of a forward-looking critic?

SB   That's probably fair enough. Before I started working on A305, I had myself been a student of the history of art, which is really my subject, but I had decided, even as an undergraduate, that the only purpose of studying the history of art was to be able to apply principles of the past to the present and to the future.

I had a personal insight in Manchester, where I first studied. Somebody was teaching me about Italian Baroque altarpieces, which I love, but I was thinking: why on earth is someone telling me about Baroque altarpieces in Italy when they should be telling me about the world outside, about Manchester? In those days—I'm talking forty, maybe fifty years ago—the study of architectural history in the UK was very primitive. The materials simply didn't exist.

So getting on the A305 team, I was brought into a world where hitherto I had been a young student at the feet of Reyner Banham, Joseph Rykwert, and Tim Benton, and suddenly I was their colleague. I used my part of A305 to talk about ideas of design, and how design can be understood not just historically but as a rationale for present and future existence. I had always been interested in vernacular things, ordinary things. My definition of excellence is the ordinary thing done extraordinarily well, and the workingman's flat—what the Germans call Existenzminimum—is the perfect test for ideas about design: can you make a modest dwelling beautiful and useful?

JM   Could you take us a little bit through the materials that you were mobilizing in the course units?

SB   Well, we just went to find those materials ourselves. We went to Vienna to get images of Karl-Marx-Hof, they didn't exist in our photo libraries. I actually had to go out in my car with my Yashica twin-lens reflex and take these pictures myself. I was given Unit 22, The Modern Flat, and television broadcast 22, "Mechanical Services in the Cinema," because they were something Tim didn't really want to do himself, having had great fun doing Bruno Taut and Siedlungen in Germany. I was left to go around England. In some of the photographs I took for Unit 23, The Garden City, the course on the suburban style, you can even see my Fiat 128 in the frame.

This should give you some impression of the zeal and effort that went into the creation of A305. It was marshalling all this diverse material and putting it into one coherent set of knowledge, saying, "This is modern design." And I have to confess, so intense was the experience that I still have the feeling that this, A305, is the authoritative, scriptural account of what modern architecture is. I still argue that point and I still believe it, because I found myself in the company of people like Banham and Rykwert, who are now great heroes of architectural history and architectural criticism.

JM   Martin Pawley was also an important architectural critic at the time. What influence did he have on A305?

SB   Martin Pawley was, certainly in my opinion, one of the greatest English architectural critics, an inspired and genuinely independent mind. Although Martin wasn't directly involved in A305, his work, particularly Architecture Versus Housing, hugely influenced A305's last television broadcast, "The Housing Question," for example. Martin had a very practical view about design and felt that the purpose of architecture should really be tested not by the quality of architect nor by the glamour and grandeur of great monuments, but by the utility of a simple residence. He brought a very high standard of intellectual scrutiny—which hitherto hadn't existed—to the study of housing.

Martin Pawley hated postmodern architecture. He got himself into trouble by suggesting, looking at some examples of recent English history, that postmodern architecture leads to financial collapse. But in 1974, it seemed entirely sensible to posit these two extremes of how modern architecture might develop. Martin also believed that architects designing housing could benefit from looking at aircraft factories. Like all great heroes of modernism, including Le Corbusier, Martin was fascinated by aviation—and machinery in general. I think Martin Pawley was amongst the first in Britain to talk about Henry Ford's production lines and how the experience of those might possibly influence modern architecture. So much of the history of architecture, at least in this country, had been hitherto anecdotal, more like belles-lettres or essays. But Martin Pawley understood mechanics, machinery, sculptures, which is quite rare amongst architectural critics, and I think *Architecture Versus Housing* was one of the great books —reforming, visionary, and humane.

One of the extraordinary things worth emphasizing now, in the early twenty-first century, is that when we were doing A305, a lot of the main protagonists of the high-modern period of the late 1920s and 1930s were still alive. We could go see them, interview them, peer into their recollections.... It was another thing which gave A305 part of its credibility: we had access to the original sources. I think it's fair to say that A305 represented the most consistent and impressive body of knowledge about modern architecture that had been created up to that moment in Britain, and perhaps ever since.

JM   Did you interview Ernö Goldfinger?

SB   I did interview Ernö Goldfinger, one of the great *bêtes noires* of modern architecture, certainly in England. Goldfinger, the James Bond villain, was actually inspired by Ernö Goldfinger. Ian Fleming was acquainted with him and he found him such a rogue and a rascal that he named his famous anti-hero after him. That's probably the greatest prominence an architect has ever achieved. But I found Ernö Goldfinger to be an agreeable, humorous, generous, and interesting man.

JM   In presenting the Trellick Tower in the television broadcast, "The Housing Question," you also seem to have been inspired by the historicism of Nikolaus Pevsner.

SB   I'm inclined to think that history is a continuous process, and everything is, to a degree, a reference to something else. The pursuit of novelty is fascinating but, I think, a delusion. Because things don't exist *de novo*, even though architects sometimes believe they do. And of course, that's something that characterizes the whole modern movement. They felt that they were finding absolute truth and timeless answers in building design. Of course, they weren't; which makes it elegiac and charming but not less noble, or less fascinating, because their inspiration was of the highest moral and aesthetic order.

Looking at questions of historicism, we can ask: Was Ernö Goldfinger's Trellick Tower in London possibly influenced by Antonio Sant'Elia? And it's quite clear that Ernö Goldfinger had been looking at Sant'Elia, whose prodigious creativity had just been rediscovered after a period of total obscurity.

JM   Other modern buildings like Park Hill in Sheffield, and the Unité d'habitation in Marseilles, were able to find their audience, in the literal sense of meeting people that were interested in living there. Quarry Hill, on the other hand didn't find that audience in time somehow, and was demolished in 1978. Housing is the classic example for teaching architecture and design because it is volatile as an idea. People's ambitions change what good housing is, and the idea of good housing is different for different people. I'm curious about the role of housing in A305, as the instrument to communicate with students through an everyday experience they would recognize immediately. You wrote the conclusion to A305 precisely on this topic.

SB   Yes, housing was a way of communicating to students how ideas about architecture were relevant to them, of applying aesthetic and practical principles to the everyday.

JM   The conclusion of the course also refers to works built after 1939. The last images in the booklets are of buildings by Venturi and Stirling.

SB   Hm. Venturi and Stirling. You've got to remember that in 1974, when we wrote *The Garden City* course unit booklet, Venturi's ideas had still not been discredited by some truly terrible buildings which he inspired. Venturi's ideas about complexity and contradiction seemed, in those days, genuinely fresh and up-to-date, that's why we had included them.

JM   I was going through the student reports, and a lot of them are about cinemas. It seems that "Mechanical Services in the Cinema" was a very successful television programme, explaining how cinemas created an artificial atmosphere of fantasy using ornament and mechanical services.

SB   We went to the Finsbury Park Astoria as part of our examination of mechanical services, particularly electric lighting and ventilation. We chose the cinema as a building type because it is obviously of the twentieth century, it didn't exist hitherto and I don't think that people are building many cinemas now. In the classic, glorious cinemas of the 1920s and 1930s, you can see that they mix fantasy—retro-kitsch fantasies of the Alhambra or whatever—with highly advanced mechanical services, such as forced ventilation. Cinemas just seemed an obvious thing to study and it gave Nick Levinson, the very talented producer, an opportunity to build in lots of archive film, crazy bits of *Fu Manchu*, and all the various other exotic references which you can find in Finsbury Park, of all places.

JM   And if we move toward the second to last television broadcast, "The Semi-Detached House," we see that you carefully go through the internal typologies and development of the suburbs.

SB   I'd always been interested in the suburbs, because I have a taste for the vernacular, the ordinary thing. I don't think we should disdain the suburbs—though a lot of high modernists, of course, did. Somebody once said that the design of an ordinary house is at the outer limits of human capability, and I actually do think that. If you wanted, in the context of a course about modern architecture and design, a little bit of a heterodox way to look at the suburbs and the garden city, you could say it is actually Britain's unique contribution to the history of world architecture. That seemed to me to be something worth saying in A305, and mildly heterodox as well, because at the time, settled opinion was that the Corbusian approach to housing was probably wiser than the garden city. But of course, government policy in Britain is now coming around to promoting garden cities again.

JM   This brings us to "The Housing Question," which is a loaded phrase. You start with footage of Yamasaki's Pruitt-Igoe being demolished, a monumentalized death of the modern architecture, to the sound of *Ionisation*, by Edgar Varèse.

SB   [Chuckles] Well, the demolition of Pruitt-Igoe was an epochal image, which of course Charles Jencks popularized. So we started with that, then we wanted to look at Ernö Goldfinger's Trellick Tower because, in those days, Goldfinger was demonized by the conservative establishment. Brutalism was not a term of opprobrium yet as it has now become in the popular press in Britain, but even in the 1970s, Goldfinger's then-new Trellick Tower was cited as one of the grossest intrusions in London's skyline. And now, of course, it's an immensely popular building.
     And then we went on to Ralph Erskine's Byker, discussing the arguments about so-called defensible space which were very popular in architecture at the time, saying that the housing problem—the problem of cities—could, to a degree, be solved by making more agreeable, more domestic scale environments with softer materials. That seemed, at the time, extremely interesting. I'm not sure it's an experiment that worked, but there's no point in making experiments if you know what the results are going to be.

Episode Eight

Still the Housing Question

Joaquim Moreno

By the time A305 was broadcast in 1975, the question of housing was as central in architectural debates as it had been in the early twentieth century, the main period A305 studied. The state of crisis into which many modernist, high-rise residential projects fell after the 1960s reinforced debates over mass housing versus individual detached houses;

> over the vilification
> of vertical, collective living
> versus the celebration
> of horizontally spread,
> single-family neighbourhoods.

Modernist housing, as one of the most contested points of friction between

> architecture,
> culture,
> and society,

was being demonized in the media, the court of public opinion, to make space in political agendas for the literal demolition of that housing.

Despite its historical focus, A305 could not exempt itself from engaging this conflict and the outcomes of the modern architecture that the course was broadcasting to a vast audience.

[A]

According to Charles Jencks, modernist housing, and thus modern architecture as a whole, had imploded along with Pruitt-Igoe in 1972. Situating itself in the moment, the Course Team used the footage of Pruitt-Igoe's demolition to open A305's final television programme,
TV 24 "The Housing Question,"
along with the sound of *Ionisation*,
a dissonant percussion piece written by Edgar Varèse in 1931. The effect was that of a tragic scene
—the expiring breath of an idea—
a collapse played in slow motion
to a composition inspired by
Futurist music's fascination with noise.
Around the same time, and in a similarly dramatic fashion, Tim Benton opened "The Rise and Fall of

Quarry Hill," his article published in *The Architect* in 1975, by saying:

> Any day now they're going to start demolishing Quarry Hill flats, one of the biggest and most spectacular housing experiments of the 1930s.

[B]

The history of modern architecture was finally being broadcast by A305, but at the same time so was its revision and rewriting along populist lines —the course was thus acknowledging media as a mirror. But it also insisted on a wider understanding of the housing question:

by documenting the demise
of monumental mass housing
like the Quarry Hill estate,
explaining the rationale
behind the suburb and the charm
of the semi-detached house,
and opening a window
onto future possibilities,

such as Ralph Erskine's new housing model proposed for the Byker complex in Newcastle.

Benton's article, together with TV 14,
"English Flats of the Thirties,"
the accompanying notes in *Broacasting Supplement*,
Part 2,
and Unit 22, "The Modern Flat,"
in the Unit 21–22 course booklet *Mechanical Services*, were the last witnesses to Quarry Hill, which was demolished in 1978.
Seen from today's distance,
the story of Quarry Hill
appears almost like a plot
constructed specifically for television.
In fact, the massive council estate became a recognizable televisual presence as the backdrop for the British sitcom, *Queenie's Castle*, which aired from 1970 to 1972.

 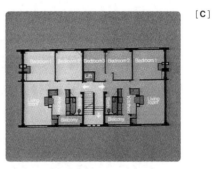

[C]

Quarry Hill was a gigantic housing complex in Leeds, built in 1938, made up of almost one thousand flats that were once home to more than three thousand people. As Benton explains in *Broadcasting Supplement, Part 2*, Quarry Hill evoked the formal qualities and infrastructure for collective living of the Karl-Marx-Hof,

Vienna's famous Austro-Marxist housing super-block. Quarry Hill's horseshoe shape and the sense of community imparted by its internal gardens, also evoked the Hufeisensiedlung in Berlin, while the new building technologies it employed drew from those applied at the Cité de la Muette in Drancy.

[D]

The Chairman of the Leeds Housing Committee, Reverend Charles Jenkinson, and the Chief Architect and Housing Director of Leeds, R. A. H. Livett, had both visited these precedents during the planning process of Quarry Hill. *In Broadcasting Supplement, Part 2*, Benton details how the new Leeds estate was engendered by agencies and models built around the idea of a totalizing lifestyle that could replace that of the hardship previously shared across the original neighbourhood, which had been cited in the late nineteenth century as one of the worst slums in Europe.

The influence of European architecture on the work of British architects in the 1930s took various forms. In addition to the purely stylistic influence of the International Style in architecture and design, we can trace the spread of certain basic attitudes towards the role of architecture in improving living conditions on the widest level.

By filming the humble splendour of Quarry Hill in TV 14, A305 was broadcasting the abandonment of a significant piece of British modern architecture while also establishing a fundamental distinction between a project that failed and one that had been made to fail.

[E]

Indeed, A305 argued that
the life of the model estate was cut short
due to bad maintenance,
bad management,
and political vengeance
more than due to design flaws or technical shortcomings.

[F]

Images of cracked windows,
broken walls,
and paved-over playgrounds
covered in litter
spoke to the demise of Quarry Hill.

[G]

A broader sense of dashed heroic ambitions
becomes evident when the course details the
parallel tragic lives of Quarry Hill's notable precedents. The Karl-Marx-Hof, for example, was as
much a project of propaganda as one of housing:
an effective piece of formal rhetoric,
or more explicitly, a visual fiction,
much more so
than a typologically or technically
innovative construction.
Known as the Red Fortress, it became a symbol of
working-class insurrection when it came under
attack and was besieged during the 1934 Austrian
Civil War. In the Unit 22 course booklet, "The Modern Flat," Course Team member Stephen Bayley
chooses to reproduce a passage from the

International Press Correspondence to narrate this story about the significance of the Karl-Marx-Hof.

[H]

[The Karl-Marx-Hof flats] were really citadels, but not because ... these houses, which had been planned by bourgeois architects, had been built to serve as "armed fortresses." They were strong fortresses because the workers defended them with their fists, with their breasts, with their last drop of blood. For three days the attacks of the government troops, who were armed to the teeth, broke against the iron resistance of the Vienna proletariat.

Bayley even presents a cartoon printed in 1934 in the *Daily Worker*, a newspaper backed by the British Communist Party, showing Engelbert Dollfuss, the right-wing Austrian Chancellor, holding a sign reading "pardon for deserters" while under machine-gun fire from the windows of an occupied Karl-Marx-Hof. As Tim Benton says in TV 14,

> "some of this militant symbolism" and pathos appeared to have "rubbed off" on the ideological underpinning of Quarry Hill more generally as a housing solution.

Just as the Red Fortress stood in opposition to rising fascism in 1930s Austria, Quarry Hill was similarly perceived by its contemporaries as a political battleground.

> For conservatives, mass housing posed a threat to the British State,
> in that it might catalyze Labour policies by helping to mobilize the New Left and unite the working class.

[1]

As with the Karl-Marx-Hof, the Cité de la Muette also became a stage for political struggles in the 1930s and 1940s. Construction of the celebrated project, which had begun in 1932, stopped in 1935 due to economic constraints, such that it sat vacant until 1938 when portions were leased to the French paramilitary. The remaining vacant portions were requisitioned during World War II for use as a prisoner internment camp, first by the French government and then by the German occupation, and eventually as a major transit camp for the deportation of Jews.

While the Austrian and German precedents were important formal and ideological influences on Quarry Hill, they lacked the modern technologies implemented by Eugene Beaudoin and Marcel Lods at the Cité de la Muette. Beaudoin and Lods had experimented with the Mopin façade system,
a prefabricated steel frame
clad in precast concrete panels,
which promised that
industrial building technology
could materialize mass housing.

 [J]

Quarry Hill also relied on the Garchey refuse collection system implemented in the Cité de la Muette, which sucked domestic waste through the kitchen sink into a complex dehydration and incineration system, using the biomass energy thus produced to power collective amenities like washers and dryers. As Stephen Bayley details in his analysis, the Garchey and Mopin systems appeared to form a perfect combination:

the assembling of symbolic efficiency
with expedient and economical
prefabrication and mass production.

These influences reached Leeds through exactly
the right channels:
  the community advocate,
  Charles Jenkinson,
  brought symbolic form to the project,
and the municipal architect, R. A. H. Livett,
  brought mass production
  and infrastructural amenities.
However, the passing of time brought to light
the difficulties that resulted from importing
technologies
  into different contexts,
  with a different way of working,
  a different knowledge base,
  and a different political structure.
At Quarry Hill, the Garchey disposal system
stopped functioning properly and the smoke produced by the incineration chimney inconvenienced
neighbouring residents. But most critically, as
an A305 student reported in his documentation
of the estate's demolition, a poorly managed
restoration of the Mopin system overloaded the
steel framing with heavier cladding panels than
it was designed to support, preventing the proper
assessment of metal corrosion and making
it impossible to maintain or restore the system—

effectively condemning the entire estate to eventual decrepitude.

> The A305 students watching
> the eventual demolition of Quarry Hill
> and the ideological battles
> surrounding it would have had a
> shared reference against which
> to contrast this ruination of modernity:
> *Queenie's Castle*.

The television series revolved around two characters: Queenie Shepherd, a petty criminal, and Quarry Hill, the castle that protected Queenie and the mostly illegal activities of her "subjects." But the estate also housed her enemy, Mrs. Petty, who ran a cake shop on the ground floor. In the series, instead of being staged as a version of an Austro-Marxist, working-class fortress, Quarry Hill was thus the lair of a gangster with a platinum-blond bouffant and a fur coat, who reigned over the estate and transformed its occupants into accomplices. This caricature portrayed collective housing as a shelter for illegal activity, transforming, for the sake of entertainment, the council estate into a bandit's castle. What the audience watching could infer from this transformation was that mass housing led to moral corruption, thereby confusing the character with the context and architecture with social evils that pervaded much broader issues.

Modern architecture
tried to change ways of life,
and in *Queenie's Castle*,
it was blamed for both
the unchanging ways of life
and the social degradation
that occurred within the estate.
In this case, Quarry Hill had no agency, only guilt.
There was little that A305 could do to disassemble
this fabricated narrative.

Because Quarry Hill was one of the projects
included in the course that students were most
likely to recognize, it created an important bridge
between
the history and practice
of modern architecture
and the environments
in which many students were likely living. But more
than a bridge,
the concurrence between
architecture history
and a fictional series
showed how media
could create
a clash of realities,
or of representations of reality.
Quarry Hill was demolished soon after it appeared
in the course, and so, after 1978, the course was
broadcasting a vanished building, making TV 14

a testament to the complex interactions between public housing, public opinion, and mass media. A305 was a real-time window into the media landscape of the moment.

The erasure of this estate, like the demolition of Pruitt-Igoe, was an episode in the battle
between flats
and semi-detached houses;
between homes in the air
and homes on the ground;
between high-density, centrally located
and low-density, peripherally located;
between elite, avant-garde taste
and popular, vernacular taste.

[K]

Stephen Bayley was responsible for staging this conflict
in TV 23, "The Semi-Detached House,"
and TV 24, "The Housing Question,"
as well as in *The Garden City*, the Unit 23–24 course booklet. Bayley clearly states his approach

to the suburbs in the notes for TV 23 in *Broadcasting Supplement*, *Part 2*:

> In this programme I want to explain the origins of the suburban style in England. This style has found its most potent form of expression in the semi-detached house.

Bayley establishes a stylistic opposition to modern architecture by saying that the semi-detached house was "a living example of the persistent British taste for the vernacular and picturesque." He states that the architecture of the suburbs was as much a product of the innovation and change that occurred during the course's 1890–1939 period of analysis as modernist buildings were, but that suburbs were nonetheless "a unique expression of popular culture independent of the Modern Movement." Bayley notes that, in apparent opposition to a modern architecture based on a desire for formal abstraction, the development of English vernacular and suburban forms was nevertheless prompted by

the same economy,
technical innovation,
and social progress
as modernist aesthetics were.

Bayley stages this inversion through follow-up questions that students were expected to address after watching TV 23, in which he asks what roles railway and legislation played in suburban development, and whether a modern flat or, rather, a semi-detached house "better represents the aspirations and ambition of ordinary people."

[L]

This dislocation of the analysis from a working-class perspective to a middle-class one underlines the rise of a new historical voice, so important for the postmodern ideological construction.

The Cheap Trains Act was the single greatest influence on the improvement of the housing problem because it enabled the less well-to-do to live in healthy surroundings while at the same time being in a position to gain speedy access to their work and source of income. Legislation also effected the change from renting property to buying it.

The less well-to-do mentioned by Bayley were nevertheless too well-off to qualify for council housing. The new legislation and the new modes of transportation that were giving rise to the suburb were also creating the figure of the commuter. And the personal taste of this new citizenry was for a dignified, albeit shrunken, version of vernacular and picturesque architecture. Even if small, the semi-detached suburban home was an image of the aspiration of its dweller, much more so than was the anonymity of a modern flat designed according to the standards of *Exitenzminimum*.

Suburban houses,
a consumer choice synonymous
with a particular kind of taste,
were built according
to shared financial constraints
as much as shared ambitions
—mostly uniform yet aspiring
to a certain sense of grandeur.

These houses were thus often described, particularly in popular media, according to moral values instead of formal characteristics

—through such terms as
decent, dignified, or sober.

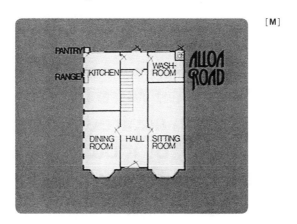

[M]

While the image of the semi-detached house was couched in the foundational myth of the garden city, Stephen Bayley points out that the suburb was the very embodiment of the urban sprawl the garden city intended to counteract.

Semi-detached suburban houses were neither functionalist nor rationalist, even if they were described as

        ideally suited
        for a servant-less family dwelling
        or as the product
        of the economic rationale
        of cheap land and fast transportation.

These suburbs were a distinctively British contribution to the history of modern architecture, with their respectable formal references to classical architecture—a genuine manifestation of bourgeois popular culture.

        Bayley closes the programme
        with a challenging question
        much in the same vein:

        Look at the Villa Savoye of Le Corbusier and at
        a semi-detached house (perhaps your own). Which do
        you honestly think is the better machine for living in?

These "decent" houses were those in which most people in Britain aspired to live, and which were criticized mainly by modernist architects. As a machine in which the audience could already imagine itself living, the semi-detached house was thus portrayed as

        honest,
        dignified,
        vernacular,
        and innovative,
        yet with a certain heritage.

They were familiar homes, through which A305's students could see their own world represented on the television.

To emphasize the currency of the debate over the opposition between the house and the flat, Bayley chooses to conclude "The Housing Question," and therefore the course,
> by examining a building
> still under construction at the time,
> the Byker Wall,
built by Ralph Erskine, Vernon Gracie & Associates in Newcastle-upon-Tyne between 1969 and 1982. The vast complex is presented as a way forward and as an alternative compromise, instead of an opposition,
> between the models
> of modernist mass housing estates
> and suburban semi-detached houses.

[N]

Bayley's commentary departs from the historic and theoretical distance of the course and shifts to a critical proposal that tries to bring the building closer to the audience by making it more likeable and easier to accept. In his reading notes in *Broadcasting Supplement, Part 2*, Bayley frames his analysis of Byker in comparison to LCC Architects' Roehampton and Ernö Goldfinger's Trellick Tower.

> Far from having its roots in architectural theories born between the wars it appears to me to be a response to some peculiarly contemporary enthusiasms for individuality, participation and variety. ... Rather than opt for a neat, clean and cool aesthetic the architects of Byker have decided on expression. The expression is achieved through the use of bright colours allied to unusual shapes and groupings of buildings.

The building was far from the vernacular or the picturesque, but it was also far from the "dogmatic" aesthetic of modern architecture during the inter-war period. As Vernon Gracie says in TV 24, in an excerpted response to a question from Bayley about the use of timber:

> One wants a new environment to be a soft environment... give it the appearance, if you like, almost of being delicate and in need of being cared for. ... Although it's a darn sight tougher than it looks.

Bayley's own description of Byker evokes this "soft environment":
> the perimeter block,
> nicknamed the "Wall,"
> is a protective sound barrier
> from the nearby highway;
> the cantilevered balconies
> and the access galleries

are sun gardens
or suspended conservatories;
the top units are maisonettes,
almost as if they are on the ground;
and the lower units
organize quiet, semi-private areas.

[O]

All of these spatial types provided the entire complex with very different scales and atmospheres from those of other mass housing projects. Bayley's narrative approach in TV 24 amounted to a warm description rather than a historical evaluation.

The lack of uniformity, the sheer expression of colour and form producing such visual interest make Byker contrast strongly with any other housing estate. Ralph Erskine and Vernon Gracie have not given Newcastle whimsical imitations of cottage styles but, instead, Byker is full of real machines-for-living-in and the form really follows the function which people have decided for it.

The real alternative that was proposed through the Byker Wall was the notion of user participation, which was gaining real political currency at the time. The planning and design process at Byker was giving an active voice to the users of mass housing, letting them participate as real protagonists in its development
  —much like A305 students were, too, real protagonists in the open process of their own education.

Index of A305

History of Architecture and Design
1890–1939

Television programmes
Course unit booklets
Radio programmes
Supplementary material
Anthology

What is Architecture?: An Architect at Work

Television programme 1 of A305, presented by Geoffrey Baker, produced by Edward Hayward, BBC for The Open University, aired 15 February 1975.

The Universal International Exhibition, Paris, 1900

Television programme 2 of A305, presented by Tim Benton, produced by Nick Levinson, BBC for The Open University, aired 1 March 1975.

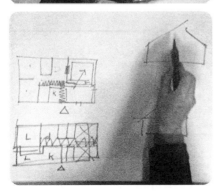

Charles Rennie Mackintosh: Hill House

Television programme 3 of A305, presented by
Sandra Millikin, produced by Nick Levinson,
BBC for The Open University, aired 8 March 1975.

Industrial Architecture: AEG and Fagus Factories

Television programme 4 of A305, presented by
Tim Benton, produced by Nick Levinson, BBC for
The Open University, aired 15 March 1975.

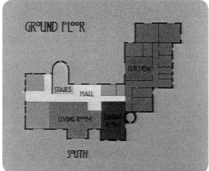

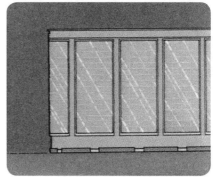

Frank Lloyd Wright: The Robie House

Television programme 5 of A305, presented by
Sandra Millikin, produced by Edward Hayward,
BBC for The Open University, aired 5 April 1975.

R. M. Schindler: The Lovell Beach House

Television programme 6 of A305, presented by
Sandra Millikin, produced by Edward Hayward,
BBC for The Open University, aired 12 April 1975.

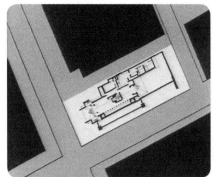

Erich Mendelsohn: The Einstein Tower

Television programme 7 of A305, presented
by Dennis Sharp, produced by Nick Levinson,
BBC for The Open University, aired 19 April 1975.

The Bauhaus at Weimar, 1919–1923

Television programme 8 of A305, presented
by Tim Benton, produced by Edward Hayward,
BBC for The Open University, aired 3 May 1975.

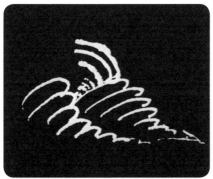

Berlin Siedlungen

Television programme 9 of A305, presented
by Tim Benton, produced by Nick Levinson,
BBC for The Open University, aired 10 May 1975.

The Weissenhof Siedlung, 1927, Stuttgart

Television programme 10 of A305, presented
by Tim Benton, produced by Edward Hayward,
BBC for The Open University, aired 17 May 1975.

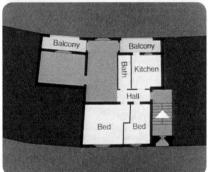

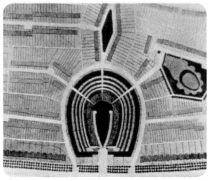

The International Exhibition of Decorative
Arts, Paris, 1925

Television programme 11 of A305, presented
by Tim Benton, produced by Nick Levinson,
BBC for The Open University, aired 31 May 1975.

Adolf Loos

Television programme 12 of A305, presented
by Tim Benton, produced by Edward Hayward,
BBC for The Open University, aired 7 June 1975.

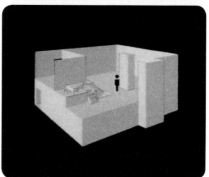

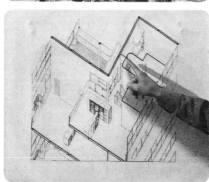

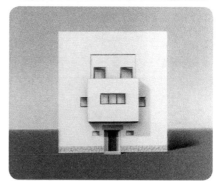

Le Corbusier: Villa Savoye

Television programme 13 of A305, presented by
Tim Benton, produced by Nick Levinson, BBC
for The Open University, aired 14 June 1975.

English Flats of the Thirties

Television programme 14 of A305, presented by
Tim Benton, produced by Edward Hayward, BBC
for The Open University, aired 12 July 1975.

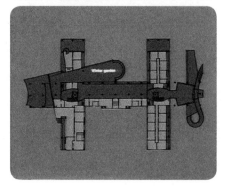

English Houses of the Thirties

Television programme 15 of A305, presented
by Geoffrey Baker, produced by Edward Hayward,
BBC for The Open University, aired 19 July 1975.

Hans Scharoun

Television programme 16 of A305, presented
by Tim Benton, produced by Nick Levinson,
BBC for The Open University, aired 26 July 1975.

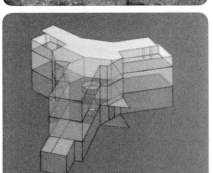

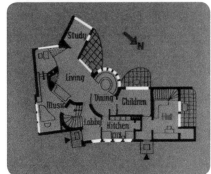

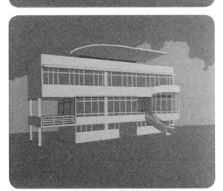

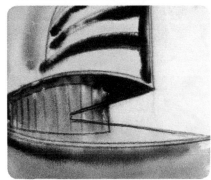

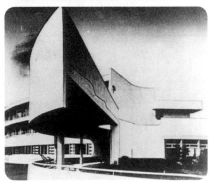

Wood or Metal? English Furniture in the Thirties

Television programme 17 of A305, presented by
Tim Benton, produced by Bennett Maxwell, BBC
for The Open University, aired 9 August 1976.

Edwin Lutyens: Deanery Gardens

Television programme 18 of A305, presented by
Geoffrey Baker, produced by Edward Hayward,
BBC for The Open University, aired 16 August 1975.

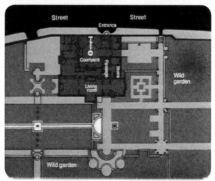

The London Underground

Television programme 19 of A305, presented by
Geoffrey Baker, produced by Edward Hayward,
BBC for The Open University, aired 30 August 1975.

Moderne and Modernistic

Television programme 20 of A305, presented by
Geoffrey Baker, produced by Nick Levinson, BBC
for The Open University, aired 13 September 1975.

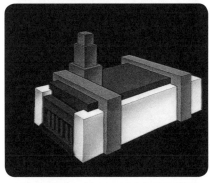

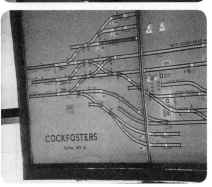

The Other Tradition

Television programme 21 of A305, presented by Geoffrey Baker, produced by Miriam Rapp, BBC for The Open University, aired 20 September 1975.

Mechanical Services in the Cinema

Television programme 22 of A305, presented by Stephen Bayley, produced by Edward Hayward, BBC for The Open University, aired 27 September 1975.

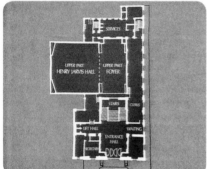

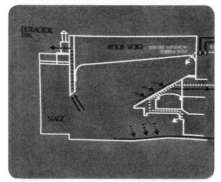

The Semi-Detached House

Television programme 23 of A305, presented by Stephen Bayley, produced by Patricia Hodgson, BBC for The Open University, aired 11 October 1975.

The Housing Question

Television programme 24 of A305, presented by Stephen Bayley, produced by Miriam Rapp, BBC for The Open University, aired 18 October 1975.

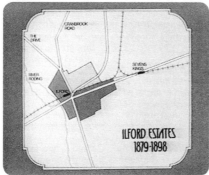

Course unit booklets

Baker, Geoffrey, and Tim Benton. *Introduction*. Course booklet for Units 1–2 of A305, History of Architecture and Design 1890–1939. Milton Keynes: The Open University Press, 1975 (full course title hereafter abbreviated to A305).

Benton, Tim, and Sandra Millikin. *Art Nouveau, 1890–1902*. Course booklet for Units 3–4 of A305. Milton Keynes: The Open University Press, 1975.

Benton, Tim, Stefan Muthesius, and Bridget Wilkins. *Europe 1900–1914: The Reaction to Historicism and Art Nouveau*. Course booklet for Units 5–6 of A305. Milton Keynes: The Open University Press, 1975.

Baker, Geoffrey, Lindsay Gordon, and Sandra Millikin. *USA 1890–1939*. Course booklet for Units 7–8 of A305. Milton Keynes: The Open University Press, 1975.

Benton, Tim. *Expressionism*. Course booklet for Units 9–10 of A305. Milton Keynes: The Open University Press, 1975.

———. *The New Objectivity*. Course booklet for Units 11–12 of A305. Milton Keynes: The Open University Press, 1975.

Benton, Charlotte, and Tim Benton. *The International Style*. Course booklet for Units 13–14 of A305. Milton Keynes: The Open University Press, 1975.

Benton, Charlotte, Tim Benton, and Aaron Scharf. *Design 1920s: German Design and the Bauhaus 1925–32, Modernism in the Decorative Arts, Paris 1910–30*. Course booklet for Units 15–16 of A305. Milton Keynes: The Open University Press, 1975.

Curtis, William. *Le Corbusier, English Architecture 1930s*. Course booklet for Units 17–18 of A305. Milton Keynes: The Open University Press, 1975.

Forty, Adrian, and Geoffrey Newman. *British Design*. Course booklet for Units 19–20 of A305. Milton Keynes: The Open University Press, 1975.

Banham, Reyner, and Stephen Bayley. *Mechanical Services*. Course booklet for Units 21–22 of A305. Milton Keynes: The Open University Press, 1975.

Bayley, Stephen. *The Garden City*. Course booklet for Units 23–24 of A305. Milton Keynes: The Open University Press, 1975.

Radio programmes

Benton, Tim, presenter. "What Is Design?" Radio programme 1 of A305, *History of Architecture and Design 1890–1939*. Produced by Edward Hayward, BBC for The Open University, first aired 18 February 1975 (full series title hereafter abbreviated to A305).

Benton, Tim, presenter. "Magazine of Decorative Art in the 1890s." Radio programme 2 of A305. Produced by Nick Levinson, BBC for The Open University, first aired 25 February 1975.

Benton, Tim, presenter. "Gaudi's Architecture and Design." Radio programme 3 of A305. Produced by Edward Hayward, BBC for The Open University, first aired 4 March 1975.

Haber, Francine, Alexander John, and Robert Mill, presenters. "Hector Guimard." Radio programme 4 of A305. Produced by Edward Hayward, BBC for The Open University, first aired 15 March 1975.

Farleigh, Lynn, and Mark Jones, presenters. "Tony Garnier: La cité industrielle." Radio programme 5 of A305, 1st ed. Produced by Edward Hayward, BBC for The Open University, first aired 18 March 1975.

Jones, Mark, and Dora Wisbenson, presenters. "Tony Garnier: La cité industrielle." Radio programme 5 of A305, 2nd ed. Produced by Edward Hayward, BBC for The Open University, first aired 11 March 1977.

Collins, Peter, presenter. "Ferro-Concrete: Hennebique to Perret." Radio programme 6 of A305. Produced by Nick Levinson, BBC for The Open University, first aired 25 March 1975.

Chafee, Richard, and Blain Fairman, presenters. "Louis Sullivan." Radio programme 7 of A305. Produced by Edward Hayward, BBC for The Open University, first aired 8 April 1975.

Millikin, Sandra, presenter. "Frank Lloyd Wright: Architecture and Democracy." Radio programme 8 of A305, 1st ed. Produced by Edward Hayward, BBC for The Open University, first aired 15 April 1975.

Banham, Reyner, presenter. "Frank Lloyd Wright." Radio programme 8 of A305, 2nd ed. Produced by Edward Hayward, BBC for The Open University, first aired 20 March 1976.

John, Alexander, and Dennis Sharp, presenters. "Glass Architecture: The World of Paul Scheerbart and Bruno Taut." Radio programme 9 of A305. Produced by Nick Levinson, BBC for The Open University, first aired 15 April 1975.

Cunningham, Colin, presenters. "Another Look at Expressionism." Radio programme 9 of A305. Produced by Nick Levinson, BBC for The Open University, first aired 27 March 1976.

Benton, Charlotte, Frank Duncan, and Anthony Jackson, presenters. "Futurism." Radio programme 10 of A305. Produced by Nick Levinson, BBC for The Open University, first aired 29 April 1975.

Franciscono, Marcel, presenter. "The Debate Between Van de Velde and Muthesius." Radio programme 11 of A305. Produced by Edward Hayward, BBC for The Open University, first aired 6 May 1975.

Benton, Tim, and Jacques Paul, presenters. "Walter Gropius Before 1923." Radio programme 12 of A305. Produced by Helen Rapp, BBC for The Open University, first aired 13 May 1975.

Benton, Charlotte, presenter. "The People Deserve Their Colonnades: Soviet Architecture." Radio programme 13 of A305. Produced by Helen Rapp, BBC for The Open University, first aired 20 May 1975.

Lubetkin, Berthold, presenter. "Berthold Lubetkin: Art, Ideology, and Revolution." Radio programme 14 of A305. Produced by Helen Rapp, BBC for The Open University, first aired 27 May 1975.

Benton, Tim, presenter. "Pierre Chareau: Maison de Verre." Radio programme 15 of A305. Produced by Nick Levinson, BBC for The Open University, first aired 3 June 1975.

Benton, Charlotte, presenter. "Oriental Lacquer and French Design in the 1920s." Radio programme 16 of A305. Produced by Helen Rapp, BBC for The Open University, first aired 10 June 1975.

Benton, Tim, presenter. "Villa Savoye: Preliminary Drawings." Radio programme 17 of A305. Produced by Nick Levinson, BBC for The Open University, first aired 17 June 1975.

Benton, Tim, Dennis Sharp, and Basil Ward, presenters. "Basil Ward on Connell, Ward & Lucas." Radio programme 18 of *A305*. Produced by Helen Rapp, BBC for The Open University, first aired 28 June 1975.

Benton, Tim, and Gordon Russell, presenters. "Gordon Russell and Modern British Craftsmanship." Radio programme 19 of *A305*. Produced by Helen Rapp, BBC for The Open University, first aired 15 July 1975.

Forty, Adrian, presenter. "The Labour-Saving Home." Radio programme 20 of *A305*. Produced by Helen Rapp, BBC for The Open University, first aired 22 July 1975.

Glanville, Ranulph, presenter. "Alvar Aalto: The Failure of Total Design." Radio programme 21 for *A305*. Produced by Nick Levinson, BBC for The Open University, first aired 29 July 1975.

Posener, Julius, presenter. "Germany: The Second Tradition of the Twenties." Radio programme 22 of *A305*. Directed by Nick Levinson, produced by BBC for The Open University, first aired 5 August 1975.

Benton, Tim, presenter. "Project Case Study: 66 Frognal, Part 1." Radio programme 23 of *A305*. Produced by Nick Levinson, BBC for The Open University, first aired 12 August 1975.

Benton, Tim, Colin Lucas, and Ursula Walford, presenters. "Project Case Study: 66 Frognal, Part 2." Radio programme 24 of *A305*. Produced by Prudence Smith, BBC for The Open University, first aired 19 August 1975.

Pevsner, Nikolaus, presenter. "Frank Pick and the London Underground." Radio programme 25 of *A305*. Produced by Edward Hayward, BBC for The Open University, first aired 2 September 1975.

Wilkins, Bridget, presenter. "London Transport Design." Radio programme 26 of *A305*. Produced by Edward Hayward, BBC for The Open University, first aired 9 September 1975.

Benton, Tim, and Berthold Lubetkin, presenters. "Berthold Lubetkin: A Commentary on Western Architecture." Radio programme 27 of *A305*. Produced by Helen Rapp, BBC for The Open University, first aired 16 September 1975.

Summerson, John, presenter. "The MARS Group and the Thirties." Radio programme 28 of *A305*. Produced by Helen Rapp, BBC for The Open University, first aired 23 September 1975.

Banham, Reyner, presenter. "The Reform of the Skyscraper." Radio programme 29 of *A305*. Produced by Nick Levinson, BBC for The Open University, first aired 30 September 1975.

Pritchard, Jack, presenter. "The Work of Isokon." Radio programme 30 of *A305*. Produced by Edward Hayward, BBC for The Open University, first aired 7 October 1975.

Hitchcock, Henry-Russell, presenter. "The International Style—50 Years After." Radio programme 31 of *A305*. Produced by Edward Hayward, BBC for The Open University, first aired 14 October 1975.

Benton, Tim, presenter. "Conclusion: Thinking about Revision." Radio programme 32 of *A305*. Produced by Helen Rapp, BBC for The Open University, first aired 21 October 1975.

Supplementary material

Benton, Charlotte, and Tim Benton, eds. *Images*. Supplementary booklet for A305, History of Architecture and Design 1890–1939. Milton Keynes: The Open University Press, 1975 (full course title hereafter abbreviated to A305).

Benton, Charlotte, ed. *Documents: A Collection of Source Material on the Modern Movement*. Supplementary booklet for A305. Milton Keynes: The Open University Press, 1975.

A305 Course Team, ed. *Radiovision Booklet*. Supplementary booklet for A305. Milton Keynes: The Open University Press, 1975.

———. "Villa Savoye Preliminary Drawings." Radiovision supplement for Radio programme 17 of *A305*. Milton Keynes: The Open University Press, 1975.

———. "Project Case Study: 66 Frognal, Part 1." Radiovision supplementary for Radio programme 23 of *A305*. Milton Keynes: The Open University Press, 1975.

———. *Broadcasting Supplement, Part 1*. Supplementary booklet for A305. Milton Keynes: The Open University Press, 1975.

———. *Broadcasting Supplement, Part 2*. Supplementary booklet for A305. Milton Keynes: The Open University Press, 1975.

———. "A305 Date Chart." Reference poster for A305. Milton Keynes: Open University Press, 1975.

Anthology

Benton, Tim, Charlotte Benton, and Dennis Sharp, eds. *Form and Function: A Source Book for the History of Architecture and Design 1890–1939*. London: Crosby Lockwood Staples in association with The Open University Press, 1975.

Works cited

"Il fallimento dell'università." *Il Post*, 28 July 2010.

"Televarsities?," *The Economist*, 16 December 1961.

"University Warehouse at Wellingborough." *Open House*, no. 31 (7 January 1971).

Addison, Paul. *No Turning Back: The Peacetime Revolutions of Postwar Britain*. Oxford: Oxford University Press, 2010.

Alberti, Leon Battista. *On the Art of Building In Ten Books, 1443–1444*. Translated by Joseph Rykwert, Neil Leach, and Robert Tavernor. Cambridge, MA: The MIT Press, 1991.

Arnheim, Rudolf. *Radio*. Translated by Margaret Ludwig and Herbert Read. London: Faber & Faber, 1936.

Anderson, Lawrence B. "History's History." In *The Education of the Architect: Historiography, Urbanism, and the Growth of Architectural Knowledge*, edited by Martha Pollak, 439–44. Cambridge, MA: The MIT Press, 1997.

Banham, Reyner. *A Critic Writes: Selected Essays by Reyner Banham*. Edited by Mary Banham et al. Berkeley: University of California Press, 1996.

———. "Historical Studies and Architectural Criticism." *Bartlett Society Transactions* 1 (1962–1963): 45–7.

———. "LA: The Structure Behind the Scene." *Architectural Design* 41 (April 1971): 227–30.

———. *Los Angeles: The Architecture of Four Ecologies*. New York: Harper & Row Publishers, 1971.

———. *Theory and Design in the First Machine Age*. London: Architectural Press, 1960.

———. *The Architecture of the Well-Tempered Environment*. London: Architectural Press, 1969.

———. "Who is this 'Pop'?" In *Design by Choice*, edited by Penny Sparke, 94–6. London: Academy Editions, 1981.

Barber, James, presenter. *Open Forum 1*. Produced by BBC for The Open University. First aired 3 January 1971.

Beegan, Gerry. *The Mass Image: A Social History of Photomechanical Reproduction in Victorian London*. Basingstoke: Palgrave Macmillan, 2008.

Benevolo, Leonardo. *History of Modern Architecture*. Cambridge, MA: The MIT Press, 1980.

Benton, Tim. "Broadcasting the Modern Movement." *Architecture Association Quarterly* 7, no. 1 (1975): 45–55.

———. "The Rise and Fall of Quarry Hill." *The Architect* (June 1975): 25–7.

Berger, John. *Ways of Seeing*. London: BBC; New York: Penguin Books, 1972.

———. *Ways of Seeing*. Four-part television programme. Produced by Mike Dibb. London: BBC 2, 1972.

———. "Ways of Seeing—the first of four essays by John Berger concerns the work of art." *The Listener* 87, no. 2233 (13 January 1972).

Black, Lawrence. "'Making Britain a Gayer and More Cultivated Country': Wilson, Lee and the Creative Industries in the 1960s." *Contemporary British History* 20, no. 3 (2006): 323–42.

Black, Lawrence, Hugh Pemberton, and Pat Thane. *Reassessing 1970s Britain*. Manchester: Manchester University Press, 2013.

Blondel, François. *Cours d'architecture enseigné dans l'Academie Royale d'Architecture*. Paris, 1675.

Blondel, Jacques-François. *Cours d'architecture, ou traité de la décoration, distribution et construction des bâtiments [...]*. Paris, 1771–7.

Blunt, Anthony. *Sicilian Baroque*. With photographs by Tim Benton. New York: Macmillan, 1968.

Bogost, Ian. "MOOCs and the Future of the Humanities (Part One): A Roundtable at the LA Review of Books." Ian Bogost's professional website, 14 June 2013. http://bogost.com/writing/moocs_and_the_future_of_the_hu/.

Boudon, Philippe. *Lived-in Architecture: Le Corbusier's Pessac Revisited*. London: Lund Humphries, 1972. First published as *Pessac de Le Corbusier*, by Dunod, 1969.

Bowden, Sue, and Avner Offer. "Household Appliances and the Use of Time: The United States and Britain Since the 1920s." *Economic History Review* 47, no. 4 (November 1994): 725–48.

———. "The Technological Revolution That Never Was: Gender, Class, and the Diffusion of Household Appliances in Interwar England." In *The Sex of Things: Gender and Consumption in Historical Perspective*, edited by Victoria de Grazia, 244–74. Berkeley: University of California Press, 1996.

Briggs, Asa. *The BBC: The First Fifty Years*. Oxford: Oxford University Press, 1985.

———. *The Golden Age of the Wireless*. Volume II of *The History of Broadcasting in the United Kingdom*. Oxford: Oxford University Press, 1995.

British Broadcasting Corporation. *The BBC and the Open University*. Northampton: Belmont Press, November 1982.

Burckhardt, Jacob. *Die Kultur der Renaissance in Italien*. Basel, 1860.

Cannadine, David, Jenny Keating, and Nicola Sheldon. *The Right Kind of History: Teaching the Past in Twentieth-Century England*. Basingstoke: Palgrave Macmillan, 2011.

Carpenter, Edmund, and Marshall McLuhan, eds. *Explorations in Communication, An Anthology*. Boston: Beacon Press, 1960.

Carter, Laura. "'Experimental' Secondary Modern Education in Britain, 1948–1958." *Cultural and Social History* 13, no. 1 (2016): 23–41.

Casson, Hugh, and Patrick O'Donovan, presenters. *Brief City: The Story of London's Festival Buildings*. Directed by Jacques Brunius and Maurice Harvey. London: Richard Massingham Films, 1952.

Coffin, Frank. "The Open University." In Peter Hoggett, ed., "The Open University." Special issue, *The Arup Journal* 9, no. 2 (June 1974): 2–7.

Chenal, Pierre, director. *L'Architecture d'aujourd'hui*. Written with Le Corbusier. Paris, 1931.

Chewning, J. A. "The Teaching of Architectural History during the Advent of Modernism, 1920s–1950s." In "Symposium Papers XIX: The Architectural Historian in America." Special issue, *Studies in the History of Art* 35 (1990): 101–10.

Clark, Kenneth, presenter. *Civilisation: A Personal View by Lord Clark*. Season one, thirteen episodes. First aired from 23 February to 18 May 1969 on BBC 2.

———. *Civilisation: A Personal View by Lord Clark*. 1969; London: BBC Worldwide, 2005. Viewing notes from the four-disc DVD set.

Committee on Higher Education. *Higher Education: Report of the Committee Appointed by the Prime Minister under the Chairmanship of Lord Robbins 1961–63*. London: Her Majesty's Stationery Office, 1963.

Conrads, Ulrich. *Programmes and Manifestoes on 20th-Century Architecture*. London: Lund Humphries, 1970.

Cooper, Julian, director. *Reyner Banham Loves Los Angeles*. London: BBC, 1972.

Cox, C. Brian, and Anthony E. Dyson, eds. "Black Paper Two: The Crisis in Education." Special issue, *Critical Quarterly* 4, no. 3 (1969).

———. "Fight for Education: A Black Paper." Special issue, *Critical Quarterly* 4, no. 1 (1969).

Crinson, Mark, and Jules Lubbock. *Architecture, Art or Profession?: Three Hundred Years of Architectural Education in Britain*. Manchester: Manchester University Press, 1994.

Crook, David. "School Broadcasting in the United Kingdom: An Exploratory History." *Journal of Educational Administration and History* 39, no. 3 (2007): 217–26.

Crosland, Anthony. *The Future of Socialism*. London: Jonathan Cape, 1956.

———. "The Transition from Capitalism." In *New Fabian Essays*, edited by Richard H.S. Crossman, 33–68. London: Turnstile Press, 1952.

Crowther, Geoffrey. "Lord Crowther's Inaugural Address." Speech, on the occasion of The Open University receiving its Royal Charter from the Privy Council, 23 July 1969. Milton Keynes: The Open University, 1969. Transcript.

Cunningham, Peter. *Curriculum Change in the Primary School Since 1945: Dissemination of the Progressive Ideal*. London: Falmer, 1988.

Cusack, Patricia. "A Reprieve for Weaver's Mill." *Concrete: The Journal of the Concrete Society* 10, no. 3 (March 1976): 20–3.

Davidson, Ian, and Graham Evans, directors. *Queenie's Castle*. Written by Keith Waterhouse and Willis Hall, produced by Yorkshire Television, aired from 5 November 1970 to 5 September 1972, on ITV.

Davies, Aled. *The City of London and Social Democracy: The Political Economy of Finance in Britain, 1959–1979*. Oxford: Oxford University Press, 2017.

Desgodetz, Antoine. *Les édifices antiques de Rome [...]*. Paris, 1682.

Dorey, Peter. "'Well, Harold Insists on Having It!'—the Political Struggle to Establish the Open University, 1965–67." *Contemporary British History* 29, no. 2 (2015): 241–72.

Durand, Jean-Nicolas-Louis. *Précis des leçons d'architecture [...]*. Paris, 1802–05.

Eisenman, Peter. "Building in Meaning. Book Review: *Meaning in Architecture*, edited by Charles Jencks and George Baird." *Architectural Forum* (July/August 1970): 88–90.

Eisenstein, Sergei. *Film Form: Essays in Film Theory*. London: Harcourt, 1949.

Ellis, Sylvia. "'A Demonstration of British Good Sense?' British Student Protest during the Vietnam War." In *Student Protest: The Sixties and After*, edited by Gerard J. DeGroot, 54–69. London: Routledge, 1998.

Fawdry, Kenneth. *Everything but Alf Garnett. A Personal View of BBC School Broadcasting*. London: British Broadcasting Corporation, 1974.

Fergusson, James. *History of Modern Styles in Architecture*. London, 1862.

Field, A. M. "The Educational Value of the Film." *History* 12 (1927): 142–3.

Fielding, Steven. *Labour and Cultural Change*. Volume I of *The Labour Governments 1964–1970*. Manchester: Manchester University Press, 2003.

Fletcher, Banister. *A History of Architecture on the Comparative Method*. London, 1896.

Forty, Adrian. "Lorenzo of the Underground." *The London Journal* 5, no. 1 (1979): 113–9.

———. *Objects of Desire: Design and Society 1750–1980*. London: Thames and Hudson, 1986.

———. "Wireless Style: Symbolic Design and the English Radio Cabinet, 1928–1933." *Architecture Association Quarterly* 4 (1972): 22–31.

Frampton, Kenneth. "America 1960–1970: Notes on Urban Images and Theory." *Casabella* 35, no. 359–360 (December 1971): 39–46.

Freedman, Des. "Modernising the BBC: Wilson's Government and Television, 1964–1966." *Contemporary British History* 15, no. 1 (2001): 21–40.

Gale, Janet. "Proteus in a Kaleidoscope: The Educational Technologist in Open University Course Production." *Journal of Educational Television* 6, no. 1 (1980): 4–7.

Giedion, Sigfried. *Mechanization Takes Command: A Contribution to Anonymous History*. New York: Oxford University Press, 1948.

———. *Space, Time and Architecture: The Growth of a New Tradition*. Cambridge, MA: Harvard University Press; London: H. Milford, Oxford University Press, 1941.

Gilbert, Lewis, director. *Educating Rita*. London: Acorn Pictures, 1983. Screenplay adapted from the stage-play by Willy Russell, first performed June 1980.

Girouard, Mark. *Big Jim: The Life and Work of James Stirling*. London: Pimlico, 1998.

Gosse, Van. *Rethinking the New Left: An Interpretative History*. New York: Palgrave Macmillan, 2005.

Gropius, Walter. "In Search of Better Architectural Education." In *A Decade of Contemporary Architecture*, edited by Sigfried Giedion, 47–52. Zurich: Girsberger, 1951.

Hall, Stuart. "Absolute Beginnings." *Universities and Left Review* 7 (Autumn 1959): 17–25.

———. "Life and Times of the First New Left." *New Left Review* 61 (January/February 2010): 177–96.

———. *Selected Political Writings: The Great Moving Right Show and Other Essays.* Edited by Sally Davidson, David Featherstone, Michael Rustin, and Bill Schwarz. London: Lawrence & Wishart; Durham: Duke University Press, 2017.

———. "The Emergence of Cultural Studies and the Crisis of the Humanities." *October* 53 (Summer 1990): 11–23.

Hankin, G. T. "The Decline of the Printed Word." *History* 15 (1930): 119–23.

Hargreaves, Andy. *Teaching in the Knowledge Society: Education in the Age of Insecurity.* New York: Teachers College Press, 2003.

Hennessy, Peter. *Having It So Good: Britain in the Fifties.* London: Penguin Books, 2006.

Hinton, James. *Seven Lives from Mass Observation: Britain in the Late-Twentieth Century.* Oxford: Oxford University Press, 2016.

Historical Association. *A List of Illustrations for Use in History Teaching in Schools.* London: G. Bell & Sons, 1930.

Hitchcock, Henry-Russell. *Architecture: Nineteenth and Twentieth Centuries.* Baltimore: Penguin Books, 1958.

———. *Modern Architecture: Romanticism and Reintegration.* New York: Payson & Clarke, 1929.

Hitchcock, Henry-Russell, and Philip Johnson. *The International Style: Architecture Since 1922.* New York: W. W. Norton & Co., 1932.

Hollow, Matthew. "The Age of Affluence Revisited: Council Estates and Consumer Society in Britain, 1950–1970." *Journal of Consumer Culture* 16, no. 1 (2016): 279–96.

Hoggart, Richard. *The Uses of Literacy: Aspects of Working-Class Life.* London: Chatto & Windus, 1957.

Hughes, Jonathan, and Simon Sadler, eds. *Non-Plan: Essays on Freedom and Change in Modern Architecture and Urbanism.* Oxford: Architectural Press, 2000

Hughes, Robert. *Shock of the New: Art and the Century of Change.* London: British Broadcasting Corporation, 1980.

Korski, Daniel. "Britain's universities must change to survive. Higher education reform is the way forward." *The Telegraph*, 23 January 2017.

Kynaston, David. *Modernity Britain: A Shake of the Dice, 1959–1962.* London: Bloomsbury, 2014.

Lane, Peter. *Documents on British Economic and Social History: Book 1, 1750–1870.* London: Macmillan, 1968.

Leach, Andrew. *Manfredo Tafuri: Choosing History.* Ghent: A&S Books, 2007.

Le Corbusier. *Précisions sur un état présent de l'architecture et de l'urbanisme.* Paris: Les éditions G. Crès et cie., 1930.

———. *Vers une architecture.* Paris: Les éditions G. Crès et cie., 1923.

Lethaby, William. *Architecture: An Introduction to the History and Theory of the Art.* London: Williams and Norgate, 1912.

Leventhal, Fred M. "'The Best for the Most': CEMA and State Sponsorship of the Arts in Wartime, 1939–1945." *Twentieth Century British History* 1, no. 3 (1990): 289–317.

Leavis, Frank Raymond, and Denys Thompson. *Culture and Environment: The Training of Critical Awareness.* London: Chatto & Windus, 1933.

Lloyd, Seton, et al., eds. *World Architecture: An Illustrated History.* London: The Hamlyn Publishing Group, 1963.

Madeley, Helen. "Time Charts." Special issue, *Historical Association Leaflet*, no. 50 (1921).

Mandler, Peter. "Educating the Nation: II. Universities." *Transactions of the Royal Historical Society* 25 (December 2015): 1–26.

Marty, Eric. "La réforme de l'université, une catastrophe." *Le Monde*, 10 April 2012.

Matthews, Stanley. *From Agit-Prop to Free Space: The Architecture of Cedric Price.* London: Black Dog, 2007.

McCarthy, Helen. "Women, Marriage and Paid Work in Postwar Britain." *Women's History Review* 26, no. 1 (2017): 46–61.

McCulloch, Gary. *Failing the Ordinary Child?: The Theory and Practice of Working Class Secondary Education.* Buckingham: The Open University Press, 1998.

McKellar, Elizabeth. "Architectural History: The Invisible Subject." *The Journal of Architecture* 1, no. 2, (1996): 159–64.

McKibbin, Ross. *Classes and Cultures: England 1918–1951.* Oxford: Oxford University Press, 1998.

McLuhan, Marshall. "The Invisible Environment: The Future of an Erosion." *Perspecta* 11 (1967): 161–7.

———. *Understanding Media: The Extensions of Man.* New York: Signet, 1964.

Milland, Jeffrey. "Courting Malvolio: The Background to the Pilkington Committee on Broadcasting, 1960–62," *Contemporary British History* 18, no. 2 (2004): 76–102.

Milliken, Ernest K. "The Teaching of History by Means of Models." *History* 22 (1937): 139–48.

Mills, Dennis. "Networks in the Open University System." In *Open House*, no. 31 (7 January 1971).

Milton Keynes Development Corporation. *The Plan for Milton Keynes, Volume 1.* Milton Keynes, 1970.

Ministry of Education. *The New Secondary Education.* London: Her Majesty's Stationery Office, 1947.

Mitchell, Rosemary. *Picturing the Past: English History in Text and Image, 1830–1870.* Oxford: Oxford University Press, 2000.

Moran, Joe. *Armchair Nation: An Intimate History of Britain In Front of the TV.* London: Profile Books, 2013.

Morris, William F. *The Future Citizen & His Surroundings,* Council for Visual Education Booklet No. 1. London: B. T. Batsford, 1946.

National Committee of Inquiry into Higher Education. *The Dearing Report: Higher Education in the Learning Society.* Report 1. London: Her Majesty's Stationery Office, 1997.

Partington, Matthew. "The London Coffee Bar of the 1950s—Teenage Occupation of an Amateur Space?" In *Occupation: Negotiations with Constructed Space*. Brighton: University of Brighton, 2009.

Pawley, Martin. *Architecture Versus Housing*. London: Studio Vista, 1971.

Payne, Alina A. "Architectural History and the History of Art: A Suspended Dialogue." *Journal of the Society of Architectural Historians* 58, no. 3 (September 1999): 292–9

Perry, Walter. *Open University: A Personal Account by the First Vice-Chancellor*. Milton Keynes: The Open University Press, 1976

Pevsner, Nikolaus. *An Enquiry into Industrial Art in England*. London: Cambridge University Press, 1937.

——. *Pioneers of Modern Design: From William Morris to Walter Gropius*. New Haven: Yale University Press, 2005. First published as *Pioneers of the Modern Movement* by Faber & Faber, 1936.

——. *The Englishness of English Art*. London: Penguin Books, 1993.

Powell, Enoch. *Still to Decide: Speeches*. Edited by John Wood. London: Elliot Right Way, 1972.

Price, Cedric. *Opera*. Edited by Samantha Hardingham. Chichester: John Wiley & Sons, 2003.

Rattenbury, Kester, and Samantha Hardingham. *Cedric Price: Potteries Thinkbelt*. Supercrit no. 1. London: Routledge, 2007.

Read, Herbert. *Art and Industry: The Principles of Industrial Design*. London: Faber & Faber, 1944.

Richardson, Michael. *Countdown to the Open University*. Produced by BBC for The Open University. First aired 8 January 1978 on BBC. Post-production transcript. http://www.open.ac.uk/library/digital-archive/pdf/script/script:03ab4128fd5060485e81ccdcc-4c193b78b4d7d35.

Robinson, Marilynne. "What Are We Doing Here?" *The New York Review of Books*, 9 November 2017.

Rowland, Robert. "The University in a Palace." *The Listener*, 17 February 1977.

Roberts, Stephen. *A Ministry of Enthusiasm: Centenary Essays on the Workers' Educational Association*. London: Pluto Press, 2003.

Robinson, Emily, Camilla Schofield, Florence Sutcliffe-Braithwaite, and Natalie Thomlinson. "Telling Stories about Postwar Britain: Popular Individualism and the 'Crisis' of the 1970s." *Twentieth Century British History* 28, no. 2 (2017): 268–304.

Ruskin, John. *The Opening of the Crystal Palace: Considered in Some of Its Relations to the Prospects of Art*. London: Smith, Elder, and Co., 1854.

Rutherford, Jessica, presenter. "English Furniture: Technique and Design." Television programme 17 of A305. Produced by Patricia Hodgson, BBC for The Open University, first aired 9 August 1975.

Rykwert, Joseph. "A Healthy Mind in a Healthy Body." In *History in, of, and for Architecture: Papers from a Symposium*, edited by John E. Hancock, 44–8. Cincinnati: School of Architecture and Interior Design, University of Cincinnati, 1981.

——. "Meaning in Building." *Zodiac* 6 (1958): 193–6.

Samuel, Raphael. "History, the Nation and the Schools." *History Workshop Journal* 30 (Fall 1990): 75–80.

——. *History Workshop: A Collectanea 1967–1991: Documents, Memoirs, Critiques, and Cumulative Index to History Workshop Journal*. London: History Workshop, 1991.

Sanderson, Michael. *Education and Economic Decline in Britain, 1870 to the 1990s*. Cambridge: Cambridge University Press, 1999.

Sartoris, Alberto. *Encyclopédie de l'architecture nouvelle*. Milan: Hoepli, 1948.

Scharf, Aaron. *Pioneers of Photography: An Album of Pictures and Words*. New York: Abrams, 1976.

Scott-Brown, Denise. "Learning from Pop." *Casabella* 35, no. 359–360 (December 1971): 15–46.

——. "Pop Off: Reply to Kenneth Frampton." *Casabella* 35, no. 359–360 (December 1971): 39–46.

Simon, Brian. *Education and the Social Order, 1940–1990*. London: Lawrence & Wishart, 1999.

Spigel, Lynn. *Make Room for TV: Television and the Family Ideal in Postwar America*. Chicago: University of Chicago Press, 1992.

Summerson, John. *The Classical Language of Architecture*. London: Methuen, 1963.

Swenarton, Mark. "The Role of Architectural History in Architectural Education." *Architectural History*, no. 30 (1987): 201–15.

Tafuri, Manfredo. *Theories and History of Architecture*. Translated by Giorgio Verrecchia. New York: Harper & Row, 1980. First published as *Teorie e storia dell'architettura* by Laterza, 1968.

Taylor, Mark. "End of the University as We Know It." *The New York Times*, 26 April 2009.

The Open University, Charter and Statutes. 23 April 1969; as amended by the Privy Council to December 2005. https://www.open.ac.uk/about/documents/about-university-charter.pdf.

Planning Committee. *The Open University: Report of the Planning Committee to the Secretary of State for Education and Science*. London: Her Majesty's Stationary Office, 1969.

Udemy. "Homepage." Accessed 23 November 2017. https://www.udemy.com.

University of the Air Advisory Committee. *A University of the Air*, Cmnd 2922, HMSO. London: Ministry of Education, 1966.

Vitruvius. *Vitruvius: Ten Books on Architecture*. Translated by Ingrid D. Rowland and Thomas Noble Howe. New York: Cambridge University Press, 2001.

von Erlach, Johann Bernhard Fischer. *A Plan of Civil and Historical Architecture [...]*. Translated by Thomas Lediard. London: Thomas Lediard, 1730.

Walford, Rex. *Geography in British Schools, 1850–2000: Making a World of Difference*. London: Woburn Press, 2001.

Walker, John. *Arts TV: A History of Arts Television in Britain*. London: Libbey, 1993.

Wedgwood Benn, June. "Letter to the Black Paper Editors." In C. Brian Cox and Anthony E. Dyson, eds., "Black Paper Two: The Crisis in Education." Special issue, *Critical Quarterly* 4, no. 3 (1969): 93.

Weinbren, Daniel. "Prisoner Students: Building Bridges, Breaching Walls." In *Students in Twentieth-Century Britain and Ireland*, edited by Jodi Burkett, 45–75. Balingstoke: Palgrave Macmillan, 2018.

———. *The Open University: A History*. Manchester: Manchester University Press in association with The Open University, 2015.

Wenham, Brian. *The Third Age of Broadcasting*. London: Faber & Faber, 1982.

Whyte, William H. *The Social Life of Small Urban Spaces*. Washington: The Conservative Foundation, 1980.

Williams, Raymond. *Communications*, 3rd ed. Harmondsworth: Penguin Books, 1976.

———. *Culture and Society, 1780–1950*. London: Chatto & Windus, 1958.

———. *Marxism and Literature*. Oxford: Oxford University Press, 1977.

———, ed. *May Day Manifesto*, London: Lawrence and Wishart, 2013. Originally published as *May Day Manifesto 1968* by Penguin Books, 1968.

———. *Television: Technology and Cultural Form*. London: Fontana, 1971. Republished by Routledge, 2003.

———. *The Long Revolution*. London: Chatto & Windus, 1961.

Wilson, Harold. "Labour's Plan for Science." Speech, Annual Labour Party Conference, Scarbourough, United Kindom, 1 October 1963. London: Victoria House Printing Company, 1963. Transcript.

———. "Time for Decision." Speech, Labour Party election manifesto, March 1966. http://politicsresources.net/area/uk/man/lab66.htm.

Wölfflin, Heinrich. *Renaissance und Barock*. Munich, 1888.

Worringer, Wilhelm. *Abstraction and Empathy: A Contribution to the Psychology of Style*. London: Routledge and Kegan Paul, 1948.

Wrigley, Amanda. "Higher Education and Public Engagement in Open University and BBC Drama Co-Productions on BBC2 in the 1970s." *Journal of British Cinema and Television* 14, no. 3 (2017): 377–93

Young, Hilary. "Whose Story Counts? Constructing an Oral History of The Open University at 40." *Oral History* 39, no. 2 (2011): 95–106.

Yorke, Francis Reginald Stevens. *The Modern House*. London: Architectural Press, 1934.

Yorke, Francis Reginald Stevens, and Frederick Gibberd. *The Modern Flat*. London: Architectural Press, 1937.

Yusaf, Shundana. *Broadcasting Buildings: Architecture on the Wireless, 1927–1945*. Cambridge, MA: The MIT Press, 2014.

Index

Biographies

Stephen Bayley

Stephen Bayley is an author, critic, columnist, consultant, broadcaster, and curator. He studied at the University of Manchester and the University of Liverpool. Bayley taught at the University of Kent before creating the Boilerhouse Project for the Victoria and Albert Museum. With Sir Terence Conran, Bayley established the Design Museum, and was briefly the Creative Director of the Millennium Dome. He is a Chevalier of the Ordre des Arts et Lettres, an Honourary Fellow of the Royal Institute of British Architects, a Trustee of The Royal Fine Art Commission Trust, and a Fellow of The University of Wales.

Joseph Bedford

Joseph Bedford is Assistant Professor of History and Theory at Virginia Tech. He holds a doctorate in History, Theory, and Criticism of Architecture from Princeton University and was the recipient of the 2008–2009 Rome Prize at the British School in Rome. Bedford has taught both design studios and architecture history and theory courses at Princeton University, Pratt Institute, and Columbia University. He is the founding editor of *Attention: The Audio Journal for Architecture*, and the founding director of *The Architecture Exchange*, a platform for theoretical exchange between architecture and other fields. Bedford has published numerous articles in journals such as *Architecture Research Quarterly*, *AA Files*, and *Log*.

Nick Beech

Nick Beech is Lecturer in the History of London at the School of History at Queen Mary University of London. His research interests include construction histories, architectural practice in municipal and national governments in Britain, and urban and architectural debates within the New Left in the 1950s and 1960s. He is currently working on a book, titled *From Progress to Possibility*, which examines the urban imagination of the New Left and early cultural studies in Britain.

Tim Benton

Tim Benton is Professor Emeritus of Art History at The Open University, and served as Visiting Professor in the Department of Art History and Archaeology at Columbia University in 2007 and at the Bard Graduate Center in 2003. He was the Clark Visiting Professor at Williams College in 2009 and also taught at the École polytechnique fédérale de Lausanne and at the Architectural Association. Benton served on the Conseil d'administration of Fondation Le Corbusier from 2008 to 2015.

Laura Carter

Laura Carter is a historian whose work focuses on education, popular culture, and everyday life in Britain in the twentieth century. She is currently a Postdoctoral Research Assistant at the Faculty of History at the University of Cambridge and a Research Fellow at Murray Edwards College. She has published articles in *History Workshop Journal*, *Twentieth Century British History*, and *Cultural and Social History*.

Adrian Forty

Adrian Forty is Professor Emeritus of Architectural History at the Bartlett School of Architecture at University College London, where he founded the master's programme in architectural history. He is the author of the books *Objects of Desire* (1986), *Words and Buildings: A Vocabulary of Modern Architecture* (2000), and most recently *Concrete and Culture: A Material History* (2012). Forty was the President of the European Architectural History Network from 2010 to 2014.

Ben Highmore

Ben Highmore is Professor of Cultural Studies at the School of Media, Film and Music at the University of Sussex. Previously, he taught cultural studies at the University of the West of England, Bristol, as well as art history at The Open University. Highmore's doctoral thesis at Birkbeck College at University of London was published as *Everyday Life and Cultural Theory* (2001), and he has subsequently published a number other books, including *The Art of Brutalism* (2017), *Cultural Feelings* (2017), *Culture* (2016), and *The Great Indoors* (2015).

Nick Levinson

Nick Levinson studied European art and architecture at the Courtauld Institute of Art in the early 1960s and joined the British Broadcasting Corporation's Open University Production Department at the start of its operations in 1969. Levinson worked for the BBC until his retirement in 1999, first as a research assistant and later as a television and radio producer. He worked on The Open University's arts foundation courses and various second- and third-level courses, specializing in programmes on art, architecture, history, and literature.

Joaquim Moreno

Joaquim Moreno studied architecture at Universidade do Porto, and holds a master's degree from Universitat Politècnica de Catalunya and a doctorate from Princeton University. He is Adjunct Assistant Professor at Columbia University, Universidade do Minho, and Universitat Autònoma de Barcelona. Moreno was one of the editors of the Portuguese journal *InSi(s)tu*. In 2008 he co-curated *Out Here: Disquieted Architecture* for the Venice Architecture Biennale, with José Gil, and in 2015 he co-curated *Carlo Scarpa I Túmulo Brion Guido Guidi* at Garagem Sul, Centro Cultural de Belém, with Paula Pinto. Moreno is also an active member of Jornal Arquitectos.

Joseph Rykwert

Joseph Rykwert is Paul Philippe Cret Professor of Architecture Emeritus at the University of Pennsylvania, where he has taught since 1988. Following his studies at the Bartlett School of Architecture and the Architectural Association, Rykwert taught at the Hammersmith School of Arts and Crafts and the Hochschule für Gestaltung, before becoming Librarian and Tutor at the Royal College of Art. In 1967, Rykwert became Professor of Art at the newly-created University of Essex, where he remained until 1981, when he became Slade Professor in the Fine Arts and later Reader in Architecture at the University of Cambridge. He has held fellowships at the Center for Advanced Studies in the Visual Art and at the Getty Center for the History of Art and the Humanities. He was awarded the Bruno Zevi Prize in Architectural History by the 2000 Venice Architecture Biennale, the Gold Medal of Merit in the Fine Arts in 2009, and the Royal Gold Medal by the Royal Institute of British Architects in 2014. Rykwert was appointed a Chevalier of the Ordre des Arts et des Lettres in 1984 and has been President of the International Committee of Architectural Critics since 1996.

Previous page:
A television studio for an Open University programme,
ca. 1970s. The Open University. F1673-95-2A

Bibliothèque et Archives nationales du Québec
and Library and Archives Canada cataloguing
in publication

The university is now on air, broadcasting
modern architecture/eight episodes by Joaquim
Moreno; in conversation with Tim Benton,
Nick Levinson, Adrian Forty, Joseph Rykwert,
and Stephen Bayley; with contributions by
Nick Beech, Laura Carter, Ben Highmore,
and Joseph Bedford.

Co-published by Jap Sam Books.
Includes bibliographical references and index.

ISBN 978-1-927071-54-0 (softcover)

1. Architecture, Modern - Study and teaching
(Higher) - Exhibitions. 2. Design - History -
20th century - Study and teaching (Higher)
- Exhibitions. 3. Open University - History
- Exhibitions. I. Moreno, Joaquim, 1973-,
author. II. Benton, Tim, 1945-, interviewee. III.
Levinson, Nick, interviewee. IV. Forty, Adrian,
1948-, interviewee. V. Rykwert, Joseph, 1926-,
interviewee. VI. Bayley, Stephen, interviewee.
VII. Beech, Nick, author. VIII. Carter, Laura,
1989-, author. IX. Highmore, Ben, 1961-, author.
X. Bedford, Joseph, author. XI. Canadian Centre
for Architecture. XII. Title: Broadcasting modern
architecture.

NA2000.O52 2018
720.711074
C2017-942679-6

The university is now on air, broadcasting modern architecture

This volume is published by the Canadian Centre for Architecture and Jap Sam Books, in conjunction with the exhibition *The University Is Now on Air: Broadcasting Modern Architecture*, organized by and presented at the CCA from 15 November 2017 to 1 April 2018.

The Canadian Centre for Architecture gratefully acknowledges The Open University for their collaboration, with special thanks to academic consultants, Emeritus Professor Tim Benton and Professor Elizabeth McKellar, Faculty of Arts and Social Sciences.

Publication

Editor-in-charge:
Claire Lubell

Editorial assistance:
Geneviève Godbout
Federico Ortiz
Ushma Thakrar

Graphic Design:
(Studio) Jonathan Hares
Clément Gicquel

Proofreading:
Katie Moore

Subject indexing:
Heather Macdougall

Rights and reproductions:
Stéphane Aleixandre

CCA photography:
Michel Boulet
Elise Windsor

Lithography:
Carsten Humme

Printing and binding:
Graphius Group

All images © The Open University, unless otherwise specified.

Exhibition

Curator:
Joaquim Moreno

Curatorial team:
Émilie Retailleau
Helina Gebremedhen
Ushma Thakrar

Design:
APPARATA

Graphic design:
Something Fantastic

Film director:
Shahab Mihandoust

Design development:
Sébastien Larivière
Anh Truong

The Canadian Centre for Architecture is an international research centre and museum founded by Phyllis Lambert in 1979 on the conviction that architecture is a public concern. Through its collection, exhibitions, public programs, publications, and research opportunities, the CCA advances knowledge, promotes public understanding, and widens thought and debate on architecture, its history, theory, practice, and its role in society today.

The CCA gratefully acknowledges the generous support of the Ministère de la Culture et des Communications, the Canada Council for the Arts, and the Conseil des arts de Montréal.

© 2018 Canadian Centre for Architecture

For more information on CCA publications, please visit cca.qc.ca/publications.

ISBN 978-1-927071-54-0

Canadian Centre for Architecture
1920 rue Baile
Montréal, Québec
Canada H3H 2S6
www.cca.qc.ca

ISBN 978-94-92852-01-4

Jap Sam Books
Hoge Heijiningsedijk 5
4794 AA Heijiningen
The Netherlands
www.japsambooks.nl

Legal deposit: April 2018
Printed and bound in Belgium

Guide to object photography

(1)	Toshiba Blackstripe C355C colour television, ca. 1976.
(2)	*Introduction*, course booklet for Units 1–2 of A305, with complete set of course booklets, 1975.
(3)	*Art Nouveau*, course booklet for Units 3–4 of A305, 1975.
(4)	*Expressionism*, course booklet for Units 9–10 of A305, 1975.
(5)	*The New Objectivity*, course booklet for Units 11–12 of A305, 1975.
(6)	*British Design*, course booklet for Units 19–20 of A305, 1975.
(7)	*Mechanical Services*, course booklet for Units 21–22 of A305, 1975.
(8)	Timetable of broadcasts and list of printed materials for A305 published in *AAQ*, 1975.
(9)	Box mailed to students with home-experiment kit for TAD292, Art and Environment, 1980.
(10)	*Images*, reference booklet for A305, 1975.
(11)	*Broadcasting Supplement, Part 1*, reference booklet for A305, 1975.
(12)	*Documents*, reference booklet for A305, 1975.
(13)	Hacker RP37A VHF Herald Radio used in Open University study centres, ca. 1971.
(14)	Film strips of reference images for A305 accompanying course unit booklets, 1975.
(15)	Film strip viewer produced by The Open University.
(16)	*Radiovision Booklet*, reference booklet for A305, 1975.
(17)	Draft page of *Broadcasting Supplement, Part 2* for Radio 30 of A305, "The Work of Isokon," 1974.
(18)	Draft title page of *Radiovision Booklet* for Radio 30 of A305, "The Work of Isokon," 1974.
(19)	Draft spread of *Radiovision Booklet* for Radio 30 of A305, "The Work of Isokon," 1974.
(20)	*Project Guide*, booklet with instructions for final student project report for A305, 1976.
(21)	"Third Level Course Examination," final exam booklet for A305, 1975.
(22)	Internal memorandum relaying A305 student feedback, 6 August 1975.
(23)	Data from A305 student responses to the Course Unit Report Form (CURF), 13 August 1975.
(24)	Set books (required reference texts) for A305.
(25)	*Form and Function*, anthology produced for A305, 1975.
(26)	Chart mapping the movement of key architects relevant to A305, 1975.
(27)	Letter from Raymond Andrews to Tim Benton about making A305 materials accessible, 7 January 1976.
(28)	Letter from Bruno Zevi to Charlotte Benton about distributing A305 materials in Italy, 22 February 1976.
(29)	Home-recordings on videocassette tapes of various A305 television programmes.